Maxine Hong Kingston's *The Woman Warrior*

A CASEBOOK

CASEBOOKS IN CONTEMPORARY FICTION

General Editor, William L. Andrews

With the continued expansion of the literary canon, multicultural works of modern literary fiction have assumed an increasing importance for students and scholars of American literature. Casebooks in Contemporary Fiction assembles key documents and criticism concerning these works that have so recently become central components of the American literature curriculum. The majority of the casebooks treat fictional works; however, because the line between autobiography and fiction is often blurred in contemporary literature, a small number of casebooks will specialize in autobiographical fiction or even straight autobiography. Each casebook will reprint documents relating to the work's historical context and reception, representative critical essays, an interview with the author, and a selected bibliography. The series will provide, for the first time, an accessible forum in which readers can come to a fuller understanding of these contemporary masterpieces and the unique aspects of the American ethnic, racial, or cultural experiences that they so ably portray.

Toni Morrison's
Beloved: A Casebook
edited by William L. Andrews
and Nellie Y. McKay

Maxine Hong Kingston's
The Woman Warrior: A Casebook
edited by Sau-ling C. Wong

Maya Angelou's
I Know Why the Caged Bird Sings: A Casebook
edited by Joanne M. Braxton

Forthcoming:

Louise Erdrich's
Love Medicine: A Casebook
edited by Hertha D. Sweet Wong

MAXINE HONG KINGSTON'S

The Woman Warrior

◆ ◆ ◆

A CASEBOOK

Edited by
Sau-ling Cynthia Wong

New York   Oxford

Oxford University Press

1999

Oxford University Press

Oxford   New York

Athens   Auckland   Bangkok   Bogotá   Buenos Aires   Calcutta
Cape Town   Chennai   Dar es Salaam   Dehli   Florence   Hong Kong   Istanbul
Karachi   Kuala Lumpur   Madrid   Melborne   Mexico City   Mumbai
Nairobi   Paris   São Paulo   Singapore   Taipei   Toyko   Toronto   Warsaw

and associated companies in
Berlin   Ibadan

Copyright © 1999 by Oxford University Press, Inc.

Published by Oxford University Press, Inc.
198 Madison Avenue, New York, New York 10016

Oxford is a registered trademark of Oxford University Press

Library of Congress Cataloging-in-Publication Data
Maxine Hong Kingston's The woman warrior :
a casebook / edited by Sau-ling Cynthia Wong.
p.   cm. — (Casebooks in contemporary fiction)
Includes bibliographical references.
ISBN 0-19-511654-2;   0-19-511655-0 (pbk.)
1. Kingston, Maxine Hong. Woman warrior.   2. Chinese American
women—Biography—History and criticism.   3. Autobiography—Chinese
American authors—History and criticism.   I. Wong, Sau-ling
Cynthia.   II. Series.
CT275.K5764A3   1998
973′.04951—dc21   98-11577

1 3 5 7 9 8 6 4 2

Printed in the United States of America
on acid-free paper

Credits

Acknowledgments

I WISH TO THANK William L. Andrews, editor of the Casebooks in Contemporary Fiction series of which this volume is a part, for the opportunity to work on this project and for his patient encouragement in shepherding it through; Susan Chang, editor at Oxford University Press, for her sharp critical eye and useful advice; the anonymous reviewers of the book proposal, for identifying my biases and suggesting correctives; Maxine Hong Kingston and her agent, Sandra Dyjkstra, for offering information on *The Woman Warrior's* reception; my colleagues Hertha Wong, King-Kok Cheung, Stan Yogi, and Wen-ching Ho, for taking time from their busy schedules to comment, share bibliographies, and otherwise help; my research assistants, Sandy Oh and Rosalee Shim, for their thorough work; and Leslie Crow of the Bank of Stockton Archives, Kathleen Roldan of the Berkeley Repertory Theater, photographer Ken Friedman, author Steve Warshaw (of *The Trouble in Berkeley*), and Beatrice Epstein of the Metropolitan Museum of Art Photo Library, for enabling me to select and obtain interesting illustrations. (See the captions for full photo credits.) Above all, I thank all the authors who, directly or through their publishers, allowed their pieces to be reprinted in the casebook.

Contents

Maxine Hong Kingston's *The Woman Warrior*

A CASEBOOK

Introduction

EDITING A CASEBOOK ON Maxine Hong Kingston's *The Woman Warrior: Memoirs of a Girlhood among Ghosts* is a daunting task. As one of the most widely circulated and frequently taught literary texts by a living American author,[1] *The Woman Warrior* has generated a vast scholarship.[2] This critical output, furthermore, represents a range of often antagonistic views on the book's meaning and significance: as with its counterparts in other American "ethnic canons," *The Woman Warrior* has been steeped in controversy, enthusiastically claimed, ingeniously deployed, and at times bitterly denounced by contesting interpretive communities. Anyone attempting to profile its complex reception history must therefore be prepared to give a reasonably intelligible account of how she got from hundreds of titles to a handful of article-length studies.

In choosing the essays for this volume, I have been guided by several considerations. First, I want to stay faithful to the idea of the casebook—*case* to me suggesting what has happened rather than what I wish had happened or what I think should be happening. I am fully aware of the inescapable (and not always welcome) canon-shaping potential of reference projects like this one. My notes to the selections will make it clear that, as a scholar identifying primarily as an Asian Americanist and holding strong feminist sympathies, I work from a certain set of critical values. On the

3

other hand, I also strive to be evenhanded, to allow a fair hearing to views that I find problematic but that have played a significant role in the evolution of the critical corpus on *The Woman Warrior*. That these approaches thereby get yet another hearing is, to me, a necessary and tolerable price for scholarship. Likewise acceptable to me is the documentary imperative intrinsic to the casebook, which makes for a heavier emphasis on older publications.

I am also concerned with both range and depth. To the extent allowed by the casebook format and its practical constraints, I try to identify major approaches adopted and major issues raised by critics, as well as at least sketch out some variations and developments thereof. This, I believe, is what distinguishes the casebook from a pedagogy-oriented companion like the MLA's *Approaches to Teaching Kingston's "The Woman Warrior,"* edited by Shirley Geok-lin Lim (1991), or a synoptic, "one-stop" resource like Patricia Chu's teaching unit on *The Woman Warrior* in the *MLA Resource Guide to Asian American Literature,* coedited by Stephen H. Sumida and me (forthcoming). With this in mind, for each approach or set of issues, I have chosen pieces that represent an especially illustrative instance; or a cogent, forceful, and elaborated account of existing scholarship; or an opportunity to dialog with other selections or open up lines of inquiry.

At the end of this introduction, I situate each essay in the critical tradition on *The Woman Warrior*, set forth questions raised by the author, point out the essay's resonances with other selections in the volume, direct readers to related studies not reproduced here, and, where appropriate, give some account of my choice. As much as possible I endeavor to identify naturalized premises, based on the conviction that no single position is transcendently objective. But with my own essay I must beg the reader to complete the task for me: as the Zen saying goes, the eye that sees cannot see itself. An extremely brief annotated bibliography at the end contains items that I consider complementary to the selected essays—no more; exhaustiveness is clearly not my aim.

Just as inclusion of an essay in the casebook does not imply my endorsement of all its arguments, so exclusion is not to be construed as a reflection on an essay's "quality." It is more accurate to say that my choices result from a complex balancing of many considerations, among which is a need that I keenly feel to give a "shape" (for lack of a better term) to the volume. (Narrativization of one sort or another, perhaps, is inevitable even in a form premised on juxtaposition.) In addition, I proceed from the assumption that by the late 1990s *The Woman Warrior* has become deeply embedded in American feminist and "multicultural" critical and pedagogical practices, so that a little initial dislodging might be needed to freshen our perception of the issues.

In placing certain words in quotation marks in this casebook—chief among them *ethnicity, minority, multiculturalism,* and *race,* and their derivations—I wish to indicate that they are contested terms whose denotative usefulness I accept but whose ideological connotations, in my view, should be subject to scrutiny.[3] This practice does not imply that terms that I use without quotation marks, such as *Chinese American,* are "natural" categories; I simply seek a convenient means to convey my own critical premises.

Part I: To restore perspective on Kingston's work, which by now has been so securely canonized that the determinants of its status are often obscured, I open the casebook with Ya-jie Zhang's 1986 article, "A Chinese Woman's Response to Maxine Hong Kingston's *The Woman Warrior.*" To begin with, Kingston, simply in her capacity as "a Chinese woman," has often been endowed with ethnographic authority to present a "real" Chinese culture constructed as timeless, monolithic, and unremittingly exotic—to her own exasperation ("Cultural Mis-readings by American Reviewers," Kingston 1982). How better to expose the speciousness of such essentialism than by citing another Chinese woman—one who self-identifies as, among other things, a citizen of the People's Republic of China—thus revealing the generic, decontextualized "Chinese woman" to be a fiction?

A visiting professor from the People's Republic of China, Zhang is much more openly personal than her American counterparts about her experiences with Kingston's book, especially about her conversion from skeptic to supporter and her declared intention to "take back" *The Woman Warrior* to teach in China in order, in the long run, to improve the lot of women there. This stance presupposes a much closer relationship between "art" and "society" than many American liberal humanists are comfortable about entertaining, even those who profess an intellectual preoccupation with matters political.

Alongside the diverse feminist readings of *The Woman Warrior* in this volume, Zhang's avowedly feminist essay could be used as a point of departure for investigating the dominance of poststructural-inflected feminist readings, for contemplating the possibility of transcultural feminist interests, and for discussing deployments of Kingston's text by various interpretive communities.

To fully appreciate the historicity of both Kingston's book and Zhang's response, one needs to take into account the state of U.S.-China relations during the period of *The Woman Warrior's* writing and of Zhang's visit to the

United States. Nixon's historic trip to Beijing did not take place until 1972 (four years before *The Woman Warrior* appeared); prior to that, China, to the average American, was largely shrouded in mystery. The American-born protagonist's speculations about traditional Chinese village culture and life under the Communists, with neither of which she has had any direct contact, must be read in this context. In the post-Mao, pre-Tiananmen era (1976–1989) during which Zhang's essay was produced, it was not uncommon for Chinese intellectuals to openly express a readiness to learn from the West, as Zhang did, while also retaining a strong sense of Chinese national identity.[4]

Frank Chin's "The Most Popular Book in China," a flauntingly absurdist parody of *The Woman Warrior*, mocks critics who value the book for its accounts of traditional Chinese and Chinese American cultures: what the admiring reader accepts as imaginative and personally authenticated details are to Chin irresponsible, cynical distortions. To those familiar with *The Woman Warrior* only as a "multicultural" curricular fixture—a formally challenging, academically respectable text bearing Chinese American and feminist credentials—the vitriol of "The Most Popular Book in China" might come as a shock. Thus, like Zhang's essay, Chin's short piece also serves a defamiliarizing function in this casebook.

Through wild exaggerations and systematic reversals of gender and East/West positioning, Chin aims to address some perennial issues found in Chinese American and to some degree Asian American or even other "ethnic" American cultural criticism (see, e.g., Palumbo-Liu 1995a): the asymmetry in power between "ethnic minority" writers and the dominant publishing industry, the critical establishment, and the popular readership; the persistence of Orientalism in cultural production and reception; gender and racial stereotypes; the vexed relationship between "literature" and "history"; the potential duplicity of the autobiographical act; the nature of tradition and of cultural transformation; and the artist's social responsibility toward her "community." These and other critical themes will be revisited again and again in this volume. Readers conversant with Kingston's other works will recognize allusions to the tale about a cross-dressing male traveler at the beginning of *China Men*. The passages concerning personal pronouns refer both to *The Woman Warrior* and to Jade Snow Wong's autobiography, *Fifth Chinese Daughter* (first published in 1945), which, according to the author, is written "in the third person from Chinese habit." "Mei-jing," the name of the author of *Unmanly Warrior*, could be a Cantonese pun: depending on the tone in which the phrase is pronounced, *Mei-jing* could be a fairly formulaic given name for girls or could mean monosodium glutamate (MSG), an artificial seasoning liberally used in Chinese American restaurants to please undiscerning palates.[5]

The third selection, my "Autobiography as guided Chinatown Tour? Maxine Hong Kingston's *The Woman Warrior* and the Chinese-American Autobiography Controversy," represents my attempt, as an Asian Americanist, to arrive at a measured understanding of the many provocative issues raised by Chin and other Asian American critics. Their concerns about cultural authenticity and artistic integrity are focused by a question of genre: *The Woman Warrior* was marketed with a "Non-fiction" label on its cover, but in the detractors' view much of the book is fiction, and compromised fiction at that.

In my essay, I tease apart several meanings of "fictionalization," contextualize the critiques in a distinctly Chinese American autobiographical tradition, and turn to both Western and Chinese scholarship on the genre to determine the validity of some of the charges made against Kingston. In the final analysis, I fully acknowledge that dominant society's Orientalist expectations are debilitating and should be resisted, but I also argue for creative space for Chinese American writers to articulate their *sui generis* experiences.[6]

Part II: Sidonie Smith's piece, "Maxine Hong Kingston's The Woman Warrior: Filiality and Woman's Autobiographical Storytelling," is the concluding chapter of her 1987 book, *A Poetics of Women's Autobiography*. Finding prevailing autobiography criticism androcentric and inadequate, Smith's theoretical framework shows how "the autobiographer who is a woman must suspend herself between paternal and maternal narratives, those fictions of male and female selfhood that permeate her historical moment" (19).[7] Next, Smith reads a set of women's autobiographies in English that to her bear the imprint of that pattern: among them, Kingston's *The Woman Warrior*. In this poetics, *The Woman Warrior* is considered exemplary for its powerful engagements with "fictions of self-representation."

Smith's gendered conceptualization of "self-authoring" may be compared to and contrasted with Eakin's (1985) "self-invention" as reflexive consciousness and existential act. Insistence on inextricable linkages between gender and genre is, of course, a staple of Anglo-American feminist criticism (with regard to *The Woman Warrior*, see Juhasz (1979), Shueller (1989), and Chu (1992)). Since Smith posits a continuity between Kingston and the fifteenth- to nineteenth-century female autobiographers in her study—"ultimately, every woman who writes autobiography ends up interrogating the prevailing ideology of gender, if only unconsciously and clumsily" (Smith 175)—readers might want to assess the concept of a transhistorical female subjectivity overriding socioeconomic, cultural, and "racial" differences.

I include Leslie Rabine's closely argued essay, "No Lost Paradise: Social Gender and Symbolic Gender in the Writings of Maxine Hong Kingston," as an illustration of the application of "theory" (in particular, French feminist and psychoanalytic theory) to American "ethnic minority" texts, epitomizing both the exciting possibilities and the serious limitations of this widely used approach. "Theory," in Rabine's hand, provides conceptual magnets for textual insights (hence sharper argumentative rigor), greater confidence in the congruence of her interpretations with the larger intellectual climate, and, last but not least, an imprimatur of legitimacy in the American academy. Rabine's espousal of poststructuralism is not wholesale; she deplores the "collapsing" of social into symbolic gender issues. However, despite her appreciation of the social, the hegemonic hold of poststructuralism has apparently created blind spots in Rabine toward her own decontextualizations. For example, to have one's analysis of Chinese culture mediated by Kristeva's *Les Chinoises* is, to say the least, questionable. The picture of Kingston as radical deconstructionist may also be overstated, an artefact of investment in the believability of voice-as-masculine/writing-as-feminine mapping. This poststructuralist schema simply has little resonance with Chinese cultural history: in traditional China a literary education was reserved for men as the prescribed path to officialdom, and writing carried no connotations of secondariness or marginality. Rabine's concept of "social gender" thus strikes me as not much less textual or academic than the deplored "symbolic gender."[8]

Part III: Given *The Woman Warrior*'s secure status in the American feminist canon, the "Chinese Americanness" of the book is often understood chiefly as sexism in the Chinese American immigrant family, a subset of universal sexism. Thus "race" frequently gets elided in the critical literature produced by non-Asian Americans.[9] This tendency to elevate feminist issues at the expense of "racial" ones has been critiqued by Schueller (1989) and Goellnicht (1991).

In contrast to this tendency, Elaine Kim contends that "*The Woman Warrior* is primarily about the Chinese American's attempt to sort fact from fantasy in order to come to terms with the paradoxes that shape her life as a member of a racial minority group in America" (1982: 199). Critics in the Asian American critical tradition pioneered by Kim and others have been contesting approaches to Asian American literature that are "color-evasive" and "power-evasive."[10]

King-Kok Cheung's "The Woman Warrior versus the Chinaman Pacific:

Must a Chinese American critic choose between Feminism and Heroism?,"
is written from the perspective of an Asian Americanist who acutely feels
the implicit or explicit "whiteness" of much feminist criticism no less than
the implicit or explicit "maleness" of Asian American rehabilitative cultural nationalism. Concerned that the complexities of Chinese American
history and cultural tradition might be lost in the polemical fray, she
makes a plea for all parties concerned to work toward "notions of gender
and ethnicity that are nonhierarchical, nonbinary, and nonprescriptive."
Elsewhere, in a similar vein, Cheung objects to the widespread labeling of
The Woman Warrior as "feminist" and of *China Men* as "ethnic" (1993: 74–125).

By gesturing toward reconciliation, Cheung raises the question of
whether gender and ethnic differences serve structural functions in
American society and are, therefore, more than matters of personal soul-
searching and interpersonal understanding. If they do serve such a function, there is also the question of whether they constitute equal categories.
Lee (1995) argues that differential treatment of "feminist" as opposed to
"ethnic" texts reflects institutional containment of touchier "racial" matters; hence the readier canonical incorporation of *The Woman Warrior* compared to *China Men*. To the extent that most of the pieces in this volume are
products of the American academy, they invite exploration of the political
limitations of professionalized criticism.

As Cheung observes in a footnote to this essay, the controversy surrounding *The Woman Warrior* is paralleled by Ishmael Reed's attack on Alice
Walker's *The Color Purple*, which is also a crossover hit popular with white
feminists and a staple of the "multicultural" curriculum. Cheung's comparative study suggests that cross-readings of "ethnic minority" literary
works, bypassing the dominant center of the Anglo-American canon,
might be a fertile direction for criticism. Ho (1987) is another example of
such comparatism. However, as no critical approach is automatically his-
toricized, its promises and liabilities must, again, be carefully considered.

In her survey essay, "Chinese American Woman Writers: The Tradition
behind Maxine Hong Kingston," Amy Ling refutes the widespread perception that *The Woman Warrior* represents the meteoric rise of a singular talent
emerging from a creative vacuum, and insists that *The Woman Warrior* be understood in its own tradition (however one defines "own"), counteracting
reductionist appropriation and tokenism in the "multicultural" American
academy.

Ling's overview of Chinese American women writers preceding Kingston poses some interesting theoretical questions about the formation of a
literary tradition. For example, Ling maintains that the very ability to write

and publish despite sexist Chinese cultural norms holds all these writers together. Beyond this, however, Ling has not expounded on other bases by which such a varied group of writers might be placed into the same tradition, especially when some of them may not have been aware of their predecessors' or peers' existence and work, or, if aware, do not consider them significant influences.[11]

After acknowledging the diversity of the group she labels "Chinese American women writers," Ling speculates that nativity has a determining effect on what and how they write. This point is well taken even if the specific ways in which Ling differentiates between Chinese- and American-born writers might be disputed. Because of their stereotype as "unassimilable aliens," Chinese and other Asian American writers are frequently assigned the "immigrant" label regardless of nativity. I can recall many instances where *The Woman Warrior* is called an "immigrant autobiography" and Kingston an "immigrant writer." It would be interesting to investigate how immigration and nativity functions in American literary ideology.

Besides Ling, Lim (1992) also argues, from feminist motivations, for a tradition of Chinese American women's "lifestories" extending back to the early twentieth century. On the other hand, elaborating on a comparison between Jade Snow Wong's *Fifth Chinese Daughter* and Kingston's *The Woman Warrior*, Lim notes a "breath-taking leap in female consciousness" (263) between the two books: discontinuity rather than continuity. Again, the issue of what makes a literary tradition is raised.

The last selection in this casebook, Reed Way Dasenbrock's "Intelligibility and Meaningfulness in Multicultural Literature in English" (excerpts), focuses not so much on the content of *The Woman Warrior* as on the acts of intercultural communication that it may enable or disable. Dasenbrock's analysis, excerpted here,[12] begins with the fact that "literature in English is an increasingly international, even global, phenomenon," which creates questions of cross-cultural (mis)understanding. Dissatisfied with the "universalism versus localism" debate in which these questions have been cast, Dasenbrock borrows from speech act theory and assails a common tendency among dominantly positioned readers to expect all "foreignness" of a work glossed and smoothed over for their convenience. But Dasenbrock's approach could also give some of these readers a justification for remaining ignorant about another culture. While Dasenbrock maintains that "The difficulty experienced by a less informed reader, far from preventing that reader from experiencing the work justly, is what creates meaning for that reader," readers occupying more privileged reading positions may not react with nearly as much openness and zeal. Though

Dasenbrock's essay addresses a situation that many contemporary critics would identify as postcolonial, it acts to privatize reading, placing it in a realm where concepts like colonialism are rendered irrelevant.

Dasenbrock's article is neither the first nor the last to apply speech act theory, and communications theory in general, to *The Woman Warrior* (see Myers 1986 and Ludwig 1996a; 1996b).[13] Speech act theory and other linguistic theories, with their drive toward austere theoretical axioms, appear an attractive source of theoretical underpinning for border-crossing literary analyses.[14]

One possible consequence of dislodging an "ethnic minority" literary work from that context is for the individual as experiential unit to gradually take precedence over the group as contextualizing entity: to effect a movement away from broad historical conditions toward individual-to-individual encounters (implicitly conceived of as exchanges between equal participants "beyond identity politics"). Such an approach is obviously at odds with studies like Holaday (1978), Li (1988), or the essays in Lim (1991: 26–63), which respect cultural specificity as a necessary and important source of insight into the text.

The application of communications theory to "multicultural" works opens up a line of inquiry that will take on increasing relevance as transnational cultural flows intensify. Over two decades after its first publication, it would not be hard to make the case that *The Woman Warrior* has become an international text. The internationalization of Asian American literature is already a documented phenomenon. (See, for example, Cheung 1997: 8, 19; Davis 1996.)[15] Kingston herself is committed to the idea of a "global novel" for her next artistic enterprise (Hornung and Ruhe 1992: 313). Standing against all this is the fact that "Chinese-Americans" are overtly singled out by Kingston as her audience at the very beginning of *The Woman Warrior* (1976: 6). Whether the tension between these two types of realities can be resolved, and if so, how, might be the next challenge facing critics in the era of U.S. and global "multiculturalism."

Part IV: I conclude this casebook with Susan Brownmiller's interview with Kingston, which caught Kingston in the first flush of *The Woman Warrior*'s sensational success, before she became an icon and the book acquired an air of hoary venerability. (The original appeared in the pages of *Mademoiselle* surrounded by advertisements for push-up bra pads, facial hair removers, and modeling agencies.) Though it is hardly the most substantial interview available, I chose it partly for its historical value and partly to, again, keep in view the fact that *The Woman Warrior* was not "born," but "made," the subject of a casebook.

Brownmiller's wide-ranging conversation with Kingston conveys a sense of the buzz in the publishing industry surrounding the debut of this hitherto unknown author. It also reveals how, virtually immediately upon publication, *The Woman Warrior* got entangled in various discourses (Anglo-American feminism, Orientalism, immigrant success stories, etc.) that preoccupy the critics in this volume.[16]

Notes

1. According to Rita Holmes of the Sandra Dyjkstra Agency, Kingston's agent, as of September 1996 over 900,000 copies of *The Woman Warrior* (both hardcover and paperback) have been sold. Kingston mentions in an interview (Fishkin 1991: 787) that as late as 1989, *The Woman Warrior* was on the trade paperback bestseller list. M. Chin (1989–90: 68) notes that Kingston was reputed to be the living author whose books are most frequently taught in college, and that *The Woman Warrior* was being used not only in literature departments but also in courses on American studies, anthropology, ethnic studies, history, women's studies, and even Black studies. In 1997, on the occasion of Kingston's receiving the National Humanities Medal, Poet Laureate Robert Hass again referred to *The Woman Warrior* as "the book by a living author most widely taught in American universities and colleges" (Scalise 1997:1). Kingston, in a personal communication to me (June 23, 1997), said that some twenty translations of *The Woman Warrior* have been made.

2. An electronic search of the MLA Bibliographic Database by subject, conducted just before the submission of the casebook manuscript, yielded 132 items under "The Woman Warrior," 185 under "Kingston."

3. As "multiculturalism" appears in one of my section headings, the reader is referred to Goldberg (1994) for a collection of contrasting views on the term.

4. Readers interested in pursuing some of the questions raised by Zhang's essay might be interested in Wu (1991-92), which brings up comparable issues regarding Kingston's *China Men,* and Deeney (1993), which analyzes a range of often contradictory reader responses from mainland China, Hong Kong, and Taiwan—all "Chinese" cultural locations—toward Kingston's *Tripmaster Monkey* and David Henry Hwang's play *M. Butterfly.*

5. Years ago I heard or read this interpretation but have forgotten the source. It could have been a comment made by Jeffery Paul Chan at a conference in the early 1980s.

6. Readers concerned with authenticity and the peculiar predicament of the "ethnic minority," especially Asian American, writer are referred to Woo and her concept of "dual authenticity" (1990). Eakin (1985), a key study of the autobiographical act as necessary self-invention, has been an obvious influence on my stand on

the controversy; the *Woman Warrior* section, on the mutual constitution of self and language (255–75), is especially relevant. Among scholarship on the generic status of *The Woman Warrior*, Homsher (1979) is an early study of genre-crossing, while an interesting angle is provided by Quinby (1992), who emphasizes the term "memoirs" in Kingston's subtitle. The affinity of this conclusion to bourgeois-romantic ideals of art (presumably unfettered freedom of individual expression) is potentially problematic for "ethnic minority" writers. I have given the issue a fuller treatment in "The Asian American *Homo Ludens*: Work, Play, and Art" (Wong 1993: 166–211). For a Critique of Asian American critics' preoccupation with *The Woman Warrior's* generic status, see Kang on "generic fixations" (1995: 35–90).

7. In this note, page numbers in parentheses refer to quotations from Smith's book outside the Kingston chapter reprinted in the casebook. Those drawn from the selection itself will not be identified by page number.

8. For further study, readers might want to compare and contrast several explorations of "postmodern historiographic metafictional" elements in Kingston. For example, Hutcheon, on affinities between *The Woman Warrior* and other "postmodern" works (1988: 72–73); my essay on ethnic dimensions of postmodern indeterminacy in *The Woman Warrior* (Wong 1992b) and a related discussion on the "postmodern" label in which Kingston took part (Hornung and Ruhe 1992: 313–22); and Cheung (1993), in her Kingston chapter (74–125), on "double-voiced" strategies in *China Men* (100–25), which gesture toward historiographic metafiction. Palumbo-Liu (1995b) critiques unreflecting adoption of the "post" label by Asian American critics.

9. I am indebted to Sandy Oh for noting this pattern in, for example, Hunt (1985) and Rubenstein (1987).

10. These terms are borrowed from Frankenberg (1993: 14–15).

11. On many occasions, when asked about her "literary identity," so to speak, Kingston either refers to nonminority Anglo-American literary forebears or else shows pride in having been considered by mainland Chinese to be a Chinese writer (e.g., M. Chin 1989–1990; Fishkin 1991; Hornung and Reuhe 1992: 313–22). Kingston once told an interviewer, "I am not sure that I got help from a former generation of Chinese-American writers, except for Jade Snow Wong: actually her book [*Fifth Chinese Daughter*] was the only available one" (Carabi 11; quoted in Lim 1992: 256) How being Chinese American and being female might be factors in the creation of a literary tradition—from which an individual writer might explicitly distance herself, and of whose existence she need not even be consciously aware—calls for additional theoretical probing.

12. The "Works Cited" list has been left intact for the reader's information.

13. Ludwig (1996b) is based on a section on *The Woman Warrior* in Ludwig's book (1996a).

14. Of course, border-crossing texts are hardly new—"great works" exported

from colonizing nations were keystones of colonial educations—but when the global dominance of Western culture was unquestioned, self-reflexiveness about the intercultural communicative act was not called for.

15. Asian American literary studies in Europe present a particularly thought-provoking case: unlike the study of Chinese American literature in Taiwan or the study of Japanese American literature in Japan (which have also produced "non-American" scholarship), appeal to cultural origin or cultural commonality is not a significant factor in its rise.

Kingston study is strong in Taiwan. The Institute of European and American Studies at the Academia Sinica has been hosting biennial conferences on Chinese American literature since 1993 and publishing the proceedings in Chinese; many of these essays are on Kingston, especially *The Woman Warrior*, as are many master's and doctoral theses at Taiwan universities. The "natural" connection here is, of course, cultural.

16. Lim (1991: 14–15) summarizes other interviews with Kingston that academics might find useful. Marilyn Chin's interview with Kingston (1989–90), not listed in Lim, was conducted after *Tripmaster Monkey* came out and revolves around that book, but it also contains extensive sections on *The Woman Warrior* and Kingston's views on culture and literature in general.

PART I

Setting Forth
Issues and Debates

A Chinese Woman's Response to Maxine Hong Kingston's *The Woman Warrior*

YA-JIE ZHANG

◆　◆　◆

*T*HE WOMAN WARRIOR, a favorite book of many of my American friends, should have been a very interesting book for me, as I was a visiting professor from the People's Republic of China.

However, it did not appeal to me when I read it for the first time, because the stories in it seemed somewhat twisted, Chinese perhaps in origin but not really Chinese any more, full of American imagination. Furthermore, some of Kingston's remarks offended my sense of national pride as well as my idea of personal discretion.

The first chapter, "No Name Woman," reads as if it could have been true in old China, but a Chinese writer would have told it differently without the imagined situations. In the chapter, "The White Tigers," Kingston has actually interwoven two ancient Chinese stories: the story of Yue Fei, a very famous hero and general in the Song Dynasty, and Hua Mu Lan. These two stories are well known to every Chinese, man and woman, old and young. In addition to that, I felt that Kingston held too much bitterness against her mother and her Chinese origin, accusing the mother of telling her too many ghost stories.

In the Chinese language, the word "ghost" may imply many different concepts. Children brought up in China cannot fail to understand it. But Kingston used the word in too many places without different connotations, so that it may arouse confusion among Westerners and give them a wrong impression: that Chinese abuse the word "ghost."

And I disagreed with Kingston on some other points in the book. For instance: "The Japanese though 'little' were no ghosts, the only foreigners considered not ghosts by Chinese." This is not true; actually we Chinese did use the derogatory meaning of ghost for Japanese invaders as well.

When I read the part in which Kingston says "the Chinese are too loud" and "tell lies," I was personally offended. This is simply not true, I thought. To me, Americans are just as loud or louder. What Kingston calls "lies" are nothing more than courteous ways of putting things. Don't the Americans also have many hypocritical ways of saying things? When they ask, "How are you?" for example, do they really want to know? At this point, I decided not to teach this book to my Chinese students when I returned home.

However, when Kingston's book was studied in Professor Amy Ling's American Ethnic Literature course at Rutgers, especially after the professor's lecture and the discussion among the students, I completely changed my ideas. Thanks to the Chinese-American professor and the American students, I could see the book in a different light. It is, after all, an American story, not a Chinese one. Some of my assumptions were wrong from the very beginning because I am Chinese.

Kingston's purpose is to make use of all these stories to show how a Chinese-American finds her own identity, how much she has to struggle through—the old culture as well as the new—and how she uses words and stories to rebel against the old and to contribute to the new.

Viewing the book from this perspective, I can accept her distortions of the stories which have always been so lofty and sacred in my homeland.

People from every country have their own ways of happiness and sorrow, laughter and tears. The expressions of these emotions are only or mostly understandable among the people within a given culture. Once people emigrate, they become a new people influenced by their new country; and it then becomes difficult for those from the "Old Country" to share the emotions and thoughts of the emigrants.

Chinese emigrants must have gone through tremendous difficulties, bearing the old world's superstitions and mysteries, entering into the new world's liberty, reason, science, and technology. What a mixture. No wonder it is hard for me, a Chinese, to share the imagination of a Chinese-American. Yet now I want to take back this story to teach. I also want to do something to add to the voice of Maxine Hong Kingston. I have things to say to both Chinese and Chinese-Americans.

In mixing ancient Chinese stories with her own imagination, Kingston has created a new woman warrior who actually challenges old and new. This warrior, Kingston herself, is bold, daring, and rebellious. She reveals what should be kept secret in the old world; at the same time, she points out how her new life in the free world seems so uninteresting, haunted by "ghosts," newsboys and garbage collectors. She must break away from both worlds, use her own words as swords to avenge wrongs, to fight, and to build.

There's no profit in raising girls. Better to raise geese than girls. When you raise girls, you're raising children for strangers. Although this concept is from old China, I am ashamed to admit that negative feelings for women have not yet been completely wiped out from Chinese minds in "New China." Disregard for women is deeply rooted in the thousands of years of feudal history. Now in New China, laws have given equal rights to women. Currently Chinese women have in many respects more independence and freedom than ever before. Women now work for equal pay; economic independence is the most essential element in women's emancipation. Also children at eighteen may now choose either their mother's or father's family names.

However, just as the British proverb says, "Old Ways Die Hard"; ideas rooted for centuries in a people's mind are not wiped out easily, quickly, and completely either by law or even revolution. Feudalism which had dominated China for thousands of years pulses in the blood of every Chinese. Therefore, even after thirty-seven years of liberation by the Chinese Communist Party, it still casts its shadow here and there.

Nowadays, thanks to the "open door policy," I can see a great many young men and women holding hands, embracing, or even kissing each other in the streets or on a bus. Such public displays were impossible ten years ago and even criminal in olden times. I happen to think it delightful that our young people can feel free to show their affection openly. Yet, how many people are throwing a disapproving glance at them, thinking in their small minds "what a cheap girl." Some even voice such thoughts in an undertone. However, never does anyone say, "What a cheap boy."

"No Name Woman" reminds me of dozens of true stories I know about—to which I would like to add at this time.

Once I lived in a Beijing compound of many courtyards. The son of a neighbor had a woman come to sleep with him every night. Mind you, this was in the late seventies, not the time of "No Name Woman." We neighbors couldn't say or do anything against it, but a lot of gossip arose. Actually, it was the young man who was not sincere; he used the woman for some time, grew tired of her, and started to beat her. What I heard from the neighboring elderly ladies was again, "The girl is cheap. It serves her right." Ergo: the fault is always the woman's.

In my childhood, I had a wet-nurse whom I called "Mama." Ever since I can remember, the life story of Mama has haunted me. She was a genuinely kind woman. Whenever I felt bored, I would beg her to tell me again and again the story of my counterpart, "Little Plaits," her daughter. She gave birth to her daughter a few days before my mother had me. Her husband, a poor idle kind of peasant, a ne'er-do-well, took to drinking and gambling and did not feed his family. Not wanting to see her first child die, Mama looked for a post as wet-nurse in the city so that she could earn a living for herself and pay for someone else to feed her daughter in the country. Thus, sadly, she parted with her own baby and came to care for me. Once when she told me that Little Plaits was having her feet bound and could not walk without pain, I cried big tears, begging to be allowed to see her and talk her out of the idea. Once a month, Mama's husband came to my home to ask for money; I would run out with a stick and try to scare him away, because every time he came, I would see Mama in tears. She hated him, and therefore I hated him too. She was reluctant to give him money to squander, but as he was her husband, she had to support him for all his idling, drinking and gambling at the cost of her own suffering and labor.

When I myself became a mother, I longed to see Mama and Little Plaits and wrote a letter to the address from my childhood's memory. When finally an answering letter arrived, Little Plaits told me that Mama was dead. After her husband had died, she had continued to support the family including an elder brother of her husband. Gossip concerning her relationship with this brother-in-law grew to such an extent that she hanged herself.

In "No Name Woman," Mrs. Kingston imagined, "Adultery, perhaps only a mistake during good times, became a crime when the village needed food." That is true yet not true. In China, if anything happens or even nothing happens but just gossip, the blame usually falls on woman. Disregard for women is still in people's minds, not in printed documents which always refer to men and women as equals. This is the stubborn, undying feudal influence of ancient ways, of eternal China. Yet just this influence, this intangible, invisible concept can grow in human minds to a degree sufficient to claim people's lives.

Kingston knows people and how to tell stories. She found her voice and fought like a real warrior by telling the sad stories of her two aunts, No

Name Woman and Moon Orchid. Who is going to sing the stories of our own women, thousands of Chinese women, living or dead, withering or already withered under the invisible but nevertheless smothering "moral system"?

Ever since 1949, our artists and playwrights have paid a great deal of attention to the subject of marriage. Many plays and operas deal with the problem of freedom of love, choosing lovers for oneself rather than one's parents' choice. Gradually, people are becoming tired of this theme. Many current writers are interested in the Cultural Revolution, in the injured generation or the current issues in China.

Few writers are interested in the plight of women. Yet women need more than the freedom to choose their own lovers, because they don't just get married and live happily ever after. Women should have the right to live a rich and rounded life, like men. They should be treated as independent beings, not just the housekeepers or the pets of men. Their equality should become one of fact, not just of law.

Women intellectuals, for instance, love to think and reason; yet how much understanding do they receive from society? And how much support do they obtain even from other women?

In China, we badly need books about women, dealing with the subject of womanhood in some depth, not just "Xiao Er Hei Got Married" or "Niao Nui Xu" (two operas quite popular in the '50s and '60s). We need books like *The Woman Warrior*. How many "No Name Women" were there in China, or Moon Orchids who never came to the United States but suffered as widows from the prime of their lives to their graves? Many, many . . . yet, who cares? Who has spoken for them? For there are always more 'important' problems to be discussed by writers.

The Woman Warrior is indeed a good book. I will not teach this book to my students after my return to China, but, as Maxine Hong Kingston did, will search for my own reed pipe and sing for my own kind.

The Most Popular
Book in China

FRANK CHIN

◆　◆　◆

THE MOST POPULAR book in China is the autobiography of a white woman born and raised in a French hand laundry in south China. The meek, sycophantic nature of the French of her childhood clashed with the aggressive, individualistic nature of the un-revolutionized Chinese, who embraced her as one of themselves.

A female and raised a French Catholic, she is, by the terms of her thousand-year-old religion, the meekest of the meek, the mildest of the mild, basking in the grace of God. She is forbidden by French culture to speak of herself except in the third person, and must limit her use of the first-person pronoun "I" to quoting the exact words spoken by card-carrying Judeo-Christian white men.

She cunningly transcends the religious ban on female first-person expression by writing of herself in metaphor. "Once upon a time, in a once-upon-a-time China, there lived a once-upon-a-time little French girl in a little French hand laundry, in the little Frenchtown on the edge of the mighty port city of Canton," the book opens. Very quickly this unusual autobiography of a Christian convert in China becomes a poetic evocation of a heroine of French feminism. She wrote a book about her imagined French ancestor Joan of Arc.

The old people of Frenchtown on the edge of Canton didn't like the book. They didn't have Smith Meijing's grasp of the Chinese language, the Chinese who loved her book said. The people of old Frenchtown said her book falsified history. They are conservative and old fashioned and don't appreciate good writing, the Chinese who loved the book said.

The picture of Joan of Arc as a man forced to dress and act like a girl and castrated after ceremonial incestuous relations with his father to satisfy the perverse sexual lusts of her parents was not historically accurate and was so inaccurate as to demonstrate that the woman had gone mad, the French people of Frenchtown on the edge of the port city said. The French girl is writing not history, but art, the Chinese who loved the book said, and continued: She is writing a work of imagination authenticated by her personal experience.

The French people of Frenchtown said, her own experience is an insane, paranoid distortion of basic knowledge common to all French. She mangles what no sane Frenchman could get wrong without going mad: Joan of Arc! the people of Frenchtown protested.

And the Chinese who loved the book said, her personal experience was authentically French and her unique understanding of both the French and Chinese views of life brings the Chinese the closest, most human understanding of the French ever produced in the Chinese language. Her book gives the Chinese insights into the French mind and the French character, not French books, the Chinese who loved the book said, and declared Smith Mei-jing the hope of French literature written in Chinese.

She violates French history, culture and language, heaps contempt on her ancestry, and depends on the ignorance of her Chinese readers for her Chinese literary success, the old people of Frenchtown said, and waved old books over their heads.

Sour grapes, the Chinese who loved the book said. She's not writing history or about history, therefore the accuracy of any of her history is irrelevant to the question of her artistry, authenticity and psychological reality, her Chinese admirers said.

The French autobiographer's name is Smith Mei-jing, her autobiography, *The Unmanly Warrior*. The Chinese *Children's Digest* version of the book has been translated into English with the hope it will be adopted as an aid in teaching American fourth and fifth graders a little about France, French culture and the relevance of Joan of Arc in the world of personal experience.

UNMANLY WARRIOR by Smith Mei-jing

Once upon a time, in a once-upon-a-time China, there lived a once-upon-a-time little French girl in a little French hand laundry, in the little Frenchtown on the edge of the mighty port city of Canton. A lone white girl in the splendor and civilization of China. Am I so alien to my vague Europe? My far France? The French are a distant people. She dreams about my French self. How strange it is to be French in China. Surely the grandest place in the world to be born. In France they burned women. They held a lottery, and each year more and more women were burned.

Joan of Arc was the last woman to be burned by my ancestors. Surely Joan imagined herself Chinese, in China where ancient woman warriors abound in the heroic tradition from ancient times. And she thought herself born again someday in me. Poor Joan of Arc. Born a son to a family that craved a daughter. They dressed their boy as a girl. They forced him into homosexual relationships with the surrounding court society, while young and naked virgins pranced through the deer park singing Vivaldi with ribald discretion.

Joan of Arc grew up a strong and muscular boy. Yet his parents dressed him in gowns and wigs and powdered him and admonished him to seduce princelings and influential priests at the crown balls. Joan took to bright lipstick and shiny satin masks and riding rescue, snatching women from the flames of the lottery.

Soon Joan mounted an army of masked women fed up with the silliness of court life that threatened to topple France, determined to make it a nation ruled by women rescued from the flames of French male bigotry.

The Church would not be denied its divine right to burn women, and mounted a Catholic army of the church militant and all male aristocracy to destroy Joan's army, capture the female general, and burn her in a public place at rush hour.

Men who formed around Joan called themselves the Nazi party and named Joan their leader. No one knew Joan of Arc was actually a six-foot-four, 225-pound man. At the head of his army, Joan was free of the homosexual affairs forced on him by his social-climbing parents. The inevitable happened. Fighting side by side with the sexiest and fiercest women of France, in battle after battle from Hastings to Waterloo, Joan fell in love with one of them. She fell in love with a militant lesbian of an aberrant Christian sect. The young girl warrior was at first seduced by the lovely Joan she had admired and defended and come to love, fighting side by side in the clang and gallop of battle as women.

The first kiss that night they kissed made them sigh. Their tongues touched and they shivered. The night the young lesbian militant grabbed Joan's naked male member vibrating at full tumescence, her mind snapped. A yelp squirted out of her throat. Her hand clenched in a death-grip around Joan's throbbing hardon. She chanted Hail Marys and tried to face west, but had lost all sense of direction. Joan's member shrank out of the grasp of the only girl Joan of Arc ever loved. If Joan had only known the Chinese were using compasses at this time, she might have turned her dead comrade-in-arms' and lover's face to the west. Joan became the elected ruler of the new Franco-Germany created by a Nazi referendum, and became the first leader of a European democracy. She pitted her army of freed women, excommunicated nuns, and fed-up ladies of the court against the armies of the Roman Church.

Joan's parents betrayed her just as she was making advances on the body of a young lapsed nun who had confessed to years of desiring intimate contact with a male organ at full tumescence. The Christian concept of original sin made no sense to Joan of Arc. She would not accept its intimidating, bullying claim to prior ownership of himself. Yet the odd notion had a strange grip on the bodily functions and thought processes, and perversions about the mother we Europeans who have been more or less Christian since possibly the death of Jesus Christ all share. Christ lived about the time the Han was peaking. Five generations later, the Three Kingdoms period came on China and the mandate of heaven was renewed almost daily, for a hundred and fifty years. By then Christianity was in its first Dark Age.

Women in the Nazi Party wanting more power in the structure betrayed Joan to his parents, who betrayed him to the church militant of Rome. They captured him, castrated him in public, in the middle of Paris, then dressed him in underwear from Frederick's of Hollywood, and high fashion from Oscar de la Renta, Gucci shoes and coochie-coos. Priests of the Pope painted his face. They put false eyelashes on his eyelids, wigged him, pierced his ears, gave him a nose job, and cut half-moons under his breasts and slipped in bags of silicone to give him the breasts of a woman. They painted his nails, stockinged his legs. He bled from the nose job. He bled out of his nose and mouth. He bled from the half-moons cut under his breasts. He bled from the groin where he had been castrated. The faithful of the church chanted and rocked their censers and crucifixes, back and forth, back and forth. The army of women had abandoned Joan when there was no doubt about Joan of Arc being a man. The women set the torch to the faggots surrounding Joan's body, and they burned him.

I identify with me, Joan of Arc tells me. He might have been a great-great-grandfather. How could he stand to read the scrawly, wormy, patsy writing of the French? Their first-person pronoun looks like a child's earring. Where are the solid weapons of the Chinese "I" I wonder, and pity the people confined to communicate with each other with an unarmed, uninhabited, passive first-person pronoun to assert themselves with, Joan would think if he were in China now.

Joan suffered for lack of a proud "I." Humiliated, he defended the honor and equality of French women, and they betrayed him. His parents betrayed him to better their positions in court society. The rituals and traditions of the Roman Church demanded he be burned as a woman. After they realized that they had burned a man—no matter that they had burned him as a woman, they had *burned a man*—they ended the burning of women. Thus Joan of Arc lived and died the daughter her parents had always wanted.

How lucky I am to be in China where civilization is whole and healthy. If only my own parents had been more adaptable and not brought all this misery to me. They make me feel so foreign. Their superstitions for every occasion have me dizzy. I like to think Joan of Arc would not have put up with this fanatical fear of life outside the small precinct of the white ghetto. Luckily the Chinese comfort and understand me. They treat me as a human being. The French do not. I come home at night and avoid my parents hunched over their Webster's Dictionary playing Scrabble again, and climb into bed and say, as I say every night, good night to my ancestor. "You're a good man, Joan of Arc."

NONE OF THE historical facts and legendary heroes and touchstones violated beyond recognition by Maxine Hong Kingston and David Henry Hwang for white approval and entertainment are anywhere near as obscure and esoteric to the Chinese as Joan of Arc is to the French.

The violation of history and of fact and of Joan of Arc makes no difference to the pleasure and stimulation the Chinese get from *Unmanly Warrior*, so why should the falsification of history, the white racist stereotypes and slurs in Kingston's prose and Hwang's theater mean anything to the pleasure whites derive from reading and seeing their work? They don't, of course. People who know nothing about China, about Chinese-Americans, the railroad, the opera and who don't want to know more than they know—know Kingston and Hwang, and that's all they care to know. How Kingston and Hwang make them feel about Chinese and Chinese-Americans.

Well, folks, it's that same old feeling. Fu Manchu, Charlie Chan, Pearl Buck, Shangri-la of the Thirties has become Maxine Hong Kingston and David Henry Hwang in the Eighties, providing whites with an escape from the immediate and pressing terror of hard times, of empty gas tanks and payments to make. Whites have been using the Chinese as the metaphorical out for all their perversions and debilitating insecurities since the thirteenth century. The popular stereotype of the Chinese in white publishing, white religion, Hollywood and TV is a sickening pastiche of white perversions and socially unacceptable fantasies made speakable by calling them Chinese. Kingston and Hwang confirm the white fantasy that everything sick and sickening about the white self-image is really Chinese. That is their service to white ego. Reviewers and critics ripe for the cycle of Christian Chinese-American autobiography and Charlie Chan become accomplices to making the fake China and Chinese America of Kingston and Hwang real with the force of history. The source of their vision of Chinese-American art and history is white fantasy, not Chinese-American history. They're more Charlie Chan than Chang Apana.

Charlie Chan was short and fat and walked with the light, dainty steps of a woman, in white fantasy. Chang Apana was tall and wiry, and he walked through sun and shadow with a bullwhip over his shoulder, in Chinese-American myth and history.

Autobiography as
Guided Chinatown Tour?

Maxine Hong Kingston's The Woman Warrior
and the Chinese American Autobiographical Controversy

SAU-LING CYNTHIA WONG

◆   ◆   ◆

AXINE HONG KINGSTON's autobiography, *The Woman Warrior*, may be the best-known contemporary work of Asian-American literature. Winner of the National Book Critics Circle Award for the best book of nonfiction published in 1976, *The Woman Warrior* remains healthily in print and on the reading lists of numerous college courses; excerpts from it are routinely featured in anthologies with a multicultural slant. It is safe to say that many readers who otherwise do not concern themselves with Asian-American literature have read Kingston's book.

In spite—or maybe, as we shall see, because—of its general popularity, however, *The Woman Warrior* has by no means been received with unqualified enthusiasm by Kingston's fellow Chinese Americans. A number of Chinese-American critics have repeatedly denounced the *The Woman Warrior*, questioning its autobiographic status, its authenticity, its representativeness, and thereby Kingston's personal integrity. Though often couched in the emotionally charged, at times openly accusatory, language characteristic of what the Chinese call "pen wars," the critical issues raised in this debate are not merely of passing interest. Rather, they lie at the heart of any theoretical discussion of ethnic American autobiography in particular and ethnic American literature in general. It would therefore be instructive to set out the terms of the controversy and explore their theoretical ramifications, with a view to understanding the nature of Kingston's narrative enterprise in *The Woman Warrior*.

The most fundamental objection to *The Woman Warrior* concerns its generic status: its being billed as autobiography rather than fiction, when so much of the book departs from the popular definition of autobiography as an unadorned factual account of a person's own life. Responding to a favorable review of the book by Diane Johnson in the *New York Review of Books*, Jeffrey Chan notes how a "white reading public will rave over ethnic biography while ignoring a Chinese American's literary art" and attacks Knopf, "a white publishing house," for "distributing an obvious fiction for fact" (6). The thrust of Chan's message is that the autobiographical label is a marketing ploy in which the author, to her discredit, has acquiesced. Chan's stricture is echoed by Benjamin Tong, who finds *The Woman Warrior* "obviously contrived," a work of "fiction passing for autobiography" ("Critic of Admirer" 6). By way of contrast, while the unusual generic status of *The Woman Warrior* is also widely noted by non–Chinese-American critics, it is seldom cited as either a weakness or a matter of personal, as opposed to artistic, purpose.[1]

How far is Kingston personally responsible for the nonfiction label on the covers of *The Woman Warrior*? According to her, very little:

> The only correspondence I had with the published concerning the classification of my books was that he said that Non-fiction would be the most accurate category; Non-fiction is such a catch-all that even "poetry is considered non-fiction."

And poetry is something in whose company she would be "flattered" to see her books.[2] The entire matter might have rested here—but for some theoretical issues raised by the controversy which command an interest beyond the topical.

Although Kingston's detractors do not use the term, at the heart of the controversy is the question of fictionalism: to what extent "fictional" features are admissible in a work that purports to be an autobiography. The Chinese-American critics of *The Woman Warrior* focus their attention on the social effects of admitting fictionalization into an autobiographical work. Their concern, variously worded, is summed up most concisely, if baldly, by Katheryn Fong:

> I read your references to mythical and feudal China as fiction. . . . Your fantasy stories are embellished versions of your mother's embellished versions of stories. As fiction, these stories are creatively written with graphic im-

agery and emotion. The problem is that non-Chinese are reading your fiction as true accounts of Chinese and Chinese-American history. (67)

Thus stated, *The Woman Warrior* "problem" is seen to rest ultimately on the readers, not the author; the basis for denouncing *The Woman Warrior* is pragmatic, response-contingent, and reader-specific. Why, then, has Kingston been implicated at all in the misreadings of her audience? It is possible to reject the very question as irrelevant, in that authors have little control over how their published works will be read. On the other hand, when critics like Chan, Tong, or Fong hold Kingston responsible for her readers' failings, they do so from a set of assumptions about ethnic literature that are grounded in a keen awareness of the sociopolitical context of minority literary creation. Such an awareness is precisely what is missing in many white reviewers' remarks on *The Woman Warrior;* moreover, the autobiographical genre, with its promise (perceived or real) of "truthfulness," by nature encourages preoccupation with a work's sociopolitical context. Thus the charge of unwarranted fictionalization must be addressed.

The Woman Warrior can be considered fictionalized in a number of ways. On the most obvious formal level, it violates the popular perception of autobiography as an ordered shaping of life events anchored in the so-called external world. It aims at creating what James Olney calls "a realm of order where events bear to one another a relationship of significance rather than chronology" ("Some Versions" 247). According to an early student of the genre, autobiographies must contain, "in some measure, the germ of a description of the manners of their times" (Pascal 8–9). Although recent scholars have found the referential grounding of autobiography much more problematic and its defining essence much more elusive (e.g., Olney, "Autobiography and the Cultural Moment" 3; Bruss 2; Eakin 5), the term *autobiography* usually does evoke, at least among general readers, a chronologically sequenced account with verifiable references to places, people, and events. As one critic puts it, in more abstruse language: "Texts bound by the real insist upon an epistemological status different from works of the imagination in which the real is more nearly hypothetical" (Krupat 25). But what if the "real" that an autobiography is bound by is the "imagination" of the protagonist?[3] This is the thorny problem of generic differentiation posed by *The Woman Warrior.*

By an outwardly oriented definition of autobiography, *The Woman Warrior* is at best only nominally autobiographical: to borrow a phrase from Pascal, it is a work "so engrossed with the inner life that the outer world becomes blurred" (Pascal 9), told by a narrator who, as a child, regularly sees "free movies" on "blank walls" and "[t]alks to people that aren't real inside [her] mind" (221). The prose slips from the subjunctive to the declarative with but the slightest warning: the No Name Woman story begins with *perhaps*'s and *could have been*'s (7) but soon dispenses with these reminders of conjecture. Likewise, while the Fa Mu Lan segment in "White Tigers" is initially marked as an enumeration of the possible and desirable—"The call *would* come from a bird. . . . The bird *would* cross the sun. . . . I *would* be a little girl of seven. . . ." (24–25; my italics)—the bulk of the narration is in the simple past tense, as if recounting completed events in the actual world. Two divergent accounts are given of Brace Orchid's encounter with the Sitting Ghost (81–84, 85–86), neither of which could have been definitive since the event (or alleged event) predates the birth of the daughter/narrator. "At the Western Palace," presented as a deceptively conventional, self-contained short story, is revealed in the next chapter to be a third-hand fiction (189–90). In short, the referential grounding of *The Woman Warrior* is tenuous and presented in a potentially misleading manner. A few public places and events in the "outer" world are recognizable from what we know about author Kingston's life; all else is recollection, speculation, reflection, meditation, imagination. Verifiability is virtually out of the question in a work so self-reflexive. Presumably, then, readers who do not pay sufficient attention to the narrative intricacies of *The Woman Warrior*, especially white readers with biased expectations, will mistake fiction for fact.

The critics of *The Woman Warrior* also detect fictionalization—in the sense of "making things up"—in the way Kingston has chosen to translate certain Chinese terms. A central example is the word *ghost*, based on Cantonese *kuei* or *gwai,* a key term in the book appearing in the subtitle as well as several important episodes.[4] Kingston renders *kuei* as *ghost*. Chan and Tong ("Critic of Admirer" 6), while conceding that the character can indeed mean "ghost" (as in "spirit of the dead"), insist that it be translated as *demon* (or *devil* or *asshole*.) They object to the connotations of insubstantiality or neutrality in Kingston's translation, finding it unsanctioned by community usage and lacking in the hostility toward whites indispensable to true works of Chinese-American literature.[5]

Tong further elevates the rendition of *kuei* as *ghost* into a "purposeful" act of pandering to white tastes and adds another example of "mistranslation" ("Critic of Admirer" 6): referring to "frogs" as "heavenly chickens" (77), which should have been "field chickens" in Cantonese. *(Tien,* "sky" or "heaven," and *tien,* "field" or "meadow," differ only in tone, which is phonemic in Chinese dialects.) Tong suggests that Kingston must have knowingly selected the wrong term, the one with the "familiar exotic touristy flavor" relished by "whites checking out Chinese America" ("Critic of Admirer" 6).

A more serious charge of fictionalization concerns the way Kingston handles not just single Chinese terms but Chinese folklore and legends. The story of Fa Mu Lan,[6] the woman warrior invoked as the young protagonist's patron saint, is recognizable only in bare outline to a reader conversant with traditional Chinese culture. The section on the girl's period of training in the mountains draws extensively on popular martial arts "novels" or "romances" (*wuxia xiaoshuo*) as well as from traditional fantasy lore on *shenxian* ("immortals").[7] As for the way Kingston makes use of the traditional Fa Mu Lan story, at least the version fixed in the popular "Mulan Shi" or "Ballad of Mulan,"[8] deviations from it in *The Woman Warrior* are so numerous that only a few major ones can be noted here. The tattooing of the woman warrior is based on the well-known tale of Yue Fei, whose mother carved four characters (not entire passages) onto his back, exhorting him to be loyal to his country. Also, the spirit-marriage to the waiting childhood sweetheart, a wish-fulfilling inversion of the No Name Woman's fate (7), is utterly unlikely in ancient China, considering the lowly place of women. The traditional Fa Mu Lan is never described as having been pregnant and giving birth to a child while in male disguise. The episode of the wicked baron is fabricated. The Fa Mu Lan of "Mulan Shi" is a defender of the establishment, her spirit patriarchal as well as patriotic, a far cry from a peasant rebel in the vein of the heroes of *Outlaws on the Marsh*.[9]

Because of these and other liberties Kingston has taken with her raw material, *The Woman Warrior* has been criticized by a number of Chinese Americans varying in their knowledge of traditional Chinese culture. Chinese-born scholar Joseph S. M. Lau dismisses the book as a kind of mishmash, a retelling of old tales that would not impress those having access to the originals (Lau 65–66). Writer Frank Chin, who is fifth-generation, attacks Kingston for her "distortions" of traditional Chinese culture. In a parody of *The Woman Warrior* filled with inversions and travesties, Chin creates a piece entitled "The Unmanly Warrior," about a little French girl growing up in Canton and drawing inspiration from "her imagined French ancestor Joan of Arc."

> [Her] picture of Joan of Arc . . . was so inaccurate as to demonstrate that the woman has gone mad, the French people of Frenchtown on the edge of the port city said. The French girl is writing not history, but art, the Chinese who loved the book said, and continued: She is writing a work of imagination authenticated by her personal experience. ("Most Popular Book" 7)

Clearly, the personal authority of an autobiographer is not easy to challenge. Perhaps sensing this, some of Kingston's critics concede it but blend the charge of fictionalization with that of atypicality. Again, the projected reactions of the white audience are kept constantly in sight. Speaking of the protagonist's account of not knowing her father's name, Chan calls this experience "unique" and expresses fears that Kingston "may mislead naive white readers" by not giving any background on the system of naming unique to Chinese Americans. Fong complains: "Your story is a *very personal* description of growing up in Chinese America. It is *one* story from one Chinese American woman of one out of seven generations of Chinese Americans" (67; italics in original). Like Chan, she feels that a narrative as personal as Kingston's must be made safe for white consumption by means of a sobering dose of Chinese-American history; the historical information to be incorporated should emphasize the "causes" behind the "pains, secrets, and bitterness" portrayed in *The Woman Warrior* (67).[10] Fong lists various excerpts that she finds especially dangerous and glosses each with a summary of experiences considered canonical to an ideologically correct version of Chinese-American history. Without such a corrective, she suggests, Kingston will reinforce the white readers' stereotype of Chinese Americans as eternally unassimilable aliens, "silent, mysterious, and devious" (67). Tong feels that Kingston's upbringing in the one-street Chinatown of Stockton, an agricultural town in California's Central Valley (instead of in a bigger, geographically more distinct and presumably more "typical" Chinatown) disqualifies her from attaining "historical and cultural insight" about Chinese America ("Chinatown Popular Cluture" 233).

According to Kingston's critics, the most pernicious of the stereotypes that might be supported by *The Woman Warrior* is that of Chinese-American men as sexist. Some Chinese-American women readers think highly of *The Woman Warrior* because it confirms their personal experiences with sexism (e.g., Suzi Wong, Nellie Wong). Others find Kingston's account of growing up amidst shouts of "Maggot!" overstated, yet can cite little to support the charge besides *their* own personal authority.[11] Contrasting *The Woman Warrior*'s commercial success with the relatively scant attention received by books like Louis Chu's *Eat a Bowl of Tea* and Laurence Yep's *Dragonwings*, both of which present less negative father images, Fong implies that Kingston's autobiography earns its reputation by "over-exaggerat[ing]" the ills of Chinese-American male chauvinism (68). She is willing to grant that a more understanding response from white readers might have given Kingston more creative license but finds the existing body of Chinese-American literature small enough to justify a more stringent demand on the Chinese-American writer, especially the woman writer.

If Chinese-American women disagree about the accuracy of Kingston's portrayal of patriarchal culture, it is hardly surprising to find male Chinese-American critics condemning it in harsh terms. Chan attributes the popularity of *The Woman Warrior* to its depiction of "female anger," which bolsters white feminists' "hallucination" of a universal female condition; and Tong calls the book a "fashionably feminist work written with white acceptance in mind" ("Critic of Admirer" 6). If Chinese-American literature is, according to the editors of *Aiiieeeee!*, distinguished by emasculation (Chin et al. xxx–xxxi), then Chinese American writers cannot afford to wash the culture's dirty linen in public. Frank Chin declares that personal pain—merely a matter of "expression of ego" and "psychological attitudinizing"—must be subordinated to political purpose ("This is Not an Autobiography" 112).

For Chin, the very form of autobiography is suspect because of its association with the Chinese tradition of confession. Although *The Woman Warrior* does not deal with Christianity, Chin places it in a tradition of Christianized Chinese-American autobiographies from Yung Wing's *My Life in China and America* through Pardee Lowe's *Father and Glorious Descendant* to Jade Snow Wong's *Fifth Chinese Daughter*. His rationale is that all autobiography, like religious confessions and conversion testimonials, demonstrates "admission of guilt, submission of my self for judgment," for "approval by outsiders." "[A] Chinaman can't write an autobiography without selling out." In fact, claims Chin, the autobiography is not even a native Chinese form, and Chinese-American writers have no business adopting it. Unfortunately, however, "[t]he Christian Chinese American autobiography is the only Chinese American literary tradition" ("This is Not an Autobiography" 122–24).

Some of the generalizations made by Kingston's critics, such as the exclusively Western and Christian origin of autobiography, may be called into question by existing scholarship. According to one student of the genre, a complex autobiographical tradition does exist in Chinese literature, its origins traceable to the first century A. D., in the Han Dynasty (Larson: esp. chap. 1). Moreover, the confessional mode attributed by Chin solely to a guilt-obsessed Christianity can also be found in traditional Chinese writing (Wu). This does not invalidate Georges Gusdorf's important insight on the cultural specificity of the modern Western autobiography: the point is not to claim that the modern Western autobiography as we know it was practiced in ancient China (it was not) but merely to point out the oversimplification in many of the statements that have been made about *The Woman Warrior*. When Chin links the genre with Christian self-accusation, he overlooks the possibility that the late medieval *breakdown* of

Christian dogma might have been responsible for the emergence of auto-biography as an autonomous literary tradition (Gusdorf 34). Furthermore, emphasis on the confessional element represents only one school of auto-biographical scholarship, the Anglo-American; there are others (Eakin 202). Even if autobiography were an entirely Western phenomenon, ac-cording to Chin's own pronouncements on the unique, nonderivative na-ture of Asian-American literature (especially on its separateness from Asian literature), Chinese-American writers have a right to appropriate a genre not indigenous to the Chinese in China but indigenous to the Chi-nese in America. As Chin and his *Aiiieeeee!* co-editors put it in their prefa-tory manifesto on Chinese and Japanese-American literature, an "Ameri-can-born Asian, writing from the world as Asian-American," should not be expected to "reverberate to gongs struck hundreds of years ago" (Chin et al. xxiv).

Other more or less self-contained disputes on isolated assertions by Kingston's critics could be explored. On the whole, however, one may say that the entire Chinese-American autobiographical debate touches on ar-ticles of ideology so jealously held that the existence of a variety of opin-ions, scholarly or otherwise, may itself be seen as a problem rather than as a possible source of solutions. Given the peremptory tone in which much of the criticism of *The Woman Warrior* has been conducted, it is important that the tacit assumptions of the critics be articulated.

The theoretical underpinnings of the hostile criticism may be summa-rized as a series of interlocking propositions, some concerning the nature of autobiography as a genre (regardless of the author's background), oth-ers generalizable to autobiography by all American ethnic writers, still others peculiar to Chinese-American autobiography.

First of all, autobiography is seen to be self-evidently distinguishable from fiction. If the two genres blur at all at the edges, the interaction merely takes the form of fiction providing "techniques" to render the mundane material of autobiography more attractive; the epistemologi-cal status of the narrated material is not affected. In the same way that language is considered a sort of sugarcoating on dry nuggets of fact, the autobiographer's subjectivity is seen as having little or no constitutive power; rather, it is a Newtonian body moving about in a world of discrete, verifiable—and hence incontrovertible—facts, its power being limited to the choice between faithfully recording or willfully distorting this external reality. In principle, therefore, autobiography is biography which just hap-pens to be written by one's self. It claims no special privilege, poses no spe-cial problems.[12] Finally, the *graphe* part of *autobiography*, the act of writing, the transformation of life into text, is seen by Kingston's critics as a mechanical conveyance of facts from the autobiographer's mind to the reader's via a medium in the physical world, the process pleasant or not depending on the author's literary talents. In the case of *The Woman Warrior* debate, correspondence between word and thing is deemed so perfect that a Chinese term, *kuei*, is supposed to be translatable by only one English equivalent, with all other overtones outlawed. The arbiter here is to be the individual critic backed by the authority of "the Chinese American community" (as if Kingston herself were not a member of this comminity).

Recognition of a preexisting external reality, however, imposes a special obligation on the ethnic American autobiographer: to provide a positive portrayal of the ethnic community through one's self-portrayal. At the very least, the autobiographer's work should be innocent of material that might be seized upon by unsympathetic outsiders to illustrate prevalent stereotypes of the ethnic group; the author should stress the diversity of experience within the group and the uniqueness and self-definition of the individual. Ideally, an ethnic autobiography should also be a history in microcosm of the community, especially of its sufferings, struggles, and triumphs over racism. In other words, an ethnic autobiographer should be an exemplar and spokesperson whose life will inspire the writer's own people as well as enlighten the ignorant about social truths.

The collective history of the ethnic community—one does not speak of *a* history in this theoretical framework—provides the ultimate reference point for the ethnic autobiographer. Here is where the Newtonian analogy begins to break down, for the self proves, after all, to be subjective in the everyday sense of "biased" or "unreliable." Handicapped by its interiority, it cannot be the equal of other "bodies" which can be summed up as a bundle of externally ascertainable properties. The self is epistemologically underprivileged, not privileged; to discover the validity of its private truths, it must appeal to the arbitration of the community (however defined). The history of the collectivity is ballast for the ethnic autobiographer's subjectivity; it is a yardstick against which the author can measure how representative or how idiosyncratic his or her life is, how worthy of preservation in writing. Should individual experience fail to be homologous to collective history, personal authority must yield to ideological imperatives, and the details of the narrative must be manipulated to present an improved picture. According to this logic, the ethnic woman autobiographer victimized by sexism must be ready to suppress potentially damaging (to the men, that is) material; to do less is to jeopardize the united front and prostitute one's integrity for the sake of white approval. *Bios* is of

little worth unless it is "representative"—averaged out to become socio-
logically informative as well as edifying.

A series of mutually incompatible demands on ethnic autobiography
follows from the tenets outlined above. Initially, ethnic autobiography is
thought useful because its focus on the uniqueness of the individual estab-
lishes a minority's right to self-definition; a sufficient number of autobiographies will disabuse white readers of their oversimplified preconcep-
tions. Autobiography's allegedly pure factuality is also prized for its
educational value: unlike fiction, it can be counted on to "tell it like it is"
and resist charges of artistic license made by doubting readers. Nonetheless, autobiography cannot, by definition, be more than *one* person's life
story; thus it cannot be fully trusted. What if the single individual's life
happens to confirm or even endorse white perceptions instead of challenging them? Hence the insistence that ethnic autobiography be "representative." The requirement would have been easily fulfilled if the autobiographer happened—that vexatious word again!—to have already been
"representative," in the sense of conforming to a view of the group agreed
upon by the members making that determination. Short of that, the "representativeness" will have to be formed out of recalcitrant material,
through an editorial process true to the spirit but not necessarily the letter
of the "ethnic experience."

The minute this is done, however, the attempt to make absolute the
generic distinctions between autobiographer and fiction ends up dissolving
the boundaries altogether: autobiography loses its putative authority in
fact and turns into fiction. Language loses its innocuous transmitting function and assumes the unruly power of transmutation. The individual loses
his or her uniqueness and becomes a sociological category. From the effort
to counter homogenization by offering depictions of diversity, a new uni-
formity emerges: one set of stereotypes is replaced by another. In the final
analysis, the main reason the critics attack *The Woman Warrior* is not that it is
insufficiently factual but that it is insufficiently fictional: that the author
did not tamper more freely with her own life story. And ironically—given
the critics' claimed championship of self-definition and literary autonomy—the kind of fiction they would like Kingston to have written is
closely dictated by the responses of white readers.

Only when safeguards against misreadings are supplied may the autobiographical label once more be affixed with confidence, the benefits of the
genre now purged of the inconvenient admixture of potential harm. The
ignorance of white readers seems to be taken for granted as immutable by
Kingston's critics. The possibility that the less unregenerate readers may

learn to read the allusions in *The Woman Warrior*, just as generations of minority readers have learned to read the Eurocentric canon, is never once raised; nor is the possibility that a Chinese-American writer may by right expect, and by duty promote, such learning in his or her audience.

These issues naturally have their counterparts in other ethnic American literatures. The differing versions of Frederick Douglass's early life found in his autobiographies provide a classic example of how a black autobiographer might feel compelled to edit "factual" details in the interest of anticipated social effect (e.g., Gates 98–124). It is worth noting that, while critic Henry Louis Gates, Jr., justifies "crafting or making [of a 'fictive self'] by design," citing the urgent need to establish the black man's right to speak for himself, he also finds a certain flatness of aesthetic effect when Douglass begins to substitute "one ideal essence for another." "Almost never does Douglass allow us to see him as a human individual in all of his complexity" (103, 119, 109).

Though the dilemma is shared by other ethnic American autobiographies, the conflicting claims of typicality and uniqueness take a particularly acute form in Chinese-American autobiography: at stake is not only the existence of the minority writer's voice but the possible perversion of that voice to satisfy the white reader's appetite for exoticism. Indeed, it is only within the context of the Chinese-American autobiographical tradition that both the vehemence of Kingston's critics and the novelty of the narrative undertaking in *The Woman Warrior* can be understood.

To borrow a phrase applied to early African-American writers, Chinese-American writers "entered into the house of literature through the door of autobiography" (Olney, "Autobiography and the Cultural Moment" 15). Autobiographies predominate in Chinese-American writing in English.[13] Some autobiographies are by Chinese-born writers who grew up in China (Lee, Yung, Kuo, Su-ling Wong, Wei); others are by writers born and brought up in the United States (Lowe, Jade Snow Wong, Goo, Kingston). An autobiography from the former group typically focuses on the protagonist's early experiences in China, often ending very abruptly upon his or her arrival in the United States. The author tends to believe the life depicted as representing Chinese life of a certain period or social milieu, and of interest to the Western reader chiefly for this reason rather than for its uniqueness; such a conviction may easily degenerate into the accommodating mentality of a friendly guide to an exotic culture.[14] The autobiographies in the second group, those by American-born writers, are primarily set in the United States.[15] Given the distressing tendency of white readers to confuse Chinese American with Chinese in China, and to attribute a kind of ahistorical, almost genetic, Chinese essence to all persons of Chinese ancestry regardless of their upbringing, the pressure on American-born writers to likewise "represent Chinese culture" is strong. Removed from Chinese culture in China by their ancestors' emigration, American-born autobiographers may still capitalize on white curiosity by conducting the literary equivalent of a guided Chinatown tour: by providing explanations on the manners and mores of the Chinese-American community from the vantage point of a "native." This stance has indeed been adopted by some, and in a sort of involuntary intertextuality, even those works that do not share it will most likely be read as anthropological guidebooks. The curse is potent enough to extend at times to nonautobiographical literature; for a book like *The Woman Warrior*, then, it would be all but impossible to prevent some readers from taking the autobiographical label as a license to overgeneralize.

A few examples will characterize the stance of the cultural guide found among both Chinese-born and American-born autobiographers. In Lee Yan Phou's *When I Was a Boy in China*, personal narrative slows at every turn to make room for background material; seven of the twelve chapter titles—"The House and Household," "Chinese Cookery," "Games and Pastimes," "Schools and School Life," "Religions," "Chinese Holidays," "Stories and Story-Tellers"—could have come out of a general survey of Chinese society. The individual's life serves the function of conveying anthropological information; the freight, in fact, frequently outweighs the vehicle. Lee directly addresses white American readers as "you" throughout the book and consciously assumes the persona of a tour guide: "The servants were . . . sent out to market to buy the materials for breakfast. Let us follow them"; "Now, let me take you into the school where I struggled with the Chinese written language for three years" (27, 57). In Helena Kuo's tellingly titled *I've Come a Long Way*, the tour guide role seems to have become second nature to the author. Like Lee, Kuo addresses her audience as "you" and constantly takes into account their likely reactions. Her descriptions of place are filtered through the eyes of her white readers (e.g., 27); the similes she favors are pure *chinoiserie* (e.g., 23). In the midst of a narrative about her journalistic career, Kuo solicitously inserts a mini-disquisition on traditional Chinese painting, to ensure that her charges will not be lost in the future when she is no longer around (171).[16]

It is perhaps no accident that a good number of the autobiographies by Chinese-born writers are rather abruptly cut off soon after the author's arrival in the United States, in apparent contrast to the structure of immigrant autobiography described in William Boelhower's typology (*Immigrant*

Autobiography 25–52). Unlike the European works cited by Boelhower, these do not chronicle the author's experience of encountering and coming to terms with American culture. While only further study can elucidate this observed difference, one might venture a guess on its cause: the Chinese authors may have sensed how far American interest in their life writings is based on the image of otherness, on exotic scenery and alien cultural practices. As the autobiographers become Americanized, the fascination they hold for the reader would fade; hence the sketchy coverage of their experience in the United States.[17]

Some American-born Chinese autobiographers also seem to have adopted the narrative stance of a cultural guide, though the presence of the audience is more implicit in their works than in Lee's or Kuo's. *Father and Glorious Descendant*, by Pardee Lowe (a contemporary and friend of Kuo's), abounds in descriptions of Chinatown customs and rituals, such as *tong* banquets, Chinese New Year festivities, celebration of the father's "Great Birthday," preparation of unusual (by Western standards) foods, and funeral practices. The name of the Lowes' ancestral village in China, Sahn Kay Gawk, is periodically rendered by the quaint circumlocution "The-Corner-of-the-Mountain-Where-the-Water-Falls," although that etymological information has been given on the first page of the book. Two chapters are devoted to a series of letters between Father and his cousin, written in a comically florid, heavily literal prose purporting to be a translation of classical Chinese (249–58). Lowe's handling of the English language betrays a habitual awareness of the white audience's need to be surprised and amused by the mystifying ways of the Chinese. Jade Snow Wong's autobiography, *Fifth Chinese Daughter*, shares with Lowe's an emphasis on Chinatown customs and rituals; with Lee's and Kuo's, a tendency to intersperse the narrative of her life with discursive segments of information on Chinese culture. A description of a dinner party for her American friends includes a step-by-step record of how egg foo young and tomato beef are cooked; an account of a visit to a Chinatown herbalist for her cough is interrupted by a clarification of the Chinese medical theory of humors (160–62, 224).[18]

Although there is much else in Lowe's and Wong's books besides these gestures of consideration for the sensibilities of white readers, it is undeniable that both of these authors, like their Chinese-born counterparts, are conscious of their role as cultural interpreters who can obtain a measure of recognition from whites for the insider's insight they can offer. The title of a chapter in Wong's book, "Rediscovering Chinatown," aptly epitomizes one way American-born Chinese may make peace with their cultural background in the face of intense assimilative pressures: to return to one's ethnic heritage with selective enthusiasm, reassessing once-familiar (and once-despised) sights and sounds according to their acceptability to white tastes.

As a form characterized by simultaneous subjectivity and objectivity, simultaneous expression and documentation (e.g., Stone 10–11; Sands 57), autobiography easily creates in its readers expectations of "privileged access" (Olney, "Autobiography and the Cultural Moment" 13) to the experience and vision of an entire people. From an intraethnic point of view, the writing of autobiography may be valued as a means of preserving memories of a vanishing way of life, and hence of celebrating cultural continuity and identity; in an interethnic perspective, however, the element of *display*, whether intentional or not, is unavoidable. Many "outsiders" will thus approach ethnic autobiographies with the misguided conviction that the authors necessarily speak for "their people." The practice of reading autobiography for "cultural authenticity" may be a particularly serious danger for Chinese-American autobiography, given the group's unique situation in United States society. The ancestral land of Chinese Americans, due to its long history, sophisticated civilization, and complex encounters with American imperialism in recent history, casts an inordinately strong spell on the white imagination. Moreover, Chinese Americans, who have been subjected to genocidal immigration policies,[19] are placed in the situation of permanent guests who must earn their keep by adding the spice of variety to American life—by selectively maintaining aspects of traditional Chinese culture and language fascinating to whites. In the terminology of Werner Sollors, if the essence of the American experience is the formation of a society based on "consent" rather than "descent," Chinese Americans have clearly been (and still are) excluded from participation in "consent" by the dominant group's insistence on the primacy of their "descent." The irony is that many readers from within the ethnic group itself have, like the detractors of *The Woman Warrior*, inadvertently contributed to this simplified and often condescending view by likewise positing a direct pipeline of cultural authenticity between the collectivity and the individual. The idea of overdetermination by "descent" is thus left unchallenged. Demanding "representativeness," the Chinese-American critics of Kingston differ from the white literary tourists only in the version of cultural authenticity subscribed to.

This tension between "consent" and "descent" is reminiscent of W. E. B. Du Bois's well-known concept of "double consciousness."[20] The writers are aware of themselves as "insiders" with unique experiences that cannot be fully captured by ethnic categories alone. On the other hand, they cannot but sense the "outsiders'" constant gaze upon their skin color, their physiognomy, their "difference." Their American right of "consent"—here taking the form of the freedom to create literature true to their felt lives—is perpetually called into question or qualified by reader expectations based on "descent." Some Chinese-American autobiographers have, indeed, sought distinction in their exotic "descent," allowing the dominant group's perceptions to define their identity. However, it is important to recognize that Kingston has taken an altogether different path in *The Woman Warrior*. The protagonist has eschewed the facile authority which self-appointment as guide and spokesperson could confer on her. The discursive space occupied by *The Woman Warrior* is between the two poles of the "double consciousness"; the audience the narrator addresses in the second person is composed of fellow Chinese Americans sharing the protagonist's need to establish a new Chinese-American selfhood:

> Chinese-Americans, when you try to understand what things in you are Chinese, how do you separate what is peculiar to childhood, to poverty, insanities, one family, your mother who marked your growing with stories, from what is Chinese? What is Chinese tradition and what is the movies? (6)

Boelhower writes:

> In the mixed genre of autobiography, . . . the question of identity involves matching the narrator's own self-perception with the self that is recognized by others, so as to establish a continuity between the two (self and world), to give a design of self-in-the-world. ("Brave New World" 12)

If the "others" are the potential "misreaders" among her white audience, Kingston is in truth far less obsessed than her critics with "the self that is recognized by others." There are, of course, other "others" in the protagonist's lonely struggle: her Chinese family, relatives, fellow "villagers," whose perceptions of her do not match her self-perceptions either. "Descent" notwithstanding, connection to them has to be forged, which can take place only after an initial recognition of difference. Neither American nor Chinese culture, as given, offers a resting place; the protagonist of *The Woman Warrior* has to discover that there is "[n]o higher listener. No higher listener but myself" (237). Her project is to reach "an avowal of values and a recognition of the self by the self—a choice carried out at the level of essential being—not a revelation of a reality given in the advance but a corollary of an active intelligence" (Gusdorf 44). This project is so bold, so unfamiliar, that even her fellow Chinese Americans sometimes mistake it for the accommodationism of earlier autobiographers. For resemblances can indeed be found between *The Woman Warrior* and its predecessors—like Lee, Kingston retells Chinese tales heard in childhood; like Kuo, she makes general remarks on Chinese culture; like Lowe, she speaks of unusual Chinese foods; like Wong, she recounts experiences of sexist oppression. The crucial question is whether these resemblances are merely superficial or whether they bespeak a basic commonality in autobiographical stance. Only a careless reader, I submit, would be able to conclude that Kingston's stance in *The Woman Warrior* is that of the trustworthy cultural guide.

For the "native" in this case, having been born and raised in "ghost country" without benefit of explicit parental instruction in cultural practices, is barely more enlightened than an "outsider" would be: "From the configuration of food my mother set out, we kids had to infer the holidays" (215). Quite unlike the generalizations about Chinese culture in *I've Come a Long Way* or *Father and Glorious Descendant*, which are meant to be encapsulations of superior knowledge, those in *The Woman Warrior* bespeak a tentative groping toward understanding. From fragmentary and haphazard evidence, the protagonist has to piece together a coherent picture of the culture she is enjoined to preserve against American influence. The effort is so frustrating that she exclaims in exasperation: "I don't see how they kept up a continuous culture for five thousand years. Maybe they didn't; maybe everyone makes it up as they go along" (216). But the point, of course, is that the Chinese who remain in Chinese-dominant communities would have no trouble at all transmitting culture through osmosis. It is the protagonist's American-born generation who must "make it up as they go along." The emigrant parents' expectation of a "continuous culture" is, if entirely human, ahistorical and therefore doomed. (So, one might add, is the critics' similar demand for cultural authenticity. Purity is best preserved by death; history adulterates).

Given *The Woman Warrior*'s situation in the broader cultural timescape of Chinese America, then, the so-called distortions of traditional Chinese culture found in the text are simply indications of how far removed from it the protagonist has become. As Debra Woo rightly observes, "where culture is problematic as a source of identity, cultural ignorance itself is part of what is authentic about the experience" (186). Thus the substitution of "heavenly chicken" for "field chicken" is not exoticization but an example of how a young Chinese child in an English-dominant society may misunderstand a tonal language. The protagonist's cosmological speculations on the omnipresent number six (91), involving a misinterpretation of *dai luk* (which in Cantonese pronunciation can be "the big six," a nonexistent col-

location, or "the big continent/the mainland"), betray her "craving for coherence" in the face of a bewildering mass of unexplained cultural data
(Hsu 434). It is not an actual Chinese fortune-teller who confuses the ho-
mophones, which might have justified the charge of willful distortion on
Kingston's part; the phrase "the Big Six" is framed by the young girl's
meditation on her mother's life, the fortune-teller a fictive one whom she
imagines her mother consulting.

It is, in fact, essential to recognize that the entire *Woman Warrior* is a sort
of meditation on what it means to be Chinese American. To this end, the
protagonist appropriates whatever is at hand, testing one generalization
after another until a satisfactory degree of applicability to her own life is
found. As she says of the differing versions of the No Name Woman's story:
"Unless I see her life branching into mine, she gives me no ancestral help"
(10). The aphoristic statements about Chinese ways interspersed in the
narrative—"Women in the old China did not choose" (7); "Chinese communication was loud, public" (13); "Among the very poor and the wealthy,
brothers married their adopted sisters, like doves" (14)—are not offered for
the benefit of readers hungry for tidbits of anthropological information.
Rather, they are threads in a larger tapestry of inferences, some sturdy,
some thin, which the protagonist weaves for her own use. Rejecting the
theory that the aunt is a "wild woman" (9) or a passive rape victim, the
narrator decides on a version relevant to her life in an immigrant family: a
story of assertion of "private life" (14) against the harsh demands of group
survival.

Even with material that tempts with its air of certainty, the protagonist
finds it necessary to tailor-make meanings from altered details. Thus she
spurns the simplistic lesson of the traditional Fa Mu Lan tale, creating instead a potentially subversive woman warrior to whom even traditions
yield. While the heroine of "Mulan Shi" sees herself merely as a second-
best substitute for an aged father (there being no elder son to take his
place), the little girl in "White Tigers" is a *chosen* one, destined to be called
away by "immortals." Martial artists typically pass on their skills to sons or
male disciples; the old couple in the mountains, in contrast, devote years
exclusively to her training. For the traditional Mulan, the campaigns are
but a detour; at the end of the poem, the erstwhile general puts on
makeup, ready to resume her interrupted feminine life. Kingston's Fa Mu
Lan chooses wifehood and motherhood in the midst of battle. Her fellow
villagers know of her identity before her triumphant return from battle
(43); their relinquishment of their precious sons to her army is thus an affirmation of faith in her female power. Of course, the very necessity of

male disguise means that the narrator's fantasized challenge to patriarchy can never be complete; in the last analysis, she would like to be remembered for "perfect filiality" (54). Yet even Fa Mu Lan's return to her parents' house has an element of active choice. All in all, working within the constraints of internalizaed values, the protagonist has done her best to make of unpromising material an inspiring, if not entirely radical, tale.

The treatment of the T'sai Yen story (241–43) follows much the same pattern of sifting out details to arrive at a relevant meaning. Kingston's retelling omits a crucial scene in the original "Eighteen Stanzas for a Barbarian Reed Pipe":[21] T'sai Yen's painful leave-taking from her half-barbarian sons. Though by now attached to her captor and heartsick at the prospect of never seeing her children again, T'sai Yen nevertheless chooses Han lands as her real home, negating the twelve years spent in the steppes as a mere unfortunate interlude. Herself a half-barbarian to her China-obsessed parents (Whenever my parents said 'home,' they suspended America" [116]), the narrator might have found such a detail too close for comfort, and too contrary in spirit to her own undertaking of forming a Chinese-American self. Thus we find a shift of emphasis: the last pages of *The Woman Warrior* celebrate not return from the remote peripheries to a waiting home but the creation of a new center through art. Singing a song that transcends cultural boundaries, T'sai Yen can now leave "her tent to sit by the winter campfires, ringed by barbarians" (243).

As with the "Eighteen Stanzas," the moral that the protagonist draws from the assorted Chinese ghost stories diverges from the one intended by the source. No automatic authority on Chinese culture simply by virtue of "descent," the protagonist must resort to public, written texts in her quest for meanings not forthcoming in her mother's private oral tradition. Contrary to one critic's judgment that the Mandarin transliteration of some names in *The Woman Warrior* betrays how Kingston passes library research for her Cantonese mother's bedtime stories,[22] Kingston does not attempt to cover her trails, as any self-respecting cultural guide would. She provides dates with the Mandarin names and identifies the source, "the research against ghost fear published by the Chinese Academy of Science" (Zhong-guo Kexueyuan Wenxueyanjiusuo 104). The lesson she constructs to make sense of her experiences in a frugal immigrant family—"Big eaters win" (105)—bears little relation to the political allegory of the Communist-compiled anthology. But what matters is not the fit (for which Procrustean beds are notorious). The most useful lesson the protagonist can learn from her research is that a passive staking of her life on some preestablished reality, like looking up *Ho Chi Kuei* (237–38) in a dictionary filled with decontextualized definitions, will always prove fruitless.

The narrator's methodology of self-redemption is thus remarkably consistent. Over and over, we find her forgoing the security of ready-made cultural meanings, opting instead to painstakingly mold a new set suited to her condition as a Chinese-American woman. The many questions about "facts" plaguing the narrator—Were there an Oldest Daughter and Oldest Son who died in China (120)? Did Brave Orchid cut her frenum (190)? Did the hulk exist or was he made up (239)?—function much like a series of Zen *koan*, frustrating because impossible to answer by appeal to an external authority (mother, in this case). In the end, realization of their very impossibility frees her to explore the fecund uncertainties of her Chinese-American existence.

The readers who fault *The Woman Warrior* for not being more responsible toward "facts" would do well to meditate on their own *koan*. To read departures from traditional material found in *The Woman Warrior* as Kingston's cynical manipulations of naïve white readers, as her critics have done, is not only to fly in the face of textual evidence but to belittle the difficulty and urgency of the imaginative enterprise so necessary to the American-born generation: to make sense of Chinese and American culture from its own viewpoint (however hybrid and laughable to "outsiders"), to articulate its own reality, and to strengthen its precarious purchase on the task of self-fashioning. The Fa Mu Lan story itself, which many of Kingston's critics take to be a fixed and sacred given, actually exists in a multitude of Chinese texts differing from each other in purpose as well as detail.[23]

Kingston's critics have been measuring *The Woman Warrior* "against some extra-textual order of fact," not realizing that this order is "based in its turn on other texts (dignified as documents)" (Eakin 23): an ideologically uplifting version of Chinese-American history revising earlier racist texts, a version of the Fa Mu Lan legend sufficiently hoary to be considered "historical." The critics' concern is understandable in view of widespread ignorance about the sociopolitical context of Chinese-American literary creation, the inherent duality of the autobiographical genre (which encourages reading for "cultural authenticity"), the existence of autobiographies by both Chinese- and American-born writers promising privileged glimpses into the group's secret life and the apparent similarities between them and Kingston's work. These issues are, indeed, vital ones generalizable to other ethnic American autobiographies, even to all ethnic American literatures. Nevertheless, intent on liberating Chinese-American writers from one set of constraints, Kingston's detractors have imposed another, in the meantime failing to take note of the most fundamental freedom of all that *The Woman Warrior* has wrested from a priori generic categories and cultural prescriptions: the freedom to create in literature a sui generis Chinese-American reality.

I am grateful to King-Kok Cheung, Samuel Cheung, Maxine Hong Kingston, Kathy Lo, Stephen Sumida, Shelley Wong, Deborah Woo, and Yiheng Zhao for their assistance in the writing of this essay, and to James Payne for his many valuable suggestions on revision. I am solely responsible for its content.

Notes

1. For example, both Juhasz and Rabine relate the unconventional narrative structure of *The Woman Warrior* to the feminist act of creating identity, although their interpretations differ.

2. Personal communication to the author from Kingston, 21 May 1988; quoted with her permission.

3. On the "real" and the "imaginary," Kingston writes: "My idea [in *The Woman Warrior* and *China Men*] was to invent a new form for telling my stories and thoughts. I needed a form in which I could have real, true human beings who have very imaginative minds tell their lives and dreams. My real characters have artful minds, the minds of fiction writers and storytellers." Personal communication to the author, 21 May 1988; quoted with Kingston's permission.

4. For example, Brave Orchid's encounter with the "Sitting Ghost"; the Chinese stories of big eaters who devour ghosts and other monsters (104–6); the protagonist's girlhood interactions with many types of "ghosts" (113–16); and Moon Orchid's reunion with her husband, both now having entered the "land of ghosts" (178).

5. For a reading of the multilayered significance of the term *ghost*, see Sato, who demonstrates how Kingston's rendering of *kuei* focuses many aspects of Chinese-American life and is hardly a "whitewashed" usage.

6. This version of the name appears to be a composite of Cantonese and Mandarin transliterations, *Fa Muk Lan* and *Hua Mu Lan*—another "impurity"?

7. The prolonged training in still "stances" and feats of balance (like sleeping on a rope), the copying of animal movements, and the gaining of control over normally involuntary bodily functions are standard fare in *wuxia xiaoshuo*. The "calling" of a chosen one for spiritual discipline, the hermit's retreat on misty mountains, the magic water gourd, and the cultivation of immortality are images from *shenxian* stories, which have passed fully into the Chinese popular mind. These and other

features from folk traditions found in *The Woman Warrior* would be familiar to children growing up in a Chinese community.

8. A translation of "The Ballad of Mulan" may be found in Liu and Lo 77–80 (cited in Chua).

9. *Outlaws of the Marsh*, a classic in Chinese literature, is based on oral tales depicting peasant heroes who form "righteous armies" to defy the corrupt imperial government. The earliest extant written version dates from the sixteenth century. The English title of Shapiro's recent translation, rather than the older *Water Margin*, is used here.

10. Note that in her next book, *China Men*, Kingston has included a list of discriminatory legislation against Chinese-Americans. "The reviews of my first book made it clear that people didn't know the history—or that they thought I didn't. While I was writing about *China Men*, I just couldn't take that tension any more" (Pfaff 26; cited in Kim xvii).

11. Fong cites her relationship with a "warm, generous and loving father" (68–69) to support her complaint against *The Woman Warrior*.

12. The critics of *The Woman Warrior* supply almost a textbook example of the assumptions about autobiography, common prior to the recent shifting of critical focus from *bios* to *autos*, described by Olney, "Autobiography and the Cultural Moment" 20.

13. Chinese-American literature has a large Chinese-language component, the exclusive domain of immigrant writers, which is only beginning to be studied and translated. This component falls outside the scope if this essay, but one should note that it contains very few autobiographies.

A Partial list (in chronological order) of works explicitly presented as autobiography, of varying literary interest and popularity, include Lee Yan Phou's *When I Was a Boy in China* (1887), Yung Wing's *My Life in China and America* (1909), Helena Kuo's *I've Come a Long Way* (1942), Pardee Lowe's *Father and Glorious Descendant* (1943), Jade Snow Wong's *Fifth Chinese Daughter* (1945), *Su-ling Wong* (pseud.) and Earl Herbert Cressy's *Daughter of Confucius: A Personal History* (1952), Jade Snow Wong's *No Chinese Stranger* (1975), Thomas York-Tong Goo's *Before the Gods* (1976), Maxine Hong Kingston's *The Woman Warrior* (1976), and Katherine Wei and Terry Quinn's *Second Daughter: Growing Up in China, 1930–1949* (1984).

14. See Kim's discussion of "ambassadors of goodwill" in her chapter on early Asian immigrant writers (24–29).

15. Goo, who undergoes assimiliation into Chinese culture in China, is an exception to this pattern.

16. A passage in Korean American Younghill Kang's fictionalized autobiography, *East Goes West* (1937), provides an interesting gloss on the practice of "cultural guiding," which is apparently generalizable from Chinese to other Asian-American

autobiographies. Kim, an older Korean exile, advises the protagonist Chungpa Han to retain his classical Oriental learning: "You have to eat. And to eat, you must enter into the economic life of Americans. . . . In making a living, Oriental scholarship may help you more than your American education. . . . [I]n such a field, you would have the advantage. There would be less competition. . . . *You must be now like a Western man approaching Asia.* . . . As a transplanted scholar, this is the only road I could point to, for your happy surviving" (277–78; my italics). Despite his rhetoric of cultural catholicity, what Kim is suggesting is really a kind of self-Orientalization.

17. This possibility is further explored in my "Immigrant Autobiography: Some Questions of Definition and Approach."

18. Recipes are again included in the sequel to *Fifth Chinese Daughter, No Chinese Stranger* (e.g., 187–88). In the latter, Wong and her husband lead tours to the Far East, thus making cultural interpretation their trade.

19. The Chinese Exclusion Act, passed in 1882 to keep out Chinese laborers, as well as subsequent anti-Chinese measures (including antimiscegenation laws and laws prohibiting laborers' wives from entering), created a "bachelor society" unable to reproduce itself. The situation did not begin to change until the Exclusion Act was repealed in 1943.

20. This concept has been related by more than one scholar (e.g., Rubin 75; Rampersad 13) to the duality of autobiography.

21. Rorex and Fong provide a complete translation of the poem as well as color illustrations from a traditional scroll. Kingston's use of the T'sai Yen material is discussed in greater detail in my forthcoming "Kingston's Handling of Traditional Chinese Sources."

22. Statement delivered by Marlon Hom at the round-table discussion, "Asian American Literature: State of the Art and Criticism," Fifth National Conference of the Association for Asian American Studies, 26 Mar. 1988, Washington State University, Pullman.

23. According to Zhao 77-79, since the Tang dynasty (618–907) there have been many versions of the Fa Mu Lan story, some poetic, others operatic or novelistic. One Qing dynasty (1644–1911) version features a sister; another adds a cowardly cousin. During the Anti–Japanese War (1937–45), the Fa Mu Lan story was frequently staged as plays, with the moral modified to emphasize nationalism (even though the "original" heroine was not Han but a member of a northern tribe). I have seen a film version from the 1960s sung in *huangmeidiao*, a variety of popular Chinese opera, available in videotape rental outlets serving Chinese-American communities. This version includes statements on the equality of the sexes reflecting modern, Westernized ideas.

Works Cited

Boelhower, William. "The Brave New World of Immigrant Autobiography." *MELUS 9*, no. 2 (1982): 5–23.

————. *Immigrant Autobiography in the United States.* Verona: Essedue, 1982.

Bruss, Elizabeth. *Autobiographical Acts: The Changing Situation of a Literary Genre.* Baltimore: Johns Hopkins UP, 1976.

Chan, Jeffrey Paul. "Jeff Chan, Chairman of SF State Asian American Studies, Attacks Review." *San Francisco Journal,* 4 May 1977, 6.

Chang, Diana. *Frontiers of Love.* New York: Random, 1956.

Chin, Frank. "The Most Popular Book in China." *Quilt* 4 (1984): 6–12.

———— "This is Not an Autobiography." *Genre* 18, no. 2 (1985): 109–30.

Chin, Frank, Jeffrey Paul Chan, Lawson Fusao Inada, and Shawn Wong, eds. *Aiiieeeee! An Anthology of Asian-American Writers.* 1974. Rpt. Washington, DC: Howard UP, 1983.

Chu, Louis. *Eat a Bow of Tea.* Seattle: U of Washington P, 1961.

Chua, Cheng Lok. "Golden Mountain: Chinese Versions of the American Dream in Lin Yutang, Louis Chu, and Maxine Hong Kingston." *Ethnic Groups* 4 (1982): 57.

Chuang Hua (pseud.). *Crossings.* New York: Dial, 1968.

Eakin, John Paul. *Fictions in Autobiography: Studies in the Art of Self-Invention.* Princeton: Princeton UP, 1985.

Fong, Katheryn M. "To Maxine Hong Kingston: A Letter." *Bulletin for Concerned Asian Scholars* 9, no. 4 (1977): 67–69.

Gates, Henry Louis, Jr. *Figures in Black: Words, Signs, and the "Racial" Self.* New York: Oxford UP, 1987.

Goo, Thomas York-Tong. *Before the Gods.* New York: Helios, 1976.

Gusdorf, Georges. "Conditions and Limits of Autobiography." Trans. James Olney. In Olney, *Autobiography* 28–48.

Hsu, Vivian. "Maxine Hong Kingston as Psycho-Autobiographer and Ethnographer." *International Journal of Women's Studies* 6, no. 5 (1983): 429–42.

Johnson, Diane. "Ghosts." Rev. of *The Woman Warrior,* by Maxine Hong Kingston. *New York Review of Books,* 3 Feb. 1977, 19+.

Juhasz, Suzanne. "Maxine Hong Kinston: Narrative Technique and Female Identity." In Rainwater and Scheik 173–89.

Kang, Younghill. *East Goes West: The Making of an Oriental Yankee.* Chicago: Follett, 1937.

Kim, Elaine H. *Asian American Literature: An Introduction to the Writings and Their Social Context.* Philadelphia: Temple UP, 1982.

Kingston, Maxine Hong. *China Men.* New York: Knopf, 1980.

————. *The Woman Warrior: Memoirs of a Girlhood among Ghosts.* 1976. New York: Random, 1977.

Krupat, Arnold. "The Indian Autobiography: Origins, Types, and Function." *American Literature* 53, no. 1 (1981): 22–42.

Kuo, Helena. *I've Come a Long Way*. New York: Appleton, 1942.

Larson, Wendy Ann. "Autobiographies of Chinese Writers in the Early Twentieth Century." Diss. U of California, Berkeley. 1984.

Lau, Joseph S. M. [Liu Shaoming]. "Tangrenjie de xiaoshuo shijie" ["The Fictional World of Chinatown"]. *Ming Pao Monthly* 173 (1980): 65–66.

Lee, Yan Phou. *When I Was a Boy in China*. Boston: Lothrop, 1887.

Lim, Genny, ed. *The Chinese American Experience: Papers form the Second National Conference on Chinese American Studies (1980)*. San Francisco: Chinese Historical Society of America and Chinese Culture Foundation, 1980.

Liu, Wu-Chi, and Irving Yucheng Lo, trans. *Sunflower Splendor: Three Thousand Years of Chinese Poetry*. Bloomington: Indiana UP, 1975.

Lowe, Pardee. *Father and Glorious Descendant*. Boston: Little, 1943.

Olney, James. "Autobiography and the Cultural Moment: A Thematic, Historical, and Bibliographical Introduction." In Olney, *Autobiography* 3–27.

———. "Some Versions of Memory/Some Versions of Bios: The Ontology of Autobiography." In Olney, *Autobiography* 236–67.

———, ed. *Autobiography: Essays Theoretical and Critical*. Princeton: Princeton UP, 1980.

Pascal, Roy. *Design and Truth in Autobiography*. Cambridge: Harvard UP, 1960.

Pfaff, Timothy. "Talk with Mrs. Kingston." *New York Times Book Review*, 18 June 1980.

Rabine, Leslie W. "No Lost Paradise: Social Gender and Symbolic Gender in the Writings of Maxine Hong Kingston." *Signs: Journal of Women in Culture and Society* 12, no. 3 (1987): 471–92.

Rainwater, Catherine, and William J. Scheik, eds. *Contemporary American Women Writers: Narrative Strategies*. Lexington: UP of Kentucky, 1985.

Rampersad, Arnold. "Biography, Autobiography, and Afro-American Culture." *Yale Review* 73, no. 1 (1983): 1–16.

Rorex, Robert A., and Wen Fong. *Eighteen Songs of a Nomad Flute: The Story of Lady Wen-Chi*. New York: Metropolitan Museum of Art, 1974.

Rubin, Steven J. "Ethnic Autobiography: A Comparative Approach." *Journal of Ethnic Studies* 9, no. 1 (1981): 75–79.

Sands, Kathleen Mullen. "An American Indian Autobiography." In *Studies in American Indian Literature: Essays and Course Designs*. ed. Paula Gunn Allen. New York: MLA, 1983. 55–65.

Sato, Gayle K. Fujita. "Ghosts as Chinese-American Constructs in Maxine Hong Kingston's *The Woman Warrior*." In *Haunting the House of Fiction: Feminist Perspectives on Ghost Stories by American Women*, ed. Lynette Carpenter and Wendy K. Kolmar. Knoxville: U of Tennessee P, 1991. 193–214.

Shapiro, Sidney, trans. *Outlaws of the Marsh*. Beijing: Foreign Language Press, 1980.

Sollors, Werner. Beyond Ethnicity: Consent and Descent in American Culture. New York: Oxford UP, 1986.

Stone, Albert. "Autobiography in American Culture: Looking Back at the Seventies." *American Studies International* 19, no. 3–4 (1981): 3–14.

Tong, Benjamin R. "Chinatown Popular Culture: Notes toward a Critical Psychological Anthropology." In Lim 233–41.

———. "Critic of Admirer Sees Dumb Racist." *San Francisco Journal*, 11 May 1977, 6.

Wei, Katherine, and Terry Quinn, *Second Daughter: Growing Up in China, 1930–1949.* New York: Holt, 1984.

Wong, Jade Snow. *Fifth Chinese Daughter.* 1945. Rev. ed. New York: Harper, 1950.

———. *No Chinese Stranger.* New York: Harper, 1975.

Wong, Nellie. Review of *The Woman Warrior. Bridge* 6, no. 4 (1978–79): 46–48.

Wong, Sau-ling C. "Immigrant Autobiography: Some Questions of Definition and Approach." In *American Autobiography: Retrospect and Prospect*, ed. Paul John Eakin. Madison: U of Wisconsin P, 1991. 142–70.

———. "Kingston's Handling of Traditional Chinese Sources." *Approaches to Teaching Kingston's The Woman Warrior*, ed. Shirley Geok-lin Lim. New York: MLA, 1991.

Wong, Shawn. *Homebase.* New York: I. Reed, 1979.

Wong, Su-ling (pseud.)., and Earl Herbert Cressy. *Daughter of Confucius: A Personal History.* New York: Farrar, 1952.

Wong, Suzi. Review of *The Woman Warrior. Amerasia Journal* 4, no. 1 (1977): 165–67.

Woo, Deborah. "Maxine Hong Kingston: The Ethnic Writer and the Burden of Dual Authenticity." *Amerasia Journal* 16, no. 1 (1990): 173–200.

Wu, Pei-Yi. "Self-Examination and Confession of Sins in Traditional China." *Harvard Journal of Asiatic Studies* 39, no. 1 (1979): 5–38.

Yep, Laurence. *Dragonwings.* New York: Harper, 1975.

Yung, Wing. *My Life in China and America.* New York: Holt, 1909.

Zhao, Jingshen. *Minzu wenxue xiaoshi [A Brief History of National Literature].* N.p.: Shijie Shuju, 1940.

Zhongguo Kexueyuan Wenxueyanjiusuo [Chinese Academy of Science, Institute of Literary Studies]. *Bupagui de gushi [Stories of Those Who Are Not Afraid of Ghosts].* Hong Kong: San Lian, 1961.

PART II

Gender, Genre, and
"Theory"

Filiality and Woman's Autobiographical Storytelling

SIDONIE SMITH

◆　◆　◆

> It is hard to write about my own mother. What-
> ever I do write, it is my story I am telling, my ver-
> sion of the past. If she were to tell her own story
> other landscapes would be revealed. But in my
> landscape or hers, there would be old, smoldering
> patches of deep-burning anger.
>
> —Adrienne Rich, *Of Woman Born*

SINCE HARRIET MARTINEAU wrote her autobiography in 1856,
many hundreds of women have contributed the story of their lives to
the cultural heritage. Writers, artists, political figures, intellectuals, busi-
nesswomen, actors, athletes—all these and more have marked history in
their own way, both as they lived their lives and as they wrote about them. A
tradition so rich and various presents a challenge to the critic of twentieth-
century autobiography. There is much to be written about the works; indeed, studies of twentieth-century autobiography are beginning to emerge.
Articles now abound. I do not want to conclude this study of women's autobiographies without attention to a contemporary work; but I also realize
that there are many choices that would have served my critical purposes.
Nonetheless, for me at least, no single work captures so powerfully the relationship of gender to genre in twentieth-century autobiography as Maxine
Hong Kingston's *Woman Warrior*.

And so it is fitting to conclude this discussion of women's autobiography
with *The Woman Warrior: Memoirs of a Girlhood among Ghosts*, which is, quite com-
plexly, an autobiography about women's autobiographical storytelling. A
postmodern work, it exemplifies the potential for works from the marginalized to challenge the ideology of individualism and with it the ideology of
gender. Recognizing the inextricable relationship between an individual's

sense of "self" and the community's stories of selfhood, Kingston self-consciously reads herself into existence through the stories her culture tells about women. Using autobiography to create identity, she breaks down the hegemony of formal "autobiography" and breaks out of the silence that has bound her culturally to discover a resonant voice of her own. Furthermore, as a work coming from an ethnic subculture, *The Woman Warrior* offers the occasion to consider the complex imbroglios of cultural fictions that surround the autobiographer who is engaging two sets of stories: those of the dominant culture and those of an ethnic subculture with its own traditions, its own unique stories. As a Chinese American from the working class, Kingston brings to her autobiographical project complicating perspectives on the relationship of woman to language and to narrative.

Considered by some a "novel" and by others an "autobiography," the five narratives conjoined under the title *The Woman Warrior* are decidedly five confrontations with the fictions of self-representation and with the auto-biographical possibilities embedded in cultural fictions, specifically as they interpenetrate one another in the autobiography a woman would write.[1] For Kingston, then, as for the woman autobiographer generally, the hermeneutics of self-representation can never be divorced from cultural representations of woman that delimit the nature of her access to the word and the articulation of her own desire. Nor can interpretation be divorced from her orientation toward the mother, who, as her point of origin, commands the tenuous negotiation of identity and difference in a drama of filiality that reaches through the daughter's subjectivity to her textual self-authoring.

Preserving the traditions that authorize the old way of life and enable her to reconstitute the circle of the immigrant community amidst an alien environment, Kingston's mother dominates the life, the landscape, and the language of the text as she dominates the subjectivity of the daughter who writes that text. It is Brave Orchid's voice, commanding, as Kingston notes, "great power" that continually reiterates the discourses of the community in maxims, talk-story, legends, family histories. As the instrument naming filial identities and commanding filial obligations, that voice enforces the authority and legitimacy of the old culture to name and thus control the place of woman within the patrilineage and thereby to establish the erasure of female desire and the denial of female self-representation as the basis on which the perpetuation of patrilineal descent rests. Yet that same voice gives shape to other possibilities, tales of female power and authority that seem to create a space of cultural significance for the daughter; and the very strength and authority of the material voice fascinates the daughter because it "speaks" of the power of woman to enunciate her own representations. Hence storytelling becomes the means through which Brave Orchid passes on to her daughter all the complexities of and the ambivalences about mother's and daughter's identity as woman in patriarchal culture.[2]

Storytelling also becomes the means through which Kingston confronts those complexities and ambivalences. In dialogic engagement with her mother's word, she struggles to constitute the voice of her own subjectivity, to emerge from a past dominated by stories told to her, ones that inscribe the fictional possibilities of female selfhood, into a present articulated by her own storytelling. Her text reveals the intensity of that struggle throughout childhood and adolescence and the persistance of those conflicts inherent in self-authoring well into adulthood; for, not only is that effort the subject in the text; it is also dramatized by the text. In the first two narratives she re-creates the stories about women and their autobiographical possibilities passed on to her by her mother: first the biographical story of no-name aunt, an apparent victim and thus a negative model of female life scripts, and then the legendary chant of the warrior woman Fa Mu Lan, an apparent heroine and positive model. But as she explores their fates, Kingston questions the very basis on which such distinctions are predicated. Uncovering layer by layer the dynamics and the consequences of her mother's interpretations as they resonate with the memories of her past, the daughter, as she too passes them on to posterity, circles around them, critiquing them, making them her own. Next she reconstructs out of the autobiographical fragments of Brave Orchid's own Chinese experience a biography of her mother, discovering by the way the efficacies of powerful storytelling for the woman who has fallen in status with her translation to another culture. In the fourth piece, an elaborate fabrication played on actual events, she becomes even more keenly attentive to all autobiographical and biographical representations, including her own. Looking back to the beginnings of her own struggle to take a voice, she traces in the final narrative the origins of her own hermeneutics. The apparent line of progress, which as it ends returns us to the beginning, becomes effectively a circle of sorts, a textual alternative to the constricting patriarchal circle Kingston has had to transgress.

"'You must not tell anyone,' my mother said, 'what I am about to tell you. In China your father had a sister who killed herself. She jumped into the family well. We say that your father has all brothers because it is as if she never had been born.'"[3] With the interdiction of female speech, uttered in the name of the father, Kingston's mother succinctly elaborates the circumstances of the sister's suicide. The concise maternal narrative concludes with forceful injunctions and powerful maxims inscribing the filial obligations of daughters in the patriarchal order: "'Don't let your father know that I told you. He denies her. Now that you have started to menstruate, what happened to her could have happened to you. Don't humiliate us. You wouldn't like to be forgotten as if you had never been born. The villagers are watchful'" (5). Kingston thus situates the origins of her autobiography in her recollection of the story her mother used to contextualize the moment of transition ineradicably marking female identity and desire. That event, as it proclaims woman's sexual potency, proclaims also woman's problematic placement within the body social, economic, politic, and symbolic.[4] While her body, the locus of patrilineal preservation, will be contracted out to male authority to serve as the carrier of legitimate sons and of the order those sons perpetuate, it will always remain a potential source of disruption and disintegration in the community: It may provide no sons for the line of descent; or it may entertain strangers and thus introduce illegitimate children and an alternative genealogy into the order.[5] Should a daughter opt for the latter (infilial) alternative, warns the mother, the patriarchal order will work efficiently to punish her transgression of the contract, eliminating her body and name from the world of things and of discourse. Kingston's aunt has suffered this fate: Her family, like the villagers, has enacted its own cleansing ritual; and Kingston's mother has perpetuated the ritual in the very way she tells the story. The aunt's name remains unuttered; and her interpretation of events is sacrificed, within the mother's text, to concern for the villagers' actions. Only her body assumes significance as it reveals the sign of its transgression, as it plugs up the family well,

The mother's cautionary tale at once affirms and seeks to cut off the daughter's kinship with a transgressive female relative and her unrepressed sexuality.[6] Kingston acknowledges the effectiveness of that strategy by revealing later in the narrative that for a long time she accepted her mother's interpretation and kept her counsel, thereby colluding in the perpetuation of both her own silencing and the erasure of her aunt's name:

> I have believed that sex was unspeakable and words so strong and fathers so frail that "aunt" would do my father mysterious harm. I have thought that my family, having settled among immigrants who had also been their neighbors in the ancestral land, needed to clean their name, and a wrong

word would incite the kinspeople even here. But there is more to this silence: they want me to participate in her punishment. And I have. (18)

Now, however, at the moment of autobiographical writing, Kingston resists identification with mother and father by breaking the silence, returning to the story that marked her entrance into sexual difference and constituting her own interpretation of events. She comes to tell another story,
seeking to name the formerly unnamed—the subjectivity of her aunt. As
she does so, she imagines her aunt in a series of postures toward that excess
of sexuality signified by the growth of her womb. Initially dismissing the
probability that "people who hatch their own chicks and eat embryos and
the heads for delicacies and boil the feet in vinegar for party food, leaving
only the gravel, eating even the gizzard lining—could . . . engender a
prodigal aunt" (7), she imagines her aunt the victim of rape, fearful, silent,
and vulnerable before her victimizer. But she suspends that narrative line,
apparently dissatisfied with its unmitigated emphasis on female powerlessness and willlessness. Beginning again, Kingston enters her aunts's subjectivity from another perspective, preferring to see her as a willful woman
after "subtle enjoyment." Contemplating this posture, she finds herself increasingly aware of the gaps in her mother's tale, which motivate her to
ask further questions of the story and to piece together an alternative textual genealogy.[7]

Instead of imagining her aunt as one of the "the heavy, deep-rooted
women" who "were to maintain the past against the flood, safe for returning" (9), and thus as victim, she imagines her as a woman attuned to "a secret voice, a separate attentiveness" (13), truly transgressive and subversive.
The fruit of her womb becomes the mark exposing the priority of her desire for sexuality and autobiographical inscription. Indeed, the expansion
of her very body and of her sense of her own authority to define herself ultimately challenges the ontological roots of her culture—"the real"; for
publicized female subjectivity points to the fundamental vulnerability of
the patrilineage by exposing it as a sustained fiction.[8] The alternative genealogy thus engendered breaks the descent line, subverting the legitimacy of male succession that determines all lines in patriarchy—descent
lines, property lines, and lines of texts.[9] "The frightened villagers, who de-
pended on one another to maintain the real," writes Kingston, "went to
my aunt to show her a personal, physical representation of the break she
had made in the 'roundness.' Misallying couples snapped off the future,
which was to be embodied in true offspring. The villagers punished her for
acting as if she could have a private life, secret and apart from them" (14).

While her journey across the boundaries that circumscribe the patriarchal order takes the aunt into the unbounded spaces of self-representation,
Kingston acknowledges also that this "rare urge west" (9) leads her into the
vast spaces of alienation, fearlessness, and death. Expelled from the family
circle, her aunt becomes "one of the stars, a bright dot in blackness, without
home, without a companion, in eternal cold and silence" (16). While the
endless night proposes limitless identities beyond the confining borders of
repetitious patriarchal representations, it promotes the "agoraphobia" attending any move beyond the carefully prescribed boundaries of ancestral,
familial, and community paradigms of female self-representation. Overwhelmed by the vast spaces of possibility, the aunt returns to the genealogical source, reestablishing her cultural "responsibility" by giving birth in the
pigsty—"to fool the jealous, pain-dealing gods, who do not switch piglets"
(16)—and then by killing herself and her child—"a child with no descent
line would not soften her life but only trail after her, ghostlike, begging her
to give it purpose" (17). From one point of view, then, the aunt enacts on her
own body and her own alternative genealogical text the punishment of the
tribe, fulfilling her filial responsibilities to her circle by eliminating the
source of contamination from its center and thereby restoring it to its unbroken configuration. She thus returns to the silence that defines her condition and her identity. From another point of view, however, the aunt's suicide continues her rebellion in a congeries of ways.[10] First, she brings back
with her to the center of her natal circle the two loci of greatest pollution in
Chinese culture—the moments of birth and death.[11] Second, by jumping
back into the circle—the family well—she contaminates, in a recapitulated
gesture of disruption, the water that literally and symbolically promises the
continuance of patrilineal descent and the symbolic order it nourishes.
Third, she takes with her the secret of paternal origins, never revealing the
name of the father. Saving the father's face, she paradoxically erases the paternal trace, betraying in yet another way the fundamental fragility of
undisputed paternal authority. Finally, by withholding from her natal
family the name of the offender whose actions have caused such disgrace,
she denies them the means to recover face by enacting their own revenge
on the violator.[12] Thus, while she seems to capitulate before the monolithic
power of the order against which she has transgressed, Kingston envisions
her as a "spite suicide," an antiheroine whose actions subvert the stability of
an order that rests on the moral imperatives of filial obligations, including
sexual repression. Her very silence becomes a powerful presence, a female
weapon of vengeance. Toward the end of this imaginative portrait, Kingston
returns once again to her mother's tale by repeating the earlier refrain:

"'Don't tell anyone you had an aunt. Your father does not want to hear her name. She has never been born'" (18). Yet while Kingston repeats her mother's words, she does so with a critical difference. Unlike her mother, she engenders a story for her aunt, fleshing out the narrative and incorporating the subjectivity previously denied that woman. Individualizing her mother's cautionary and impersonal fate, she transforms in the process both her aunt's text and her aunt's body from a maxim (a mere vessel to hold patriarchal signifiers) into a "life." Moreover, she ensures that she herself becomes more than a mere vessel perserving her mother's maxims, however deeply they may be embedded in her consciousness. For the story of this "forerunner," her "urge west" and her agoraphobia, becomes a piece in the puzzle of her own erased and erasable identity: "Unless I see her life branching into mine, she gives me no ancestral help" (10). And so, the filiations of her own story stretch backward to her aunt's, and the filiations of her aunt's story stretch forward to her own, as the two lives interpenetrate, crossing narrative boundaries in the text as Kingston interweaves her childhood experiences in the immigrant community encircling her with the imaginative biography of her aunt.

Kingston retrieves her aunt from the oblivion of sexuality repressed and textuality erased by placing her in an alternative narrative: the line of matrilineal descent to which she traces her origins and through which she gives voice to her subjectivity. Like her aunt's before her, this transgression of the injunction to filial silence challenges the priority of patrilineal descent. Allowing her imagination to give voice to the body of her aunt's text, Kingston expresses in her own way the excess of narrative (textuality) that links her intimately to that earlier excess of sexuality she identifies in her aunt. Indeed, her aunt becomes her textual "child," product of the fictions through which Kingston gives "birth" to her, and, by the way, to herself. Her story thus functions as a sign, like her aunt's enlarging belly, publicizing the potentially disruptive force of female textuality and the matrilineal descent of texts.

On the level of her mother's tale, then, the originating story of Kingston's autobiography testifies to the power of the patriarchy to command through mothers the silence of daughters, to name and to unname them, and thereby to control their meaning in discourse itself. On another level the opening piece displaces the mother's myth with the daughter's, thereby subverting the interpretations on which patrilineal descent and filial responsibilities are predicated and establishing a space in which female desire and self-representation can emerge. Yet Kingston concludes with a word of caution:

My aunt haunts me—her ghost drawn to me because now, after fifty years of neglect, I alone devote pages of paper to her, though not origamied into houses and clothes. I do not think she always means me well. I am telling on her, and she was a spite suicide, drowning herself in the drinking water. The Chinese are always frightened of the drowned one, whose weeping ghost, wet hair hanging and skin bloated, waits silently by the water to pull down a substitute. (19)

As the final sentence suggests, the identification may not be fortuitous, for autobiographical journeys and public self-representations are problematic adventures for daughters to pursue. Kingston does not yet know her aunt's name; and the subjectivity she has created for her remains only another interpretation, a fiction. Nor, by implication, can she be sure that she will ever know the truth about her own past. Her name is never uttered in the text; and her memories and stories may only be fictions too. This maternal trace, disruptive of the patriarchal order, may be potentially as threatening to Kingston as it was to her aunt. Indeed, she may be the child—"it was probably a girl; there is some hope of forgiveness for boys" (18)—that her aunt takes with her to the grave. Ultimately, the full, the "real" story of woman may lead to madness and to self-destruction rather than to legitimate self-representation.

Kingston in the second piece engages another of her mother's representations of female autobiography, a story from which she learned that Chinese girls "failed if we grew up to be but wives and slaves." Here she does not distinguish in quotation marks the words of her mother; rather, she moves directly to her own elaboration of Fa Mu Lan's chant.[13] But she goes further, appropriating not only the chant but also the very body of that legendary woman warrior: The identities of woman warrior and of woman narrator interpenetrate until biography becomes autobiography, until Kingston and Fa Mu Lan are one.[14] Through this fantasy of mythic identification, the adult daughter describes an autobiography of "perfect filiality" through which she fulfills her mother's expectations and garners her mother's unqualified love. Simultaneously, this "life" enables her to escape confinement in conventional female scripts and to enter the realm of heroic masculine pursuits—of education, adventure, public accomplishment, and fame. Ironically, however, Kingston's mythical autobiography betrays the ontological bases on which that love, power, and compliance with perfect filiality rest.

The woman warrior gains her education beyond the engendered circle of community and family in a magical, otherworldly place where male and female difference remains undelineated. Her educators are a hermaphroditic couple beyond childbearing age whose relationship appears to be one of relative equality; and the education they offer encourages her to forge an identity, not through conventional formulations of woman's selfhood, but through a close identification with the creatures of nature and the secrets of natural space.[15] In such a space female sexuality, signaled by the onslaught of puberty, remains a "natural" event rather than a cultural phenomenon situating the girl in a constellation of attitudes toward female pollution and contamination. Nonetheless, that education, while it appears to be liberating, presupposes Fa Mu Lan's total identification with the desires of her family, ubiquitously present even in its absence. For instance, she passively watches in the gourd as her own wedding ceremony takes place despite her absence, the choice of husband entirely her parents' prerogative. Ultimately, woman can be trained as warrior only in a space separate from family; but she can enter that space only because her sacrifice to the circle is the basis on which her education takes place at all. Consequently, her empowerment does not threaten to disrupt the representations of the patriarchal circle; on the contrary, it serves both the family and the discourse of gender.

When she returns home, Fa Mu Lan takes her place, not as "woman," but as extraordinary woman—as, that is, man: My parents killed a chicken and steamed it whole, as if they were welcoming home a son" (40). As surrogate son, she replaces her father in battle, eventually freeing her community from the exploitation and terrorization of the barons. Yet she must do more than enact the scenario of male, selfhood. She must erase her sexual difference and publicly represent herself as male, a "female avenger" masquerading in men's clothes and hair styes. And while her sexual desire is not repressed altogether, as in the case of the virginal Joan of Arc to whom Kingston alludes, it must remain publicly acknowledged. Hidden inside her armor and her tent, her "body" remains suppressed in the larger community.[16] It also bears the marks of her textual and sexual appropriation by man: "Now when I was naked, I was a strange human being indeed—words carved on my back and the baby large in front" (47). The lines of text on her back are not her own creation: They are the words by which the father has inscribed his law on her body, wounding her in the process. And her belly is full of a male heir whose birth will ensure the continuance of the patrilineage she serves in her heroism.[17] Finally, and most telling, the narrative's closure asserts the ultimate limitations of the warrior woman's autobiographical possibilities. Fa Mu Lan's story breaks roughly into two parts: the narratives of preparation and public action. It thus reinscribes the traditional structure of androcentric self-representation, driven by a linear-causal progression. Once the revenge carved on her back has been enacted, however, both her life as woman warrior and her autobiography end. Having returned home to unmask herself and to be recuperated as publicly silenced wife and slave, she kneels before her parents-in-law: "'Now my public duties are finished. . . . I will stay with you, doing farmwork and housework, and giving you more sons'" (53–54). There is nothing more to be said by her and of her.

Fa Mu Lan's name, unlike the name of no-name aunt, is passed on from generation to generation, precisely because the lines of her story as woman warrior and the lines of her text as woman autobiographer reproduce an androcentric paradigm of identity and selfhood and thereby serve the symbolic order in "perfect filiality." Since both life and text mask her sexual difference and thereby secure her recuperation in the phallic order by inscribing her subjectivity and her selfhood in the law of the same representation, they legitimate the very structures man creates to define himself, including those structures that silence women.[18]

The heroic figure of Fa Mu Lan thus represents a certain kind of woman warrior, a culturally privileged "female avenger." Embedded in Kingston's fantasy autobiography, however, lies a truly subversive "story" of female empowerment. Imaged as tiny, foot-bound, squeaky-voiced women dependent on male authority for their continued existence, the wives of warriors, barons, and emperors who haunt the interstices of the textual landscape are, in one sense, conventional ghosts. Yet those apparently erased ciphers become, in another sense, the real female avengers:

> Later, it would be said, they turned into the band of swordswomen who were a mercenary army. They did not wear men's clothes like me, but rode as women in black and red dresses. They bought up girl babies so that many poor families welcomed their visitations. When slave girls and daughters-in-law ran away, people would say they joined these witch amazons. They killed men and boys. I myself never encountered such women and could not vouch for their reality. (53)

Such "witch amazons" are figures of all that is unrepressed and violent in ways both sexual and textual, in the narrator herself as well as in the social order. Wielding unauthorized power, they do not avenge the wrongs of fathers and brothers; they lead daughters against fathers and sons, slaying the source of the phallic order itself.[19] Moreover, they do so, not by masking, but by aggressively revealing their sexual difference. Paradoxically, Fa

Mu Lan has liberated the women who subvert the order she serves, just as Kingston the narrator has released the rumor that subverts the story she tells.

Kingston's memories of the real, rather than mythical, childhood also subvert the fiction she has created out of her mother's expectations. Juxtaposing to this autobiography of androcentric selfhood another self-representation that undermines the priority of the fantasy of "perfect filiality," Kingston betrays Fa Mu Lan's story as a fragile fiction only coterminous with the words that inscribe it as myth. And the jarring texture of her recollected experience—its nervous, disjointed, unpoetic, frustrated prose—calls into question the basis for the seamless elegance and almost mystical lyricism of Fa Mu Lan's autobiography.

Kingston recalls the repitition of commonplace maxims that deny female significance ("Feeding girls is feeding cowbirds"; "When you raise girls, you're raising children for strangers"; "Girls are maggots in the rice"); the pressures of a language that conflates the ideographs representing the female "I" and "slave"; the images of poor people snagging their neighbors' flotage with long flood hooks and pushing the girl babies on down the river" (62). All these signs and stories of her culture equate her identity as "girl" with failed filiality and engender in her a profound sense of vulnerability and lack. Thus she remembers how she tried to fulfill her filial obligations in the only way imaginable to her: She works at being a "bad" girl—for, as she asks, "Isn't being a bad girl almost a boy?" (56). She rejects the traditional occupations of femininity: refusing to cook, breaking dishes, screaming impolitely as maxims are mouthed, defiantly telling her parents' friends that she wants to become a lumberjack, bringing home straight A's, those signs from another culture of her extraordinary public achievements. She adopts, that is, the cultural postures of a "son" by generating signs imitative of male selfhood. But her efforts to be the phallic woman do not earn the love and acceptance of her mother and community, as they do Fa Mu Lan. And so her experience gives the lie to that other autobiography: Everywhere the legend is betrayed as a misleading fiction.[20]

In the end, there remains only one residual locus of identity between Kingston and Fa Mu Lan: "What we have in common are the words at our backs. The ideographs for revenge are 'report a crime' and 'report to five families.' The reporting is the vengeance—not the beheading, not the gutting, but the words. And I have so many words—'chink' words and 'gook' words too—that they do not fit on my skin" (63). Her appropriation of the pen, that surrogate sword, and her public inscription of the story of her own childhood among ghosts become the reporting of a crime—the crime of a culture that would make nothing of her by colonizing her and, in so doing, steal her authority and her autobiography from her as her mother's legend would do. In the tale the forces of exploitation remain external to her family; but in her own experience they remain internal, endemic to the patriarchal family whose existence is founded on the colonization and erasure of women in service to the selfhood of men and boys and whose perpetuation is secured through the mother's word. By simultaneously enacting and critiquing that legendary story of female power, Kingston manages to shatter the complacencies of cultural myths, problematic heroines, and the illusory autobiographical possibilities they sanction. By "slaying" the stories of men and boys and phallic women warriors, she allies herself with the true female avengers of her tale. Fa Mu Lan may have denied her identity with such women; Kingston does not.

Whereas the first two narratives explore the consequences of Kingston's appropriation of her mother's stories, the third goes through the stories to the storyteller herself. Three scrolls from China serve as originating locus of this biography of her mother pieced together with "autobiographical" fragments. Texts that legitimate her mother's professional identity as doctor, the scrolls stimulate biography because they announce public achievements, a life text readable by culture. They also announce to the daughter another mother, a mythic figure resident in China who resisted the erasure of her own desire and who pursued her own signifying selfhood. In her daughter's text, Brave Orchid becomes a kind of "woman warrior," whose story resonates with the Fa Mu Lan legend: both women leave the circle of the family to be educated for their mission and both return to serve their community, freeing it through many adventures from those forces that would destroy it. Both are fearless, successful, admired.

Kingston's biography accretes all varieties of evidence testifying to her mother's bravery and extraordinariness. Portrayed as one of the "new women, scientists who changed the rituals" (88), Brave Orchid bears the "horizontal name of one generation" that truly names her rather than the patronym signifying woman's identity as cipher silently bonding the patrilineage. Thus Kingston's awe-filled narration of her mother's confrontation with the Sitting Ghost takes on such synecdochic proportions in the text: "My mother may have been afraid, but she would be a dragoness ('my totem, your totem'). She could make herself not weak. During danger, she fanned out her dragon claws and riffled her red sequin scales and unfolded her coiling green stripes. Danger was a good time for showing off. Like the dragons living in temple eaves, my mother looked down on plain people who were lonely and afraid" (79). The ensuing battle between woman and ghost unfolds as a primal struggle with the dynamics and the rhythms of an attempted rape. A physically powerless victim of the palpably masculine presence who "rolled over her and landed bodily on her chest" (81), Brave Orchid is initially unable to challenge his strength. But she ultimately prevails against the Boulder, defeating him with the boldness of her word and the power of the images she voices to taunt him into submission and cowardice. Such fearlessness and verbal cunning characterize subsequent adventures the daughter invokes: the coexistence with ghosts and strange monsters populating the countryside through which she travels on her way to administer to the sick; the bargain she drives with the slave dealer; her response to the birth of monster babies; and her bold orientation toward food.[21]

Embedded in the daughter's representation of her mother's extraordinariness, however, lies another, a palimpsest that tells of her mother's preoccupation with autobiographical interpretation. Even more important than the story of Brave Orchid's confrontation with the Sitting Ghost is the re-creation of her narrative of the encounter. Skillful in creating compelling stories of her experience, Brave Orchid makes of the ghost a vividly ominous antagonist, thereby authoring herself as powerful protagonist. Such imaging ensures the emboldening of her presence in the eyes and imaginations of the other women (and of her daughter): "'I am brave and good. Also I have bodily strength and control. Good people do not lose to ghosts'" (86). Kingston also suggests that her mother secured the same admiration in other ways. By studying in secret, "she quickly built a reputation for being brilliant, a natural scholar who could glance at a book and know it" (75). Returning to her village, she "wore a silk robe and western shoes with big heels"; thereafter she maintained that posture by never dressing "less elegantly than when she stepped out of the sedan chair"(90). By avoiding treatment of the terminally ill, she ensured that her powers as doctor were magnified. In linguistic and behavioral postures, Brave Orchid orchestrates her public image, inscribes, that is, her own autobiography as extraordinary woman.

The mother's mode of self-authoring complicates the daughter's effort to reconstruct her mother's biography. Brave Orchid's stories about China become the only archival material out of which Kingston can create that "life"; and yet the stories are already "representations" or "fictions" of her experiences before she reaches an America where she is no doctor, where she works daily washing other people's laundry or picking fruit and vegetables in the fields, where she is no longer woman alone but a wife and mother, where she is no woman warrior dressed elegantly in silk. "You have no idea how much I have fallen" (90), she confesses and therein suggests the efficacy of stories and storytelling as means to preserve her extraordinariness. Significantly, the dynamics of the mother's fate recall those of Fa Mu Lan's: Adventures concluded, both return to the home of the husband as wife and slave, there to become the subject of wonderful tales of an earlier glory in a faraway place.

Kingston's narrative, as it interpenetrates her autobiography with her mother's biography reveals how problematic such stories can become for the next generation. From one point of view, they can be exhilarating, creating in children the admiration that is so apparent in Kingston's text. But from another, they generate confusions and ambiguities, since as a child Kingston inflected the narratives with her own subjectivity, attending to another story within the text of female heroism. For Brave Orchid's tales of bravery and exoticism are underwritten by an alternative text of female vulnerability and victimization. The story elaborating the purchase of the slave girl reaffirms the servile status of women and actually gives legitimacy to Kingston's fears her parents will sell her when they return to China. The stories of babies identify femaleness with deformity and suggest to the daughter the haunting possibility that her mother might actually have practiced female infanticide. The story of the crazy lady, scurrying directionless on bound feet, encased in the mirror-studded headdress, caught in her own self-destructive capitulations, dramatizes communal fear of the anomalous woman who embodies the threat of uncontrolled female sexuality and subversive alliances between women—always strangers within the community—and the enemy outside.

All these tales from her mother's past, by reinforcing the representation of women as expendable, resonate with Kingston's sense of displacement in her family and in the immigrant community in America, her confusion about her sexuality, and her fears of her own "deformities" and "madnesses." They leave her with food that suffocates her, a voice that squeaks on her, and nightmares that haunt the long nights of childhood. They also complicate Kingston's sense of identification with her mother by betraying the basis on which her tales of extraordinariness are founded, that is, the powerlessness of ordinary women and children and their cruel and insensitive victimization, even at the hands of Brave Orchid herself. In fact, in her self-representation Kingston identifies herself with the "lonely and afraid," a victim of her mother's stories, and thus no true heroine after her mother's model. Paradoxically, her mother, the shaman with the power of word and food, has, instead of inspiring her daughter to health and heroism, made the daughter sick, hungry, vulnerable, fearful.

In the closing passage of this third narrative, Kingston re-creates her most recent encounter with her mother and, through it, her continuing resistance to her mother's victimizing presence. Ironically, the scene recapitulates the earlier scene of her mother's biography. The dark bedroom, the late hour recall the haunted room at the medical school. Here Brave Orchid is herself the ghost who would continue to haunt her daughter: "My mother would sometimes be a large animal, barely real in the dark; then she would become a mother again" (118). Like Brave Orchid before her, Kingston grasps the only weapon effective in overcoming that ghost—the words with which she resists her. In the syncopated rhythm of statement and rebuttal, she answers her mother's vision of things with her own, challenging unremittingly the power of her mother to control interpretations. She also offers an alternative representation of her mother in this closing scene, portraying her as an old woman, tired, prosaic, lonely, a woman whose illusions of returning to China have vanished, whose stories have become peevish, repetitious. In creating a portrait of her mother as neither fearless nor exotic, the daughter demystifies Brave Orchid's presence and diffuses the power of her word.

For all the apparent rejection of her mother as ghost, the final passage points to a locus of identification between mother and daughter and a momentary rapprochement between the two. In saying goodnight, Kingston's mother calls her Little Dog, a name of endearment unuttered for many years, and, in that gesture of affection, releases her daughter to be who she will. As a result, Kingston experiences the freedom to identify with her; for, as the daughter makes evident in her biography, her mother before her had strayed from filial obligations, leaving her parents behind in pursuit of her own desire: "I am really a Dragon, as she is a Dragon, both of us born in dragon years. I am practically a first daughter of a first daughter" (127). At this moment of closure, Kingston affectionately traces her genealogy as woman and writer to and through her mother in a sincere gesture of filiality, acknowledging as she does so that her autobiography cannot be inscribed outside the biography of her mother, just as the biography of her mother cannot be inscribed outside her own interpretations. Mother and daughter are allied in the interpenetration of stories and storytelling, an alliance captured in the ambiguous reference of the final sentence: "She sends me on my way, working always and now old, dreaming the dreams about shrinking babies and the sky covered with airplanes and a Chinatown bigger than the ones here" (127). As the motifs of the final pages suggest, both mother and daughter are working always and now old.

In the fourth narrative Kingston does not take the word of her mother as her point of narrative origin. She will reveal at the inception of the next piece that the only information she received about the events narrated in the fourth piece came from her brother through her sister in the form of an abrupt, spare bone of a story: "What my brother actually said was, 'I drove Mom and Second Aunt to Los Angeles to see Aunt's husband who's got the other wife'" (189). Out of a single factual sentence, Kingston creates a complex story of the two sisters, Brave Orchid and Moon Orchid. She admits that "his version of the story may be better than mine because of its bareness; not twisted into designs" (189); but the "designs" to which she alludes have become integral to her autobiographical interpretations.

In Kingston's designs Moon Orchid, like Brave Orchid in "Shaman," embodies her name: She is like a flower of the moon, a decorative satellite that revolves around and takes its definition from another body, the absent husband. Mute to her own desire, attendant always on the word of her husband, she represents the traditional Chinese wife, a woman without autobiographical possibilities. "For thirty years," comments her niece, "she had been receiving money from him from America. But she had never told him that she wanted to come to the United States. She waited for him to suggest it, but he never did" (144). Unlike Brave Orchid, she is neither clever nor shrewd, skilled nor quick, sturdy nor lasting. Demure, self-effacing, decorative, tidy, refined—she is as gracefully useless and as elegantly civilized as bound feet, as decoratively insubstantial as the paper cutouts she brings her nieces and nephews from the old country. Having little subjectivity of her own, she can only appropriate as her own the subjectivity of others, spending her days following nieces and nephews through the house, describing what they do, repeating what they say, asking what their words mean. While there is something delightfully childlike, curious, and naive about that narration of other people's lives, there is a more profound sadness that a woman in her sixties, unformed and infantile, has no autobiography of her own.

When her husband rejects her, giving his allegiance to his Chinese-American wife, who can speak English and aid him in his work, he denies the very ontological basis on which Moon Orchid's selfhood is predicated and effectually erases her from the lines of descent. He also undermines with his negation of her role what autobiographical representations she has managed to create for herself. "'You became people in a book I read a long time ago'" (179), he tells the two sisters, dramatically betraying the elusiveness of the "fictions" on which Moon Orchid has sustained her identity as first wife. Once having been turned into a fairy-tale figure from a time long past, this woman loses the core of her subjectivity and literally begins to vanish: She appears "small in the corner of the seat" (174); she stops speaking because the grounds for her authority to speak have been undermined— "All she did was open and shut her mouth without any words coming out" (176); later she stops eating, returning to Brave Orchid's home "shrunken to the bone." Ultimately, she vanishes into a world of madness where she creates repetitious fictions, variations on a story about vanishing without a trace. Thus she fantasizes that Mexican "ghosts" are plotting to snatch her life from her, that "'they' would take us in airplanes and fly us to Washington, D.C., where they'd turn us into ashes. . . . drop the ashes in the wind, leaving no evidence" (184). The tenuousness, evanescence, and elusiveness of identity press on her so that everywhere she sees signs (sees, that is, evidence of the legitimacy of her own interpretations) that alien males threaten to erase her from the world, leaving no trace of her body as her husband has left no trace of her patrilineal existence. To protect herself she withdraws into the "house" of her sister, that edifice that has supported her construction of an identity as first wife. There she literally makes of the house what it has always been metaphorically—a living coffin—windows shut and darkened, "no air, no light," and she makes of storytelling itself a living coffin. As Brave Orchid tells her children, "'The difference between mad people and sane people . . . is that sane people have variety when they talk-story. Mad people have only one story that they talk over and over'" (184). Only after Brave Orchid commits her to a mental institution does she find a new fiction to replace the old one, a renewed identity as "mother" to the other women ("daughters") who can never vanish. In the end the story of vanishing without leaving a trace becomes the only trace that is left of her, an impoverished autobiographical absence.

Her mother Kingston now represents, not as the "new woman" of "Shaman," but as a traditional woman intent on preserving her family from harm by maintaining the old traditions against the erosions of American culture. Through the conventions of speaking (Chinese), eating, greeting, chanting, storytelling, she keeps China drawn around her family in a linguistic and gustatory circle. More particularly, she seeks to preserve the old family constellation and, with it, the identity of woman. Thus, from Brave Orchid's "Chinese" perspective, her sister is a first wife, entitled to certain privileges and rights, even in America. Yet, in her allegiance to the old traditions of filial and affinal obligations, Brave Orchid becomes shortsighted, insensitive, and destructive. She succeeds only in making other women (her niece, who remains trapped in a loveless marriage; her sister, who dies in a mental institution) unhappy, sick, even mad; and she does so because, failing to anticipate just how misplaced the traditions and myths have become in the new world, she trusts her word too well. The stories she tells create illusions that fail of reference to any reality.

The story of the Empress of the Western Palace is a case in point. "'A long time ago,'" Brave Orchid tells her sister on the drive to Los Angeles,

> "the emperors had four wives, one at each point of the compass, and they lived in four palaces. The Empress of the West would connive for power, but the Empress of the East was good and kind and full of light. You are the Empress of the East, and the Empress of the West has imprisoned the Earth's Emperor in the Western Palace. And you, the good Empress of the East, come out of the dawn to invade her land and free the Emperor. You must break the strong spell she has cast on him that has lost him the East." (166)

The myth, however, is an inappropriate text through which to interpret Moon Orchid's experience. The Empress of the West is not conniving; the Emperor does not want freeing; and the Empress of the East cannot break the spell. Moreover, for all Brave Orchid's forceful narratives of the projected meeting among Moon Orchid, the husband, and the second wife, the actual scene is pitifully humorous, squeezed as it is in the backseat of the car. "'What scenes I could make'" (149), she tells her sister; but the only scenes she makes are in her fantasies of them (and her daughter the storyteller is the one who actually makes the scene). Though she is not entirely speechless when they confront Moon Orchid's husband, she is obviously awed by the wealthy, successful, and much younger man, and by the pressure of his young, efficient wife. Kingston creates a Brave Orchid bested in the game of fictionalizations. The husband has turned the two sisters into characters from a book read long ago, a devastating recapitulation of their efforts to turn him into the fictional Emperor. While the power of her myths to help define and situate identities has been eroded by another cultural tradition, Brave Orchid has not been destroyed because, unlike Moon Orchid, she is willful, hardworking, clever, intelligent, shrewd, stubborn, "brave"—all those qualities that have enabled her to cope with and to survive in her translation to another cultural landscape. Moreover, she can always fabricate another story, as she does when she urges her children to sabotage any plans her husband, now in his seventies, might have to marry a second wife. Nonetheless, other women are victimized by her words, their autobiographical possibilities cut off.

Through the "designs" in "At the Western Palace," Kingston confronts explicitly the problematics of autobiographical "fictions." Both Moon Orchid and Brave Orchid serve as powerful negative models for the perils of autobiography. Moon Orchid, bereft of the husband who defines her place and who sets the limits of her subjectivity within the structures of the patrilineage, succumbs to an imagination anchored in no-place, an imaginative rootlessness threatening Kingston herself. Overwhelmed by repetitious fantasies, her aunt vanishes into a world where alien males continually plot to erase her from existence, a preoccupation that resonates with Kingston's childhood fears of leaving no culturally significant autobiographical trace. A woman of no autobiography, Moon Orchid cannot find a voice of her own, or, rather, the only subjectivity that she finally voices is the subjectivity of madness. Brave Orchid, too, serves as a powerful negative model. She would write a certain biography of her sister, patterned after traditional interpretations of the identity of a first wife. In preserving her interpretations, however, she victimizes other women by failing to make a space in her story for female subjectivity in unfamiliar landscapes, by remaining insensitive to her sister's fears and desires, as she remains insensitive to her daughter's desires. Giving her unquestioning allegiance to language, she fails to recognize the danger in words, the perils inherent in the fictions that bind.

In the end Kingston, too, has created only a fiction, an elaborate story out of the one sentence passed by her brother through her sister; and she, too, must beware the danger in words as she constructs her stories of those other women, more particularly her mother. To a certain extent she seems to do so in this fourth narrative. For all the negative, even horrifying, aspects of Brave Orchid's fierce preservation and Moon Orchid's repetitious fantasies, both women come across in this section as fully human. Her mother, especially, does so; and that is because, releasing her mother to be her own character, under her own name "Brave Orchid," rather than as "my mother," the daughter penetrates her mother's subjectivity with tender ironies and gentle mercies. In doing so, she effaces her own presence in the text as character, her presence implied only in the reference to Brave Orchid's "children." Unlike her mother, then, who does not imagine the contours of her sister's subjectivity, Kingston here tries to think like her mother and her aunt. Yet even as she creates the fullness of her mother out of her word, she recognizes the very fictionality of her tale—its "designs" that serve her own hermeneutical purposes. She, too, like her mother within her story, negotiates the world by means of the fictions that sustain interpretations and preserve identities. In the persistent reci-

procities that characterize Kingston's storytelling, her mother becomes
the product of her fictions, as she has been the product of her mother's.

Kingston represents in the final piece, "A Song for for a Barbarian Reed
Pipe," her adolescent struggle to discover her own speaking voice and autobiographical authority. This drama originates in the memory of her
mother's literally cutting the voice out of her: "She pushed my tongue up
and sliced the frenum. Or maybe she snipped it with a pair of nail scissors. I
don't remember her doing it, only her telling me about it, but all during
childhood I felt sorry for the baby whose mother waited with scissors or
knife in hand for it to cry—and then, when its mouth was wide open like a
baby bird's, cut" (190). Notably, Kingston remembers, not the actual event,
but the reconstruction of the event in language, a phenomenon testifying
to the power of the mother's word to constitute the daughter's history, in
this case her continuing sense of confusion, horror, deprivation, and violation. Her mother passes on a tale of female castration, a rite of passage
analogous to a clitoridectomy, that wounding of the female body in service
to the community, performed and thereby perpetuated by the mother.[22] It
is a ritual that results in the denial to woman of the pleasure of giving
voice to her body and body to her voice, the pleasure of autobiographical
legitimacy and authority.

   In her re-creation of the confrontation with the Chinese-American girl
in the bathroom of the Chinese school, Kingston evokes her childhood
confusion about speechlessness: "Most of us," she comments, "eventually
found some voice, however faltering. We invented an American-feminine
speaking personality, except for that one girl who could not speak up even
in Chinese school" (200). A kind of surrogate home, the Chinese school
functions as the repository of old traditions and conventional identities
within the immigrant community; and the bathroom is that most private
of female spaces—only for girls, only for certain acitivities, which, as it lo-
cates the elimination of matter from the body, ultimately becomes associated with female pollution and shame. In that space, Kingston responds
cruelly, even violently, to the female image before her, abhorring the girl's
useless fragility: her neat, pastel clothes; her China-doll haircut; her tiny,
white teeth; her baby-soft, fleshy skin—"like squid out of which the glassy
blades of bones had been pulled," "like tracing paper, onion paper" (206).
Most of all, she abhors her "dumbness," for this girl, who cannot even
speak her name aloud, is ultimately without body or text. "'You're such a
nothing,'" Kingston remembers yelling at her. "'You are a plant. Do you
know that? That's all you are if you don't talk. If you don't talk, you can't

have a personality. You'll have no personality and no hair. You've got to let people know you have a personality and a brain. You think somebody is going to take care of you all your stupid life?'" (210).

Yet, while the girl stands mute before the screaming Kingston, they both weep profusely, wiping their snot on their sleeves as the seemingly frozen scene wraps them both in its embrace. Kingston remembers feeling some comfort in establishing her difference from the girl, taking pride in her dirty fingernails, calloused hands, yellow teeth, her desire to wear black. But the fierceness with which she articulates her desire for difference only accentuates her actual identity with the nameless girl: Both are the last ones chosen by teams; both are silent and "dumb" in the American school. An exaggerated representation of the perfect Chinese girl, this girl becomes a mirror image of Kingston herself, reflecting her own fears of insubstantiality and dumbness (symbolized for her in the zero intelligence quotient that marks her first-grade record). In the pulling of the hair, the poking of the flesh, Kingston captures the violence of her childhood insecurity and self-hatred. Striking the Chinese-American girl, she strikes violently at her own failure to take a voice and at all her mother's prior narratives of female voicelessness. Tellingly, her aggressive attack on that mirror image eventuates, not in the girl's utterance of her name, but in Kingston's eighteen-month illness, which ensures that she indeed does become like the other girl. Confined to bed, isolated inside the house, she is literally silenced in the public space, a fragile and useless girl. Attended always by her family, she too becomes a plant, a nothing. Ironically, she says of that time: "It was the best year and a half of my life. Nothing happened" (212). The admission betrays the tremendous relief of not having to prove to people she has "a personality and a brain," the powerful enticement of succumbing to the implications of her mother's narratives and her culture's maxims, the confusing attractiveness of not having to find a public voice, of not struggling with shame.

For, as her narrative recollection reveals, taking a voice becomes complicated by her sense of guilt. She is ashamed to speak in public with a voice like those of the immigrant women—loud, inelegant, unsubtle. She is ashamed to speak the words her mother demands she say to the druggist ghost because she considers her mother's words, as they exact compliance with traditional beliefs, to be outdated. She is ashamed to keep the same kind of silences and secrets her mother would keep because such secrets command her duplicity before the teachers she respects. For all these reasons she would not speak like her mother (and Chinese women) in her American environment; but her own efforts to take the appropriate American-feminine voice fail, and that failure too gives her cause for shame. In public her voice becomes "a crippled animal running on broken legs" (196), a duck voice; her throat "cut[s]" off the word; her mouth appears "permanently crooked with effort, turned down on the left side and straight on the right" (199). Her face and vocal chords continue to show the signs of her prior castration, and the physical mutilation and discomfort that mark her relationship to language and to any public enunciation of subjectivity.

The landscape of her childhood, as she reconstructs it, reveals the underlying logic in Kingston's failure to overcome her symbolic disability. Seeing around her the humiliating representations of woman, hearing words such as "maggots" become synonyms for "girls," suspecting that her mother seeks to contract her out as the wife and slave of some young man, perhaps even the retarded boy who follows her around with his box full of pornographic pictures, she negotiates a nightmare of female victimization by adopting the postures of an unattractive girl, the better to foil her mother's efforts and to forestall her weary capitulation. Cultivating that autobiographical signature, she represents herself as publicly as the obverse of her mother's image of the charming, attractive, pratical young girl by becoming clumsy, vulgar, bad-tempered, lazy, impractical, irreverent, and stupid "from reading too much" (226). She becomes, that is, a kind of fiction; and the psychic price she pays for orchestrating such a public posture is high. Publicly appearing as the "dumb" and awkward girl, she does not earn the affection and respect of her family and community. Moreover, she must convince herself of the reality of her mind by constantly attending to the grades she earns in the American school, those signs, unrecognized in her Chinese culture, that signal her access to other discourses. She remains "dumb" in another sense, for she recognizes even in childhood that "talking and not talking made the difference between sanity and insanity," in that "insane people were the ones who couldn't explain themselves" (216). Since she cannot give voice to her subjectivity, except by indirection and dissimulation, externalizing in an awkward masquerade the text of publicly unexpressed desires, she finds commonality with the anomalous women such as Pee-a-Nah and Crazy Mary, who retreat into imaginary worlds, there to haunt the outskirts of the immigrant community and the imaginations of its children.

The culmination of this struggle with voice comes when Kingston finally attempts to "explain" her silenced guilts, the text of which lengthens daily, and to represent her repressed desires to her mother, believing that by doing so she will establish some grounds for identification and overcome her profound isolation and dumbness: "If only I could let my mother know the list, she—and the world—would become more like me, and I would never be alone again" (230). Recapitulating the earlier castration, her mother cuts her tongue by refusing to acknowledge the daughter's stories as legitimate: "'I can't stand this whispering,' she said looking right at me, stopping her squeezing. 'Senseless gabbings every night. I wish you would stop. Go away and work. Whispering, whispering, making no sense. Madness. I don't feel like hearing your craziness'" (233). In response, Kingston swallows her words, but only temporarily. The tautness of her vocal cords increasing to a breaking point, she later bursts the silence, uttering in a cathartic moment the text of her inner life before her mother. Finally, this girl takes of voice, albeit in great confusion, and thereby authors a vision, textualizes her subjectivity, and legitimizes her own desires. She embarks, that is, on the autobiographical enterprise, articulating her interpretations against her mother's.

In this battle of words, mother and daughter, products of different cultural experiences, systems of signs, and modes of interpretation, speak two different "languages" and inscribe two different stories—graphically imaged in the sets of quotation marks that delimit their separate visions and betray the gap in the matrilineage as the circle of identity, of place and desire, is disrupted. Unable to understand the mother, unwilling to identify with her, the daughter would, in ironic reciprocity, cut off her mother's word: "'I don't want to listen to any more of your stories; they have no logic. They scramble me up. You lie with stories. You won't tell me a story and then say, 'This is a true story,' or 'This is just a story'" (235). But her mother's reluctant admission—"'We like to say the opposite'" (237)— forces Kingston to question, at the moment of their origin, her own interpretations and thus the "truth" or "fictiveness" of the autobiography she would inscribe through her memories of the past. As a result, the young Kingston comes to recognize the relativity of truth, the very elusiveness of self-representation that drives the autobiographical enterprise. "Ho Chi Kuai" her mother calls her; and, even to the moment in her adult life when she writes her autobiography, she cannot specify, can only guess, the meaning of the name her mother gave her from that culture she would leave behind. In the end she can only try to decipher the meaning of her past, her subjectivity, her desire, her own name: "I continue to sort out what's just my childhood, just my imagination, just my family, just the village, just movies, just living" (239).

Kingston closes *The Woman Warrior* with a coda, returning it to silence after telling two brief stories, one her mother's, one hers. She starts with the former: "Here is a story my mother told me, not when I was young, but recently, when I told her I also talk-story. The beginning is hers, the ending, mine" (240). Notably, her mother's story is now a gift. Passed from one storyteller to another, it signals the mother's genuine identification with the daughter. Yet the two-part story also functions as a testament to difference, the simple juxtaposition of two words rather than the privileging of one before the other. Here, at last, Kingston lets her mother's word stand without resisting it.

Her mother's story, set in the China of the previous generation, presents Kingston's grandmother as a willful and powerful woman who, convinced "that our family was immune to harm as long as they went to plays" (241), loves to attend theater performances. Unfolding in the ironies of the unexpected, the contingencies of opposites, the absence of linear logic, the story is emblematic of Brave Orchid's individual narrative style and vision, of the kinds of stories she tells. It speaks both of the horrifying vulnerability of women and their fierce and commanding power; and it tells of the power of art to sustain the continuity of life and the power of interpretations to turn adversity and victimization to triumph. Through her "gift," mother places daughter in the line of powerful "Chinese" women whose source of inspiration and whose very survival in the midst of vulnerability lie in the word of the creative imagination.

Kingston follows her mother's words with what she imagines might be the story on the stage at one of those performances. Turning toward rather than resisting her Chinese roots, she takes as her protagonist a Chinese poet who lived in the second century.[23] Forced to live among barbarians for twelve years, during which time she bears two children who cannot speak Chinese, Ts'ai Yen remains isolated beyond the boundaries that sustain her sense of place and identity. Nonetheless, she eventually discovers that even barbarians make music of life and longing, reflecting civilized, rather than merely primitive, sensibilities. In the midst of cultural difference, the poet finds a commonality of experience and subjectivity through the language of art, which enables her to give voice to her own desire for self-representation and, in doing so, to join the circle of humanity. Eventually, Ts'ai Yen is ransomed, returning to her home "so that her father would have Han descendants" (243); but the more momentous "birth" she contributes to posterity is the song of sadness, anger, and wandering created out of her experience in the alien land. Speaking of human yearning, it "translates well" through the generations and across communal boundaries. Ultimately, the story of Ts'ai Yen, the woman of words, is the tale of Brave Orchid, who finds herself hostage in the barbarian land of America where even her children, born like Ts'ai Yen's among the aliens, cannot "speak" her native language, cannot understand her. Yet the tale is simultaneously that of Kingston herself, whose sense of alienation is doubly complicated, since, as a product of two cultures, she remains outside the circle of both. Mother and daughter sing the songs of sadness, loneliness, and displacement, finding their common sustenance in the word. Thus through her storytelling Kingston can create the total identification of mother and daughter as they both become Ts'ai Yen, woman poet.

In that final juxtaposition of two stories, Kingston asserts the grounds of identification with her mother, affirming continuities rather than disjunctions in the line.[24] She is her mother's daughter, however much she may distance herself geographically and psychologically, learning from her the power and authority that enable her to originate her own storytelling. Carrying on the matrilineal trace, she becomes like her mother a mistress of the word in a culture that would privilege only the lines, textual and genealogical, of patrilineal descent.[25] With her text she gives historical "birth" to Brave Orchid, creating for her a textual space in the genealogical record, and she gives "birth" to herself as the daughter who has passed through the body and the word of the mother.

Notes

1. Albert E. Stone comments that Kingston's autobiography joins others in "this terrain of contemporary autobiography which abuts the continent of fiction" (Albert E. Stone, *Autobiographical Occasions and Original Acts* [Philadelphia: Univ. of Pennsylvania Press, 1982], p. 25).

2. For a review article on recent literature on mothers and daughters, see Marianne Hirsch, "Mothers and Daughters," *Signs: Journal of Women in Culture and Society* 7 (Summer 1981): 200–222. See also Adrienne Rich, *Of Woman Born* (New York: Norton, 1976), esp. ch. 9.

3. Maxine Hong Kingston, *The Woman Warrior: Memoirs of a Girlhood among Ghosts* (New York: Random House, 1977), p. 3. Subsequent citations appear in the text.

4. At this moment the female body, emitting the menstrual flow and promising the subsequent discharge of childbirth portended in the blood, becomes one powerful and primary source of pollution in the community: The blood emitted reaffirms the association of woman with the dangerous powers of life and death, those two events that bring into play the process of disintegration and integration within the patrilineal group and the forces of disorder and order in the community. See Emily M. Ahern, "The Power and Pollution of Chinese Women," in *Women in Chinese Society*, ed. Margery Wolf and Roxanne Witke (Stanford: Stanford Univer-

sity Press, 1975), pp. 193–214. See also Mary Douglas, *Purity and Danger: An Analysis of Concepts of Pollution and Taboo* (New York: Praeger, 1966), esp. pp. 114–28.

5. For a discussion of the subversive power of woman's womb, see Susan Hardy Aiken, "Dineson's 'Sorrow-acre': Tracing the Woman's Line," *Contemporary Literature* 25 (Summer 1984): 165–71.

6. For a discussion of *The Woman Warrior* with an attention to certain dynamics in the work that are similar to my own, see Paul John Eakin, *Fictions in Autobiography: Studies in the Art of Self-Invention* (Princeton: Princeton Univ. Press, 1985), pp. 255–75. As Eakin comments on this first "cautionary" tale, he focuses on the relation of woman to her community. I find Eakin's analysis throughout stimulating. Although we read the work in similar ways, we often give different emphases to the details.

7. Margery Wolf, "Women and Suicide in China," in *Women in Chinese Society*, ed. Wolf and Witke, p. 112. Why, for instance, was this married aunt living with her own parents rather than with her in-laws? And who had been the stranger, or was he a stranger, who had entered her house/womb? Kingston notes that a woman pregnant by someone near to, perhaps even in, her natal family would lay bare the vulnerability of the patrilineage to violations by incest.

8. Aiken, p. 167. See also Gayle Rubin, "The Traffic in Women: Notes on the 'Political Economy' of Sex," in *Toward an Anthropology of Women*, ed. Rayna R. Reiter (New York: Monthly Review Press, 1975), pp. 157–210; and Tony Tanner, *Adultery in the Novel: Contract and Transgression* (Baltimore: Johns Hopkins Univ. Press, 1979), pp. 58–66.

9. See Ahern, pp. 199–202.

10. See Wolf, pp. 113–14.

11. See Ahern, p. 198.

12. See ibid., p. 113.

13. Florence Ayscough, *Chinese Women: Yesterday and Today* (Boston: Houghton Mifflin, 1937), pp. 214–22.

14. Suzanne Juhasz makes this point also in her essay, "Towards a Theory of Form in Feminist Autobiography: Kate Millet's *Flying* and *Sita*; Maxine Hong Kingston's *The Woman Warrior*," in *Women's Autobiography: Essays in Criticism*, ed. Estelle C. Jelinek (Bloomington: Indiana Univ. Press, 1980), p. 234.

15. She does not succumb to the agoraphobia that presses so heavily her no-name aunt. Indeed, despite cold and hunger, she prospers in the midst of illimitable space and possibilities.

16. Kingston/Fa Mu Lan recognizes that her very life depends on this successful erasure of her true identity: "Chinese executed women who disguised themselves as soldiers or students, no matter how bravely they fought or how high they scored on the examination" (46). In that way traditional Chinese culture effectively denied women access to the power signified by the sword and the power signified by the surrogate sword, the pen and the knowledge it inscribed.

17. In the original legend, Mu Lan remains chaste during her years as the woman warrior. Kingston does make a space in her interpretation and her text for female sexuality, but, as I note above, it remains suppressed in the larger community.

18. Josette Féral, "Antigone or the Irony of the Tribe," *Diacritics* 8 (Fall 1978): 4.

19. The baron whom Kingston/Fa Mu Lan finally slays mistakes her for this kind of warrior. In response to his query about her identity, she tells him she is "a female avenger." His response—"'Oh, come now. Everyone takes the girls when he can. The families are glad to be rid of them'" (51)—suggests that he understands her to be an avenger of the wrongs of woman. Kingston/Fa Mu Lan specifies that the crime she seeks to avenge is, however, his impressment of her brother.

20. Her heroic space is far larger than that which provided the canvas for Fa Mu Lan's adventures: "Nobody in history has conquered and united both North America and Asia" (58). The public gestures of heroism she attempts are not uttered in a dazzling display of swordsmanship but in a self-effacing, tentative, "squeaky" voice that identifies her, not with the woman warrior, but with the "wives and slaves" tucked into the interstices of the mythical narrative. In her modern American space, the martial arts are not the grandiose gestures of heroic action: they are merely exercises "for unsure little boys kicking away under fluorescent lights" (62). Moreover, in Communist China her relatives, instead of being identified with the exploited peasants, are identified as exploiting landowners and punished as the barons in the myth.

21. As the daughter knows, "all heroes are bold toward food" (104). They demonstrate by their gustatory feats their power over the natural world, their high degree of aristocratic cultivation, and their association with the sacred. See Claude Lévi-Strauss, *The Raw and the Cooked*, trans. John and Doreen Weightman (New York: Harper & Row, 1969).

22. See Mary Daly, *Gyn/Ecology: The Metaethics of Radical Feminism* (Boston: Beacon Press, 1978), pp. 153–77.

23. For a brief biography of Ts'ai Yen, see Wu-Chi Liu and Irving Yucheng Lo, eds. *Sunflower Splendor: Three Thousand Years of Chinese Poetry* (Garden City: Anchor, 1975), pp. 537–58.

24. For a discussion of the narrative rhythms of identification and differentiation in *The Woman Warrior* and *China Men*, see Suzanne Juhasz, "Maxine Hong Kingston: Narrative Technique and Female Identity," in *Contemporary American Women Writers*, ed. Catherine Rainwater and William J. Scheik (Lexington: Univ. Press of Kentucky, 1985), pp. 173–89.

25. See Aiken, pp. 175–84.

No Lost Paradise

Social Gender and Symbolic Gender in the Writings of Maxine Hong Kingston

LESLIE W. RABINE

◆　◆　◆

THE QUESTION OF GENDER, of what it is, how it works, and how it determines our lives as men and women, receives divergent answers in contemporary feminist history. The notion that gender is a social construct rather than an innate essence[1] has been complicated in recent years by theories of feminists influenced by French critical theory and Lacanian psychoanalysis for whom gender is a symbolic construct. Whether French or Americans schooled in French theory, these feminists see gender as produced in and through language systems.[2]

Hélène Cixous, for instance, taking off from the notion that linguistic signs are not positive entities but products of a system of difference, sees our particular form of gender difference as the paradigm by which we conceive the particular pattern of difference that shapes our symbolic order. This pattern is based not on true difference but on hierarchical oppositions. One term, the masculine, posits itself as the primary term and represses the other (feminine) term, replacing it with its mirror opposite, a secondary term, derived from itself. This symbolic law of opposition, operating in different systems—"discourse, art, religion, the family, language"[3]—always comes back to the man/woman opposition,"[4] and wherever it operates, it works to absorb the other into the same. Without seeing gender as biological, Cixous, and those who in different ways also seek to subvert this law of

85

opposition, do see it as fundamental, grounding the very structures of subjectivity, representation and language.[5] For this reason, those theories, which have been called "French feminist" and which I will here call "symbolic feminist," provide tools for analyzing gender more precisely and deeply through analyses of discourses.

But the blind spot in the discursive practices of symbolic feminism is that they tend to repress the social dimension of gender by collapsing the social into the symbolic. The notion that linguistic structures and social structures are coextensive can lead to reestablishing a hierarchal opposition in which the specificity of the social is repressed and becomes the secondary, derived term of the symbolic. It may be true, as Jacqueline Rose says, that "there is no feminine outside language . . . because the 'feminine' is constituted as a division in language, a division which produces the feminine as its negative term."[6] But while the social cannot be thought outside of language, an exclusive theoretical focus on language structure can lead to strategies that seek to liberate the "feminine" while leaving intact the oppression of social women.

The strategies used by symbolic feminism to transform our phallocentric gender system bring into play both its strengths and its blind spot. In various ways the theorists seek to replace a sociosymbolic order based on the logic of opposition with one based on the logic of difference or to displace the absolute difference *between* masculine and feminine so as to reveal multiple differences *within* each sex and each speaking being.[7] In other words, the hierarchized dichotomy between a superior masculine essence embodied by men and an inferior feminine essence embodied by women would give way to an infinity of different and alternating gender positions. Fixed gender identity that protects the rigidly guarded identity of the masculine subject and denies feminine subjecthood would give way to subjects in flux. Since our oppositional order represses the feminine and substitutes for it a femininity that stands in as the secondary term derived from masculinity, the repressed feminine becomes, in the works of writers like Cixous and Luce Irigaray, the site where the play of sexual difference can emerge through discursive practices that Cixous calls "feminine writing."[8]

As Cixous and others have pointed out, masculine and feminine are not necessarily embodied by biological men and women. Therefore, men can also engage in feminine writing and in deconstructing a phallocentric gender system. What this analysis leaves out, however, is that our social order transforms biological bodies into social men and women, into occupiers of relatively privileged and relatively oppressed social positions that the oppressed cannot simply choose to abandon and that few privileged people would want to abandon. Sexed bodies become the visible signs through which a system of hierarchal social roles is enforced by economics, politics, the family, religion, and other institutional constructs so that individuals whose bodies are visibly marked "female" find themselves forced into oppressive positions. In such a social order men, or individuals whose bodies are marked male, can and do engage in feminine discursive practices while occupying positions of privilege and while continuing to exclude women from them. Strategies of feminine writing can subvert symbolic gender while leaving social gender oppression intact if they do not also adopt social feminist strategies of institutional transformation.

The following analysis of Maxine Hong Kingston's writing seeks to reconcile insights of symbolic and social feminism. If feminine writing expresses difference, then it cannot simply take the form practiced by French theorists but must also take many different forms. Although Kingston's writing does not put into play a subject in boundless flux, it is a "feminine writing" of a different kind. Two aspects of Kingston's writing, its double ambivalence to the culture her parents brought from China and to the U.S. culture that also claims her, as well as its complex textuality, make the fixed polarities of oppositional logic unstable. In various interviews Kingston has said that her writings aim to "claim America"[9] for Chinese-Americans, and she disclaims that they are representative of China or Chinese-Americans.[10] Her individual expression of a Chinese-American culture marginalized by Anglo-American culture sets the laws of gender systems into motion.

Like the feminine writing of Cixous and Irigaray, Kingston's writing violates the law of opposition, making gender dichotomies proliferate into unresolvable gender differences. In conjunction with this instability of male and female, her texts also set to spinning fixed oppositions of theme and form—between fiction and autobiography, history and myth, parents and children, and finally, writing and oral legend. Unlike Cixous and Irigaray, Kingston's proliferation of gender arrangements remains rooted in the social world and so reveals not only how gender systems change across cultural boundaries but also how the distinction between symbolic and social gender changes between cultures. These two forms of gender, distinct and interrelated, illuminate, contradict, and reinforce each other. By making their contradictions work for her, Kingston performs a writerly liberation that also has social implications. The following reading will first study Kingston's work as a unique kind of feminine writing that in its own way fractures the logic of opposition into a play of difference and will then study how this play of difference, especially between writing and oral legend, clarifies relations between social and symbolic gender.

Gender Opposition/Gender Difference

While in *The Woman Warrior* and *China Men*[11] gender determines one's place in the family and society, and certainly one's place in power relations, there are no gender essences. Women can have opposite qualities. They can be strong and aggressive, like Maxine's mother Brave Orchid, or meek and passive, like her aunt Moon Orchid. They can be both at different times, like Maxine herself, who as a child is talkative and athletic in Chinese school, silent and passive at American public school. Kingston does away with the illusion of a universal feminine, placing among her confusing and painful childhood experiences the attempts to be "American feminine."

Though neither sex possesses essential qualities, gender oppositions do play a determining role in organizing Kingston's textual world. *The Woman Warrior* tells the story of the women in Kingston's family, and *China Men* tells the stories of the men. The members of each sex are shadow creatures in the world and in the book of the other sex. But Kingston seems to emphasize gender boundaries *between* the two books all the better to reorganize and play with these boundaries *within* each book. Each book incorporates legends from the oral tradition into autobiographical, biographical, and historical stories; and in each book the starring legend concerns a character who crosses over the boundary into the other gender. *The Woman Warrior* takes its title from the legend of Fa Mu Lan, the swordswoman who disguises herself as a man by dressing in male armor so that she can take revenge against greedy landlords and barons for the injustices done to her family. *China Men* opens with the legend of Tang Ao, who in Kingston's verstion travels to the Land of Women, where he is forced to have his feet bound, his ears pierced, his eyebrows plucked, to don constricting clothing and makeup, and, in short, to become a member of the weaker sex.[12] Both legends are metaphors for a textual practice in *The Woman Warrior* and *China Men* that displaces and transforms boundaries.

This double deployment of gender, with the logic of the "difference between" genders practiced between the two books and the logic of the "difference within" each gender practiced within each text, is expressed by Kingston in two statements. One appears in an interview with Elaine Kim, and the other is a poetic statement in *The Woman Warrior*. Kim reports, "Kingston says that she wrote *The Woman Warrior* and *China Men* together, having conceived of them as an interlocking story about the lives of men and women. But the women's stories 'fell into place,' and she feared that the men's were anti-female and would undercut the feminist viewpoint."[13] Kim reports Kingston as saying: "I feel I have gone as deeply into men's psyches as I can, and I don't find them that different. I care about men . . . as much as I care about women. . . . Given the present state of affairs, perhaps men's and women's experiences have to be dealt with separately for now, until more auspicious times are with us."[14]

This statement about gender opposition as a destructive and, it is hoped, temporary condition bears a striking contrast to Fa Mu Lan's mystic vision in *The Woman Warrior* of gender difference as the basis of time and movement themselves:

> I saw two people made of gold dancing the earth's dance. They turned so perfectly that together they were the axis of the earth's turning. They were light; they were molten, changing gold—Chinese lion dancers, African lion dancers in midstep. I heard high Javanese bells deepen in midring to Indian bells, Hindu Indian, American Indian. Before my eyes, gold bells shredded into gold tassels that fanned into two royal capes that softened into lions' fur. Manes grew tall into feathers that shone—became light rays. Then the dancers danced the future. . . . I am watching the centuries pass in moments because suddenly I understand time, which is spinning and fixed like the North Star. And I understand how working and hoeing are dancing: how peasant clothes are golden, as king's clothes are golden; *how one of the dancers is always a man and the other a woman.*[15]

Gender is as necessary as it is arbitrary.

The language here replaces the logic of separation with a logic of difference. It is difference, rather than separation, that allows change, motion, integration, and connection to happen. This couple is reminiscent of the Tao in the *I Ching* where Yin, the masculine, and Yang, the feminine, are constantly in the process of changing into each other and where their changes engender chains of transformations similar to those Kingston here expresses in a poetic mode.

The logics of opposition and difference vie with each other in theme and narrative structure as well. In *China Men*, Kingston is the woman warrior who takes vengeance *for* the family by reporting the vicious racism her male relatives combatted in America and the uncredited contributions they made to building this country. In *The Woman Warrior*, Kingston takes vengeance *against* the family, expressing her rage against an institutionalized hatred for women, and especially girls.

Corresponding to this thematic opposition, the narrative structures of the two books, as Suzanne Juhasz has shown, also differ from each other.[16] The narrative structure of *China Men* is based, like much traditional male narrative, on a linear and circular quest to return to a lost paradise. In *The Woman Warrior*, which relates Kingston's girlhood memoirs, there is no lost paradise, not in China the mythical homeland, or in childhood, or in her relationship to her mother; and its absence structures the text. This absence, moreover, may have significance beyond the poetic power it anchors in *The Woman Warrior: Memoirs of a Girlhood among Ghosts*, for Kingston is not the only writer to evoke it. Other second-generation women from immigrant communities in the United States, like Anzia Yezierska and Sandra Cisneros, have also written semiautobiographical works structured on the lack of a lost paradise.[17]

The Narrative Structure of Femininity

The Woman Warrior is structured in a double and simultaneous movement that traces the girl's anguished but never totally completed struggle to break away from her girlhood world and the incomplete return after the incomplete break. The narrator, in telling her story, simultaneously relives the young girl's negative feelings for her mother, her family, the community, and its myths and also measures the distance that bestows on them their positive and irreplaceable value: "I looked at their ink drawings of poor people snagging their neighbors' flotage with long flood hooks and pushing the girl babies on down the river. And I had to get out of hating range. . . . I refuse to shy my way anymore through our Chinatown, which tasks me with the old sayings and the stories. The swordswoman and I are not so dissimilar. May my people understand the resemblances soon so that I can return to them."[18] A double voice writes these words, a voice that is at the same time both in and out of hating range, the voice of a writer who in a certain sense has already returned to write about her people, to claim and transform their stories, but who writes as the girl who cannot return. Throughout *The Woman Warrior*, these two voices, while remaining two, never really separate from each other any more than Kingston can really separate from her mother and her people. Her story, like those of Cisneros and Yezierska, is about separation and the impossibility of separation.

In the works of all three writers, women's contradictory attitude toward their culture has both social and psychological reasons. The culture of each—Chinese-American, Jewish-American, Chicano—in addition to providing their personal identity, also provides an area of resistance against the dominant culture that dehumanizes people not only through racism but also through a homogenizing and sterile rationalism. Yet the childhood culture, infused in the works of all three authors with what Kingston calls "woman hatred,"[19] provides small haven. The myths that nourish the imagination and the spirit also relegate women to an inferior position; and the community, instead of suffusing them with warmth, suffocates them, limits them to a role of serving men, and hinders their growth. "Living among one's own emigrant villagers can give a good Chinese far from China glory and a place. . . . But I am useless, one more girl who couldn't be sold."[20] A woman from an immigrant group in the United States can find that between the two cultures she has no place.

This insoluble ambivalence can be explored through psychoanalytical theories about mother-daughter relationships, theories that analyze the way that male and female infant relationships to the mother affect the development and structure of the masculine and feminine psyche.[21] Boys separate completely from the mother, developing a subjective structure based on lack (or as Freudians have said, on castration) and, therefore, on the desire to fill it. Fulfillment is fantasized as a return to the lost unity with the mother and the state of nature she represents or, in other words, to a lost paradise. But girls do not go through this complete separation, so that their subjectivity is shaped not by a linear desire for something imagined as lost, but by a conflict between two needs: they desire both to remain close to the mother and to break into autonomy.

Luce Irigaray, in her poetic work *Et l'une ne bouge pas sans l'autre*, expresses the violence and insolubility of this conflict. For the narrator, the acultural, asymbolic unity with the mother suffocates and paralyzes her: "And I can no longer run toward what I love. And the more I love, the more I become captive, held in sluggish fixity." With great effort, she gains autonomy from the mother, but her only alternative is to turn to the father. She becomes a "mechanical scholar,"[22] learning the sterile power-hungry culture of the father, which for Kingston, Cisneros, and Yezierska would also be the racist or anti-Semitic dominant culture. Irigaray explores constructing a new cultural relationship with the mother, but only as an impossbile fantasy, at least for now.

The narrator of *The Woman Warrior* weaves her ambivalence to her community and culture into her ambivalence toward her mother, who communicates to her the culture and its myths and who interprets the community for her.[23] In a scene relating an interchange between the adult Maxine and her mother, the narrator says, "How can I bear to leave her again?"[24] And in the same scene she also expresses the contrary desire to get away:

"'When I'm away from here,' I had to tell her, 'I don't get sick. . . . I can breathe. . . . I've found some places in this country that are ghost free. And I think I belong there.'"[25] Yet it is the mother's ghosts who breathe life into the daughter's writing.

Feminine Narrative/Masculine Narrative

In *The Woman Warrior* this conflictual texture provides the internal structuring principle; in *China Men* the relationship to the father forms the external framework in which Kingston molds the lives and thoughts of the men in her family and immigrant community. In *China Men*, the theme of revenge, which permeates the *Woman Warrior*, becomes secondary to the theme of being exiled from home, precisely the theme of the lost paradise, whose absence in *The Woman Warrior* so marked the structure and the female experience recounted. Both books describe with nostalgia the loving rituals accompanying the birth of boys, and both express bitterness over the silence accompanying the birth of girls. Within the texts, these rituals express parental love and make childhood an Edenic place from which girls are excluded. But there are sociohistoric reasons for this difference as well. In *China Men*, the grandfathers and great-grandfathers, admitted to the United States as agricultural and railroad workers, long to go home because the cruel treatment they receive deprives them of a worthwhile life. But in *The Woman Warrior*, the place Maxine's family calls "home" is the country where families sell their daughters into slavery and where daughters-in-law are tortured. "Home" is a place she does not want to go.

Yet Kingston's writing make permeable this boundary between the apparently mutually exclusive experiences of men and women. Most of the legends incorporated into *China Men* are about exiles who wander in search of returning home, and, in at least two of these legends, exile is symbolized by the men being transformed into women. To be a woman, whose birth is not recognized by the family, is to be a permanent exile, without any home, without a place. To be a man who loses one's home is to cross over into the feminine gender. *China Men*, about men who have been forced to cross over into the feminine gender, is written by a woman, who, in the act of writing, has also, like the woman warrior, crossed over, albeit voluntarily, into the masculine gender and assumed the voice of the men she writes about.

The Woman Warrior recounts not only how the boys' births were celebrated while the girls' were ignored but also how her brother was royally welcomed home from Vietnam by the family, while she was never welcomed home from Berkeley. That scene of bitterness in *The Woman Warrior*[26] is transformed into the triumphant conclusion of *China Men*, where the brother, having gone to Hong Kong and discovered he does not belong there, fulfills the family's quest by coming "back home" to California. In the course of the male family quest in *China Men*, the meaning of "home" for the men of the family gradually shifts from China to America. It is Great Uncle who pronounces this shift: "'I've decided to stay in California.' He said, 'California. This is my home. I belong here.' He turned and, looking at us, roared, 'We belong here.'"[27]

Ironically, it is through this hated Great Uncle, who calls his girls maggots, that Maxine finally discovers a home of sorts, a place where she "belongs." In *China Men* she describes herself hiding from her great uncle because he treats her like a servant:

> I did not want to see him or hear him or be in his bossy presence. . . . I liked hiding in the dark, *which could be anywhere*. The cellar door sloped overhead, a room within the storeroom within the basement. I listened to footsteps above the rafters. He would not come down to the basement, where he had to duck the pipes and walk stooped. I was safely tucked away among the bags of old clothes and shoes, the trunks and crates the grown-ups had brought with them from China, the seabags with the addresses in English and Chinese, the tools, the bags and bottles of seeds, the branches of seeds and leaves and pods hanging upside down, and the drying loofahs. . . . I thought over useless things like wishes, wands, hibernation. I talked to the people whom I knew were not really there. I became different, complete, an *orphan*; my partners were beautiful cowgirls, and also men, cowboys who could talk to me in conversations; I named this activity Talking Men. . . . *I belonged here.*[28]

Through this dreamlike landscape, Kingston writes her own version of what Freud calls the "family romance."[29] Giving access to a childhood imaginary realm freed from the bitter memories of childhood experience, this room within a room within a room (recalling the Jungian passageway to the unconscious) transforms old China from a threatening family law into a conglomeration of mythic symbols—crates, bags, dried plants, English and Chinese writing—evoking dream instead of duty and waiting to be transformed into fantasy and then into text. Like a dream, the memory performs the work that translates the materials of the unconscious into language. A buried, internal place that is not a place but a darkness, this place could be anywhere. A nonplace of writerly productivity, the antechamber of the unconscious, it is in the father's house (and in the father's book); in fact, it is at the foundation of the father's house but hidden from the fathers, unseen and unrecognized by them. It resembles Sarah Kofman's description of the unconscious that "doesn't have a place. Like writing it is a-topical. It disrupts the domestic economy and turns the house upside down." The unconscious, says Kofman, is *"unheimlich"*—uncanny but also without a home.[30]

While at the foundation of the family institution, Maxine is yet outside of the family, an orphan. Her situation contrasts with that of Ch'ü Yüan, China's Homer, and the subject of the last legend in *China Men*.[31] Kingston, relating Ch'ü Yüan's exile, calls him, too, an "orphan," because he "cannot go home."[32] Ch'ü Yüan's male tragedy is precisely Maxine's escape from female tragedy. The orphaned state that marks for him the loss of home marks for her the discovery of a home that does not exist anywhere. It is constructed through and exists only in the logic of ambiguity that weaves her texts, a logic that overturns the law of opposition.

Violating the Law of Gender: A Logic of Ambiguity

Kim sees the "portrayal of ambiguity as central to the Chinese-American experience," which is neither mainstream American nor Asian-Chinese.[33] This ambiguity, which instead of finding resolution is transformed into the warp and woof of Kingston's writing, is also the result of love/hate relationships to the immigrant Chinese culture and to the childhood myths and memories experienced in that culture. Without a childhood imaginary realm and the access to the unconscious it opens up, we would be little more than robots. The power of childhood imaginary realm also increases the power of marginalized cultures in the United States to resist a social order that tends to turn us all into robots. But its very necessity to us constitutes its danger since it can also draw one back into paralytic unity with the mother, as well as accommodate one to the limits of patriarchal institutions. Kingston's ambiguity shuttles between the necessity and the danger of this childhood imaginary realm.

As feminists, many of us seek in pre-Greek and pre-Judaic matriarchal myth and in an idyllic mother-daughter bond a healing alternative to patriarchal technocracy. Kingston, in writing the healing journey into myth, also encourages a questioning of myth as an unequivocally positive answer to women's oppression. The same narrator who glorifies the mythical woman warrior Fa Mu Lan also praises antimythical rationalism: "I had to leave home in order to see the world logically, logic the new way of seeing. I learned to think that mysteries are for explanation. I enjoy the simplicity. Concrete pours out of my mouth to cover the forests with freeways and sidewalks. Give me plastics, periodical tables, TV dinners."[34] *The Woman Warrior* also raises questions about the liberating quality of the mother archetype and the idyllic quality of a matriarchal community since, like other more theoretical works, it portrays in its own poetic register a Chinese cultural structure that can incorporate matriarchal relationships into a patriarchy as oppressive as any other.[35]

Even legends, as they are told within the context of an oppressive community, are at first presented as sending anything but a liberating message. *The Woman Warrior* begins by showing the traditional community and its oral tradition at its worst. The heroine's mother tells her a hair-raising story of an aunt in China, pregnant out of wedlock, whom the villagers terrorized to the point that she took revenge by drowning herself and her newborn baby (girl) in the family well. It is a cruel story, cruelly told by the mother for a cruel motive: "Don't let your father know that I told you. He denies her. Now that you have started to menstruate, what happened to her could happen to you. Don't humiliate us. You wouldn't like to be forgotten as if you had never been born."[36]

Oral culture, which on one level transmits an unquestioning acceptance of women's subservience, is anything but idealized here. Yet, like everything in *The Woman Warrior*, it branches into ambiguities. Themes and language, like the relation to the mother, split and separate within their unity. The text suggests that the mother's stated motives for telling the story also hide an opposite motive, that of telling the forbidden story in a secret pact with her daughter for the pleasure of telling it. In repeatedly enjoining her daughter from telling this story—"Don't tell anyone you had an aunt. Your father does not want to hear her name"[37]—is the mother not also seeking her own release from silence and giving Maxine the means and material to break the injunction? Kingston's motive in telling the story of the aunt, "No Name Woman," is indeed to violate the paternal/community injunctions to silence and, beyond that, to destroy their power and authority. She not only breaks the silence but also transforms the oral story into writing and by this act denies the power of the community that maintains its cohesiveness through the oral tradition. A story that is oppressive when orally transmitted within the context of family and community is liberating when transformed into writing.[38]

Yet Kingston's act is just as ambiguous as her mother's. Like the cruel mother, she, too, tells the story for the pleasure of telling it and, moreover, to preserve the culture whose authority she seeks to destroy. This act of cultural preservation, itself born of ambiguity, splits into another ambiguity. Her act preserves culture not just by keeping old stories alive but by engaging in the tradition of ancestor worship. Other ancestral spirits have "their descent lines providing them with paper suits and dresses, spirit money, paper houses, paper automobiles." Of her aunt, Kingston says, "I alone devote pages of paper to her, though not origamied into houses and clothes."[39]

She observes the customs of ancestor worship in such a way as to destroy its fundamental principle, that of maintaining patriarchal descent intact. She pays homage to the woman who ruptured the descent line and so had to be excluded from it in order to preserve it unbroken. By establishing a descent line with this woman, Kingston reaffirms the damage to the true patriarchal descent line and replaces it with a competing, illegitimate line. She adheres to it not just by offering paper to the spirit of her aunt but also by carrying on the aunt's tradition of engaging in the one act that destroys the essence of patriarchal descent: illegitimate birth. She gives birth not only to the aunt who was "forgotten as if she had never been born," but also to a book that violates the father's law. From the very first sentence of the book: "You must not tell anyone,"[40] the text performs its own transgression of the paternal law concerning language, sexuality, generation, and gender. An illegitimate conception, it imitates No Name Woman, who "crossed boundaries not delineated in space."[41] Crossing boundaries of gender and genre, both desiring and rejecting her family, her mother, her family's culture, and its traditions, Kingston's writing enacts what the swordswoman learns in her mystical vision of the dancing couple, that nothing is identical to itself but is always something else as well. The "difference between," the logic of opposition, the law of gender that protects patriarchal genealogy, gives way to the difference within.

The legendary figures in *The Woman Warrior* are also textual figures in which the logic of ambiguity spins its relays. Each of them plays a different role in elaborating a kind of feminine writing. While one such figure is of course Fa Mu Lan, another figure is Ts'ai Yen (Lady Wen-Chi), legendary poetess of the second century. The last episode of *The Woman Warrior*, which suggests Kingston's reconciliation with her mother and her culture, retells the legend in which Ys'ai Yen was kidnapped by a barbarian general, had two children by him, and fought in his army, but after twelve years she "was ransomed and married to Tung Ssu so that her father would have Han descendents."[42] According to Caroline Ong, Ts'ai Yen would have been considered, as a person who lived among the barbarians and had barbarian children, a greater outcast than No Name Woman.[43] She is legendary because she later redeemed herself by returning to China and leading a life of exemplary filial piety. According to Robert Rorex and Wen Fong, Ts'ai Yen's return is associated in the Chinese tradition with the idea of "the superiority of Chinese civilization over cultures beyond her borders; the irreconcilability of the different ways of life; . . . and above all, the Confucian concept of loyalty to one's ancestral family and state."[44]

Needless to say, Kingston changes the meaning in rewriting the legend, or, to put it more precisely, she deprives it of a single, definite meaning or truth and makes it alternate between different meanings. In concluding that Ts'ai Yen's words were later adopted by the Chinese because they "translated well,"[45] Kingston suggests that Ts'ai Yen is a parable for her own writing as translation of the Chinese oral tradition into American-English writing. Yet like many of the legends that Kingston juxtaposes in biography and autobiography, the legend of Ts'ai Yen is a parable that does not work. By inserting legend among contemporary stories, Kingston follows the conventions of parable, inviting the reader to create interpretive parallels between the two narrative chains, but at a certain point the parallels fall apart.

The mother herself, the model "talk-storier," also uses myths as analogies to interpret experience. Yet Kingston recounts her mother's proliferation of parables in a satiric way. Brave Orchid, in one of her own acts of Fa Mu Lan–style warfare, plots to avenge her sister Moon Orchid against Moon Orchid's husband and his second wife. Explaining to Moon Orchid how she will win her husband back, Brave Orchid says: "You are the Empress of the East, and the Empress of the West has imprisoned the Earth's Emperor in the Western Palace. And you, the good Empress of the East, come out of the dawn to invade her land and free the Emperor."[46] This parable wildly distorts the situation. Like Kingston's legends, Brave Orchid's myth of the empresses carries a double message: legends are meant to be interpreted as analogies for experience, and legends cannot be interpreted as analogies for experience. The message on interpretation cannot itself be interpreted except as split within itself.

This happens because contradictory analogies alternate within the legend of Ts'ai Yen and the other legends retold in *The Woman Warrior* and *China Men*. The figure of Ts'ai Yen flashes back and forth between being an analogy for Maxine Hong Kingston in relation to her mother, and for the mother, Brave Orchid, in relation to her daughter. In the mother's eyes the daughter has gone to live among the barbarians, yet it is the mother herself who has left China to live in a barbarian land and sings songs of her homesickness. When Kingston says of Ts'ai Yen that "her words seemed to be Chinese, but the barbarians understood their sadness and anger" and that "her children did not laugh, but eventually sang along,"[47] she could be speaking either about herself translating her own sadness and anger toward her mother into poetry, or she could be talking about her mother's oral stories.

Who is the real outcast poetess, who the real woman warrior, Maxine or Brave Orchid? Both legendary figures, Ts'ai Yen and Fa Mu Lan, merge the mother and daughter but also separate them since they can both fit the figure, but not at the same time. The figure of Ts'ai Yen, like the figure of Fa Mu Lan, as it alternates between embodying Kingston and embodying her mother, is different within itself. It creates both a difference and a relationship between mother and daughter. Through Ts'ai Yen, the daughter's conflict, evoked by Irigaray, between merging and separating is not resolved (how could it be?), but it is harmonized in poetry. The fantasy of the legendary poetess is on a formal level a fantasy of transforming the conflict from pain into beauty and from paralysis into harmonious movement. Like the myth of the empresses in relation to Moon Orchid's American experience, the alternating form of the Ts'ai Yen analogy distorts the relationship between mother and daughter but also clarifies a not-yet-existing possibility.

The figure of Fa Mu Lan takes this contradictory form in a different direction. Like her daughter Maxine, Brave Orchid also plots elaborate strategies of revenge—against male privilege in the episode of the sister's husband or against a society in which she does not feel at home, as in the episode of the druggist's delivery boy.[48] Like her daughter, she also fantasizes her revenge in a proliferation of extravagant stories. In contrast to her daughter, however, she puts them into practice with great theatrical flourish, although they backfire on her in equally dismal failures. Maxine identifies with Fa Mu Lan in fantasy but recoils in embarassment when her mother takes on the role of the swordswoman in real life.

The scenes in which the mother plots revenge cast identification with Fa Mu Lan into a more overtly comic and satirical light that reflects on both the vengeful mother and the embarrassed daughter. The comedy casts doubt on the use of the Fa Mu Lan legend itself as an ideal, a model, and a metaphor for Kingston's text. The woman warrior, affirmed and doubted as the metaphor of the text, embodies an ambiguity toward writing itself. She figures a quality essential to a certain kind of women's writing—a literature whose angry, poetic revenge against racial and sexual injustice is not diminished by a turning back on itself in self-questioning and self-amusement. Such self-questioning avoids dogmatism or indulgence in self-pity.

The legend that introduces *China Men*, Tang Ao in the Land of Women, also presents itself as a parable for the text while raising doubts about the parallels it suggests. Recounting with apparent relish the treatment of Tang Ao by the female rulers, it is a revenge story, since treating a man like a woman is in itself a form of revenge. The conventions of parable lead to the interpretation that for Kingston to tell her father's stories is also a form of vengeance, especially since he would never tell them to her, taking refuge in what his daughters interpret as a punishing silence alleviated by strings of antifemale curses. Kingston's revenge consists in forcing him to be interpreted by a disdained woman and to be absorbed into a woman's language. While telling his stories is on the one hand an act of love, it is, on the other hand, an act of vengeance, also a way of usurping power from the father. Since opposition to the father proves futile, Kingston, borrowing from Fa Mu Lan's store of military strategy, defeats and transforms patriarchal power by immersing herself in it.

Like the figures of Fa Mu Lan and Ts'ai Yen, Tang Ao is a metaphor both for the father and for Kingston as writer. In writing *China men*, Kingston travels to the Land of Men and assumes the voice of her male relatives. Her version of the legend, in which Tang Ao becomes indistinguishable from a woman, also suggests that the arbitrary and fictional quality of gender, both unstable and rigid, makes it dangerous to play with for both men and women, both Kingston and Tang Ao, in this double crossover.[49]

Symbolic Gender and Social Gender

The danger and necessity of crossing the gender boundary is related to the problem of crossing the genre boundary or of bringing legends from the oral tradition into a written text. Some feminine theorists for whom gender is a symbolic structure also see writing and the spoken word as gendered. Theorists like Julia Kristeva and Kofman associate writing with the feminine and voice with phallocentrism.[50] In Kingston's text, writing and orality are gendered as well but in a different way. This difference opens up the collapse between symbolic and social gender discussed earlier in this essay.

According to these French theorists, the logic of metaphysical opposition that helps to shape gender operates everywhere, even creating an opposition between speech and writing. In this opposition, the spoken word has the status of the primary, privileged term, and writing, the derived, secondary term. Western symbolic orders (as distinct from Chinese) limit writing to the concept of phonetic writing and reduce it to nothing more than a transcription of the spoken word. In colloquial usage, writing means merely the marks that transcribe sounds, but Kofman, following Derrida, reverses and displaces this opposition. She contends that writing in a more general sense, as the marks of difference, spacing, repetition, always inhabits speech. This "graphic element" makes possible the production of meaning. It is the "inscription of energy,"[51] without which a speaking subject, in a necessary disruption of its own unity and stability, could not produce language. Writing, like the feminine, is associated with difference, disruption of oneness, in a culture that represses difference. Kofman sees a "complicity between logocentrism and phallocentrism." For her, "the voice of truth," or the voice that claims absolute truth for itself, is "that of the law, of God, of the father." Conversely, writing as a "form of disruption of presence, like woman, is always abased, reduced to the lowest rung."[52]

According to this theory, the spoken word, enforced and guaranteed by the presence of the speaker, can create the illusion of emitting a single, absolute truth. It thus upholds the power of patriarchy that posits the absolute truth of the father's authority and the absolute opposition between a superior masculine essence and an inferior feminine essence. Writing opens up ambiguity, the difference within each word, person, or entity that makes it nonidentical to itself rather than the differences between pure, self-identical, unalterable essences.

For Kingston, whose writing denies the father's truth, the relation between writing and the spoken word is not so much reversed and displaced as double and contradictory.[53] In her interview with Arturo Islas, she says: "[T]he oral stories change from telling to telling.... Writing is static."[54] Yet in the texts the oral tradition, although at times a source of pleasure, transmits patriarchal authority, while writing releases the freedom of internal difference and is the medium of rebellion. An examination of the contradiction will show that in *The Woman Warrior* and *China Men*, the relation between writing and orality operates in two different ways because the texts distinguish between social gender and symbolic gender.

According to Caroline Ong, the legend of Fa Mu Lan, as transmitted in oral culture, communicates a lesson, a patriarchal "truth about absolute filial piety and the battle of absolutes, with good triumphing over evil,[55] and Kingston does at one point indicate that her mother used the legend to chide her for insufficient filial devotion. Ong shows how Kingston, in transforming the oral legend into writing, transforms it from a story about absolutes and patriarchal authority to a story glorifying feminine freedom and ambiguity. It becomes a story about the freedom to live outside the rigid categories of a patriarchal family, free from guilt and conflicts about the family. Kingston also changes it from a story communicating a single moral to a story with multiple and contradictory meanings at different levels. The orally transmitted stories of No Name Woman and Ts'ai Yen, intended to teach, respectively, a negative or positive moral about filial duty, are transformed in similar ways.

Yet it is the mother who transmits the power of "talk-story," while the father, "a silent magician," whose "magic was also different from my mother's"[56] transmits the power of the written tradition, in which he received a classical education. Kingston inherits the oral tradition from her mother: "I too had been in the presence of great power, my mother talking-story. . . . I had forgotten this chant [of the Woman Warrior] that was once mine, given me by my mother."[57] Even the stories about the fathers and grandfathers in *China Men* come from the women, guardians of the oral tradition: "Without the female story teller, I couldn't have gotten into some of the stories. . . . Many of the men's stories were ones I originally heard from women."[58]

But the writing with which she transforms the oral tradition is given to her by, or stolen from, her father. *China Men* recounts how her father took her as a young child to the gambling hall where he worked:

> We put away our brooms, and I followed him to the wall where sheaves of paper hung by their corners, diamond shaped. "Pigeon lottery," he called them. "Pigeon lottery tickets." Yes, in the wind of the paddle fan the soft thick sheaves ruffled like feathers and wings. He gave me some used sheets. Gamblers had circled green and blue words in pink ink. They had bet on those words. You had to be a poet to win, finding lucky ways words go together. My father showed me the winning words from last night's games: "white jade that grows in water," "red jade that grows in earth," or—not so many words in Chinese—"white water jade," "redearthjade," "firedragon," "waterdragon." He gave me pen and ink, and I linked words of my own: "rivercloud," "riverfire," the many combinations with *horse, cloud,* and *bird.* The lines and loops connecting the words, which were in squares, a word to a square, made designs too. So this was where my father worked and what he did for a living, keeping track of the gamblers' schemes of words."[59]

In spite of Kingston's comments on writing as static, this scene of writing, like Mallarmé's "Never Will a Throw of the Dice Abolish Chance," shows that if gamblers are poets, poets must also be gamblers, casting their lot in the infinity of chance connections writing makes between words. The very repetitiveness of writing makes the connections fall into dazzling kaleidoscopic patterns. One of the chanciest tricks of writing's combinatory power is that it always escapes the writer, always says more and otherwise than she intends it to say. The writer, absent from the act of communicaton, does not have the same illusion of authority as the speaker. Read by many different people, in many different contexts, writing also changes every time it is read, and it furthermore, as Kingston has pointed out, gives rise to new talk-stories outside the patriarchal tradition. For all these reasons, it throws the single-minded moral of patriarchal "truth" in the stories to the winds.

While many of the "talk-stories" in Kingston's books express the pleasure with which they were written, many scenes that represent talking in *The Woman Warrior* associate it—or its mirror opposite, the impossibility of talking—with the most painful memories of childhood. Writing, by contrast, as in the scene of the gambling hall, is associated with the most pleasant memories. After relating her fantasy identification with Fa Mu Lan, Kingston ironically contrasts it to her conflict-ridden girlhood in Stockton. She portrays the pain in this time in terms of a loss of the spoken word: "When one of my parents or the emigrant villagers said, 'Feeding girls is feeding cowbirds,' I would thrash on the floor and scream so hard I couldn't talk."[60] When, as a young adult, she tries to fight against racist bosses and unjust city officials, in imitation of the woman warrior, she can only squeak and whisper "in my bad, small-person's voice that makes no impact."[61] However, during the one period of her life, just before high school, when she can talk, she reproduces the cruelty, absolutism, and authoritarianism of oral culture in her behavior toward the most silent of the Chinese girls. Voice is here associated with "the worst thing I had yet done to another person."[62] The injustice of talk and the pain of silence as represented by the text contrast with the rebellious power of the text itself as it transforms talk and "talk-story" into writing.

A summary of the role of writing and the oral word in Kingston's texts brings forth the distinction between social gender and symbolic gender. On a symbolic level, writing is associated with feminine difference and the spoken word with patriarchal absolutism, but the social act of storytelling belongs to the realm of women, and the social act of writing belongs to the realm of men. It is that realm, the secret "father places" that Kingston sets out to "win by cunning."[63] Kingston says during the Fa Mu Lan story, "Chinese executed women who disguised themselves as soldiers or students, no matter how bravely they fought or how high they scored on the examinations."[64] In the culture that Kingston describes (as well as in contemporary culture), writing belongs to men privileged to express the feminine within them, while the oral tradition, although it seems the province of women, serves, as in the orally transmitted legends of Fa Mu Lan, Ts'ai Yen, and No Name Woman, to accommodate them to patriarchy. The privileged members of patriarchy can afford to give themselves a certain freedom from their own phallocentric symbolic order, but they cannot afford to give it to the oppressed who might use it to overthrow the order.

In the first part of *China Men*, Maxine's father, the intellectual, differs from his peasant brothers. He is the favorite of the mother, and as an intellectual he does not do hard farm labor so that his hands stay smooth. In an analysis of the role of intellectual castes within society, Julia Kristeva calls such an intellectual "a twin of the opposite sex," an outsider who is yet accepted by society.[65] Maxine's father, whose story is introduced by that of Tang Ao, is also a feminine man, but there is a night and day contrast between the femininity of the two men. Tang Ao is made into a social woman, an oppressed being, while the father as an intellectual is allowed to play the role of the feminine without being outcast, humiliated, or deprived of male status.

As a writer, then, Kingston is heir to her father the classical scholar. In this, too, she resembles Fa Mu Lan, who "took her father's place in battle."[66] The swordswoman, disguised as a man, resembles the male intellectual. She is outside the community yet accepted; she lives outside its laws, duties, and classifications and yet is not an outcast but an honored member. She is a twin of the opposite sex, able finally to express with freedom the feminine within herself, only because she has become a social man. Her male armor hides her forbidden pregnancy, so that in direct contrast to the horror of No Name Woman's childbearing, hers is enjoyed in tranquil bliss. Her male armor also hides the writing, the words of revenge inscribed on her back. "The swordswoman and I are not so dissimilar," says Kingston. "What we have in common are the words at our backs."[67] But Fa Mu Lan has to hide the writing under the male armor in order to be able to express it.

The writerly feminine, as mentioned at the beginning of this essay, can be in our social order the feminine of a privileged being, of a social man. And, with few exceptions, it has to be. For a social woman to write in our social order, she has to be able to don, whether legitimately or illegitimately, male privilege. To write in a public way means not only to set words to paper but also to have these words printed, published, distributed, sold, advertised, and reviewed by male-dominated institutions. Such is our present sociosymbolic order that feminine difference has to be expressed in a way acceptable to these institutions in order even to be recognized as feminine difference. Winning back from the "father places" the power of symbolic feminine freedom for social women has indeed been the task of woman warriors. But here, too, the parallel between Kingston as writer and Fa Mu Lan is both appropriate and inapplicable, for in writing *The Woman Warrior* Kingston has to a certain extent shed her male armor and, writing/fighting as a social woman, is in this respect dissimilar from the fantasy heroine.

Notes

1. See Alice Echols, "The New Feminism of Yin and Yang," in *Powers of Desire: The Politics of Sexuality*, ed. Ann Snitow, Christine Stansell, and Sharon Thompson (New York: Monthly Review Press, 1983), 440; Zillah R. Eisenstein, *Feminism and Sexual Equality: Crisis in Liberal America* (New York: Monthly Review Press, 1984); Heidi Hartmann, "The Unhappy Marriage of Marxism and Feminism: Towards a More Progressive

Union," in *Women and Revolution: A Discussion of the Unhappy Marriage of Marxism and Feminism*, ed. Lydia Sargent (Boston: South End Press, 1981); and Gayle Rubin, "The Traffic in Women: Notes on the 'Political Economy of Sex,'" in *Toward an Anthropology of Women*, ed. Rayna Reiter (New York: Monthly Review Press, 1975). The theorists they most ofen associate with a universal female principle are Mary Daly, Robin Morgan, and Adrienne Rich (see e.g., Echols, 442).

2. For some of the most prominent French theories of gender, see Hélène Cixous, *La jeune née* (Paris: Union Générale d'Editions, 1975); Luce Irigaray, *This Sex Which is Not One*, trans. Catherine Porter with Carolyn Burke (Ithaca, N.Y.: Cornell University Press, 1985); and Julia Kristeva, *La Révolution du langage poétique* (Paris: Editions du Seuil, 1974), translated as *The Revolution in Poetic Language*, by Margaret Waller (New York: Columbia University Press, 1984). For American versions of poststructuralist theories of gender, see Jane Gallop, *The Daughter's Seduction* (Ithaca, N.Y.: Cornell University Press, 1982), and *Reading Lacan* (Ithaca, N.Y.: Cornell University Press, 1985); and Kaja Silverman, *The Subject of Semiotics* (New York: Oxford University Press, 1983).

3. Cixous, 64.

4. Hélène Cixous, "Castration or Decapitation?" trans. Annette Kuhn, *Signs: Journal of Women in Culture and Society* 7, no. 1 (Autumn 1981): 41–55, esp. 44.

5. Cixous's and Irigaray's insistence that gender is fundamental has led to a debate on the extent to which they are essentialists in their notions of femininity. Toril Moy argues that their texts contain a contradiction between a deconstructive view of gender and an essentialist view and that the essentialist view constitutes a flaw in their theories (see Moy, *Sexual/Textual Politics* [London: Methuen, 1985]). Naomi Schor argues, however, that this contradiction between deconstructive and essentialist writing on gender is productive and one of the strengths of Cixous's and Irigaray's writing (see "Introducing Feminism" [paper delivered at symposium of the UCLA Faculty Critical Theory Study Group, University of California, Los Angeles, March 15, 1986]).

6. Jacqueline Rose, "Introduction—II," in *Feminine Sexuality: Jacques Lacan and the école freudienne*, ed. Juliet Mitchell and Jacqueline Rose (New York: W. W. Norton & Co., 1982), 55.

7. These terms come from Barbara Johnson, *The Critical Difference: Essays in the Contemporary Rhetoric of Reading* (Baltimore: Johns Hopkins University Press, 1978).

8. See esp. Hélène Cixous, "The Laugh of the Medusa," trans. Keith Cohen and Paula Cohen, in *New French Feminisms*, ed. Elaine Marks and Isabelle de Courtivron (New York: Schocken Books, 245–64.

9. Elaine H. Kim, *Asian American Literature: An Introduction to the Writings and Their Social Context* (Philadelphia: Temple University Press, 1982), 209.

10. Maxine Hong Kingston, interview by Arturo Islas, in *Women Writers of the West Coast Speaking of Their Lives and Careers*, ed. Marilyn Yalom (Santa Barbara, Calif.: Capra Press, 1983), 12.

11. Maxine Hong Kingston, *The Woman Warrior: Memoirs of a Girlhood among Ghosts*

(New York: Random House/Vintage Trade Books, 1977), hereafter referred to as *WW*, and *China Men* (New York: Ballantine Books, 1980), hereafter referred to as *CM*.

12. The story of Tang Ao in the Land of Women comes from the Chinese eighteenth-century classic novel by Li Ju-Chen, *Flowers in the Mirror*, trans. and ed. Lin Tai-Yi (London: Peter Owen, 1965). In the novel, it is Tang Ao's brother-in-law who is forced to become a member of the weaker sex in the Land of Women.

13. Kim, 209.

14. Ibid.

15. *WW*, p. 32 (emphasis added).

16. Analyzing the narrative techniques of *The Woman Warrior* and *China Men* in the framework of Nancy Chodorow's theory and in relation to the search for a home as I am doing here, Suzanne Juhasz comes to almost opposite conclusions on issues of narrative structure and the search for a home (Suzanne Juhasz, "Maxine Hong Kingston: Narrative Technique and Female Identity," in *Contemporary Women Writers*, ed. C. Rainwater and W. J. Soheik [Lexington: University Press of Kentucky, 1985], 173–89).

17. Sandra Cisneros, *The House on Mango Street* (Houston: Arte Publico Press, 1983); Anzia Yezierska, *The Bread Givers* (1925; reprint, New York: Persea Books, 1975).

18. *WW*, 62.

19. Maxine Hong Kingston, "Reservations about China," *Ms. Magazine* (October 1978), 67–79, esp. 67.

20. *WW*, 62.

21. The most influential of these theories is that of Nancy Chodorow, *The Reproduction of Mothering: Psychoanalysis and the Sociology of Gender* (Berkeley and Los Angeles: University of California Press, 1978). See also Dorothy Dinnerstein, *The Mermaid and the Minotaur: Sexual Arrangements and Human Malaise* (New York: Harper & Row, 1976). While these theories are grounded in Western notions of the oedipal conflict, I am mentioning them here in the hope that they can help to analyze the texts in question since the oedipal quest structure of *China Men* contrasts so strikingly to the nonlinear composition of *The Woman Warrior* and since Kingston has pointed out that her writing is unmistakably American (see Maxine Hong Kingston, "Cultural Misreadings by American Reviewers," in *Asian and Western Writers in Dialogue: New Cultural Identities*, ed. Guy Amirthanayagam [London: Macmillan, 1982], 55–65). It is significant in this respect that the heroes of *China Men* eventually decide that their "lost paradise is to be found not in China but in the United States.

22. Luce Irigaray, *Et l'une ne bouge pas sans l'autre* (And one doesn't stir without the other) (Paris: Editions de minuit, 1979), 7, 12 (my translation).

23. For a study of the ambiguity of the mother in *The Woman Warrior*, see Stephanie A. Demetrakopoulos, "The Metaphysics of Matrilinearism in Women's Autobiography: Studies of Mead's *Blackberry Winter*, Hellman's *Pentimento*, Angelou's *I Know Why the*

Caged Bird Sings, and Kingston's *The Woman Warrior*," in *Women's Autobiography: Essays in Criticism*, ed. Estelle C. Jelinek (Bloomington: Indiana University Press, 1980).

24. *WW* (n. 11 above), 118.

25. Ibid., 126–27.

26. Ibid., 56.

27. *CM* (n. 11 above), 184.

28. *CM*, 180–81 (emphasis added).

29. Sigmund Freud, "Family Romance," in *The Standard Edition of the Complete Psychological Works*, trans. and ed. James Strachey, vol. 9 (London: Hogarth Press, 1962).

30. Sarah Kofman, *Lectures de Derrida* (Paris: Editions Galilée, 1984), 55 (my translation).

31. See Jaroslav Prusek, *Chinese History and Literature* (Dordrecht: D. Reidel Publishing Co., 1970); and Dorothea Hayward Scott, *Chinese Popular Literature and the Child* (Chicago: American Library Association, 1980).

32. *CM*, 258.

33. Kim (n. 9 above), xvii. See Also Frank Chin, Jeffery Paul Cahn, Lawson Fusao Inada, and Shawn Hsu Wong, *Aiiieeeee! An Anthology of Asian-American Writers* (Washington, D.C.: Howard University Press, 1974); David Hsin-Fu Wand, *Asian-American Heritage: An Anthology of Prose and Poetry* (New York: Washington Square Press, 1974); and Kai-yu Hsu and Helen Palubinskas, *Asian American Authors* (Boston: Houghton Mifflin Co, 1972).

34. *WW*, 237.

35. The incorporation of matriarchy into patriarchy in Chinese family structure is examined in Julia Kristeva, *Des Chinoises* (Paris: Des Femmes, 1974); and P. Steven Sangren, "Female Gender in Chinese Religious Symbols: Kuan Yin, Ma Tsu, and the 'Eternal Mother,'" *Signs* 9, no. 1 (Autumn 1983): 4–25.

36. *WW* (n. 11 above), 5.

37. Ibid., 18.

38. Suzanne Juhasz has a different analysis of *The Woman Warrior* as an autobiography that integrates fantasy, in "Towards a Theory of Form in Feminist Autobiography: Kate Millet's *Flying* and *Sita*; Maxine Hong Kingston's *The Woman Warrior*," *International Journal of Women's Studies* 2, no. 2 (1979): 62–75.

39. *WW*, 18–19.

40. Ibid., 3.

41. Ibid., 9.

42. Ibid., 243.

43. Personal communication with Caroline Ong, June 1985.

44. Robert A. Rorex and Wen Fong, "Introduction," in *Eighteen Songs of a Nomad Flute: The Story Lady Wen-Chi* (a fourteenth-century handscroll in the Metropolitan Museum of Art) (New York: Metropolitan Museum of Art, 1974), 1.

45. *WW*, 243.

46. Ibid., 166.

47. Ibid., 243.

48. Ibid,. 196—98.

49. The story of Tang Ao also shows the uncanny ability of writing to produce connections. The story, part of the oral tradition, is a modified version of an episode from Li Ju Chen's *Flowers in the Mirror* (n. 12 above). Although Kingston does not make an explicit connection between the oral legend and the novel, the coincidental similarities between *China Men* and *Flowers in the Mirror* are remarkable. Li Ju Chen is known as China's feminist author. He sets off the action in his novel by a double act of revenge that "disturbs the principles of the sexes" by putting a woman emperor on the throne. Tang Ao has a daughter who spends the last half of the novel searching for her father, who will not communicate with her.

50. Julia Kristeva, "Le Texte clos," in *Semeiotike: Recherches pour une sémanalyse* (Paris; Editions du Seuil, 1969).

51. Kofman (n. 30 above), 64.

52. Ibid., 25.

53. Kingston's difference from European and Euro-American theorists in this respect may come from her incorporation of material from a Chinese symbolic order that, not based on phonetic writing, is not logocentric or is not logocentric in the same way. For a development of this hypothesis, see Kristeva, *Des Chinoises* (n. 35 above), 57—63.

54. Kingston, interviewed by Islas (n. 10 above), 18.

55. Caroline Ong, "The Woman Warrior/The Woman Writer: An Analysis of Maxine Hong Kingston's novel *The Woman Warrior* according to Julia Kristeva's essay 'The Bounded Text' from *Desire in Language*," (Irvine: University of California, Department of French and Italian, 1985, photocopy).

56. *CM* (n. 11 above), 236.

57. *WW* (n. 11 above), 24.

58. Kim (n. 9 above), 208.

59. *CM*, 240.

60. *WW*, 54.

61. Ibid., 57.

62. Ibid., 210.

63. *CM*, 238.

64. *WW*, 46.

65. Kristeva, *La révolution du langage poétique* (n. 2 above), 92 (my translation).

66. *WW*, 24.

67. Ibid., 62—63.

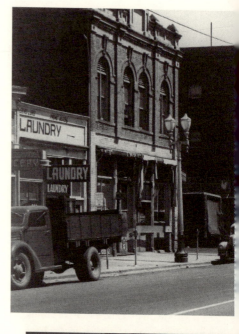

Center and Lafayette Sts., 1951. Courtesy of the Bank of Stockton Photo Collection.

"When the thermometer in our laundry reached 111° on summer afternoons, either my mother or my father would say that it was time to tell another ghost story so that we could get some good chills up our backs."

A scene from the Berkeley Repertory Theater's production of *The Woman Warrior*, adapted by Deborah Rogin from the novels of Maxine Hong Kingston. Copyright © 1994 by Ken Friedman.

The figure of the woman warrior in traditional Chinese opera garb is juxtaposed against the figure of the protagonist on her sickbed, to which she is confined by a mysterious illness after her torture of the quiet Chinese girl in the school bathroom.

"Departure from China," one of the scrolls in the Metropolitan Museum of Art collection illustrating the story of T'sai Wen-Chi [T'sai Yen], author of *Eighteen Songs of a Nomad Flute* ["Eighteen Stanzas for a Barbarian Reedpipe" in *The Woman Warrior*]. Courtesty of the Photo Library, Metropolitan Museum of Art, New York.

"It translated well."

A demonstration on the University of California, Berkeley, campus during the 1960s. Reprinted from *The Trouble in Berkeley* (Diablo Press, 1965), published with permission from the publisher.

"I went away to college—Berkeley in the sixties—and I studied, and I marched to change the world, but I did not turn into a boy."

PART III

A Chinese American Tradition in an Era of "Multiculturalism"

The Woman Warrior versus the Chinaman Pacific

Must a Chinese American Critic Choose between Feminism and Heroism?

KING-KOK CHEUNG

◆　◆　◆

THE TITLE OF THE anthology notwithstanding, I will primarily
be speaking not about topics that divide feminists but about conflicting politics of gender, as reflected in the literary arena, between Chinese
American women and men.[1] There are several reasons for my choice. First,
I share the frustrations of many women of color that while we wish to engage in a dialogue with "mainstream" scholars, most of our potential readers are still unfamiliar with the historical and cultural contexts of various
ethnic "minorities." Furthermore, whenever I encounter words such as
"conflicts," "common differences," or "divisive issues" in feminist studies,
the authors more often than not are addressing the divergences either between French and Anglo-American theorists or, more recently, between
white and nonwhite women. Both tendencies have the effect of re-center-
ing white feminism. In some instances, women of color are invited to participate chiefly because they take issue with white feminists and not because what they have to say is of inherent interest to the audience. Finally,
I believe that in order to understand conflicts among diverse groups of
women, we must look at the relations between women and men, especially where the problems of race and gender are closely intertwined.

It is impossible, for example, to tackle the gender issues in the Chinese
American cultural terrain without delving into the historically enforced

"feminization" of Chinese American men, without confronting the dialectics of racial stereotypes and nationalist reactions or, above all, without wrestling with diehard notions of masculinity and femininity in both Asian and Western cultures. It is partly because these issues touch many sensitive nerves that the writings of Maxine Hong Kingston have generated such heated debates among Chinese American intellectuals. As a way into these intricate issues, I will structure my discussion around Kingston's work and the responses it has elicited from her Chinese American male critics, especially those who have themselves been influential in redefining both literary history and Asian American manhood.

Attempts at cultural reconstruction, whether in terms of "manhood" and "womanhood," or of "mainstream" versus "minority" heritage, are often inseparable from a wish for self-empowerment. Yet many writers and critics who have challenged the monolithic authority of white male literary historians remain in thrall to the norms and arguments of the dominant patriarchal culture, unwittingly upholding the criteria of those whom they assail. As a female immigrant of Cantonese descent, with the attendant sympathies and biases, I will survey and analyze what I construe to be the "feminist" and "heroic" impulses which have invigorated Chinese American literature but at the same time divided its authors and critics.

I

Sexual politics in Chinese America reflect complex cultural and historical legacies. The paramount importance of patrilineage in traditional Chinese culture predisposes many Chinese Americans of the older generations to favor male over female offspring (a preference even more overt than that which still underlies much of white America). At the same time Chinese American men, too, have been confronted with a history of inequality and of painful "emasculation." The fact that ninety percent of early Chinese immigrants were male, combined with anti-miscegenation laws and laws prohibiting Chinese laborers' wives from entering the U.S., forced these immigrants to congregate in the bachelor communities of various Chinatowns, unable to father a subsequent generation. While many built railroads, mined gold, and cultivated plantations, their strenuous activities and contributions in these areas were often overlooked by white historians. Chinamen were better known to the American public as restaurant cooks, laundry workers, and waiters, jobs traditionally considered "women's work."[2]

The same forms of social and economic oppression of Chinese American women and men, in conjunction with a longstanding Orientalist tradition that casts the Asian in the role of the silent and passive Other,[3] have in turn provided material for degrading sexual representations of the Chinese in American popular culture. Elaine H. Kim notes, for instance, that the stereotype of Asian women as submissive and dainty sex objects has given rise to an "enormous demand for X-rated films featuring Asian women and the emphasis on bondage in pornographic materials about Asian women," and that "the popular image of alluring and exotic 'dream girls of the mysterious East' has created a demand for 'Oriental' bath house workers in American cities as well as a booming business in mail order marriages."[4] No less insidious are the inscriptions of Chinese men in popular culture. Frank Chin, a well-known writer and one of the most outspoken revisionists of Asian American history, describes how the American silver screen casts doubts on Chinese American virility:

> The movies were teachers. In no uncertain terms they taught America that we were lovable for being a race of sissies . . . living to accommodate the whitemen. Unlike the white stereotype of the evil black stud, Indian rapist, Mexican macho, the evil of the evil Dr. Fu Manchu was not sexual, but homosexual. . . . Dr. Fu, a man wearing a long dress, batting his eyelashes, surrounded by muscular black servants in loin clothes, and with his bad habit of caressingly touching white men on the leg, wrist, and face with his long fingernails is not so much a threat as he is a frivolous offense to white manhood. [Charlie] Chan's gestures are the same, except that he doesn't touch, and instead of being graceful like Fu in flowing robes, he is awkward in a baggy suit and clumsy. His sexuality is the source of a joke running through all of the forty-seven Chan films. The large family of the bovine detective isn't the product of sex, but animal husbandry. . . . *He never gets into violent things* [my emphasis].[5]

According to Chin and Jeffery Paul Chan, also a writer, "Each racial stereotype comes in two models, the acceptable model and the unacceptable model. . . . The unacceptable model is unacceptable because he cannot be controlled by whites. The acceptable model is acceptable because he is tractable. There is racist hate and racist love."[6] Chin and Chan believe that while the "masculine" stereotypes of blacks, Indians, and Mexicans are generated by "racist hate," "racist love" has been lavished on Chinese Americans, targets of "effeminate" stereotypes:

> The Chinese, in the parlance of the Bible, were raw material for the "flock," pathological sheep for the shepherd. The adjectives applied to the Chinese

ring with scriptural imagery. We are meek, timid, passive, docile, industrious. We have the patience of Job. We are humble. A race without sinful manhood, born to mortify our flesh. . . . The difference between [other minority groups] and the Chinese was that the Christians, taking Chinese hospitality for timidity and docility, weren't afraid of us as they were of other races. They loved us, protected us. Love conquered.[7]

If "racist love" denies "manhood" to Asian men, it endows Asian women with an excess of "womanhood." Elaine Kim argues that because "the characterization of Asian men is a reflection of a white male perspective that defines the white man's virility, it is possible for Asian men to be viewed as asexual and the Asian woman as only sexual, imbued with an innate understanding of how to please and serve." The putative gender difference among Asian Americans—exaggerated out of all proportion in the popular imagination—has, according to Kim, created "resentment and tensions" between the sexes within the ethnic community.[8]

Although both the Asian American and the feminist movements of the late sixties have attempted to counter extant stereotypes, the conflicts between Asian American men and women have been all the more pronounced in the wake of the two movements. In the last two decades many Chinese American men—especially such writers and editors as Chin and Chan—have begun to correct the distorted images of Asian males projected by the dominant culture. Astute, eloquent, and incisive as they are in debunking racist myths, they are often blind to the biases resulting from their own acceptance of the patriarchal construct of masculinity. In Chin's discussion of Fu Manchu and Charlie Chan and in the perceptive contrast he draws between the stock images of Asian men and those of other men of color, one can detect not only homophobia but perhaps also a sexist preference for stereotypes that imply predatory violence against women to "effeminate" ones. Granted that the position taken by Chin may be little more than a polemicist stance designed to combat white patronage, it is disturbing that he should lend credence to the conventional association of physical aggression with manly valor. The hold of patriarchal conventions becomes even more evident in the following passage:

> The white stereotype of the Asian is unique in that it is the only racial stereotype completely devoid of manhood. Our nobility is that of an efficient housewife. At our worst we are contemptible because we are womanly, effeminate, devoid of all the traditionally masculine qualities of originality, daring, physical courage, creativity. We're neither straight talkin' or straight

shootin'. The mere fact that four of the five American-born Chinese-American writers are women reinforces this aspect of the stereotype.[9]

In taking whites to task for demeaning Asians, these writers seem nevertheless to be buttressing patriarchy by invoking gender stereotypes, by disparaging domestic efficiency as "feminine," and by slotting desirable traits such as originality, daring, physical courage, and creativity under the rubric of masculinity.[10]

The impetus to reassert manhood also underlies the ongoing attempt by Chin, Chan, Lawson Inada, and Shawn Wong to reconstruct Asian American literary history. In their groundbreaking work *Aiiieeeee! An Anthology of Asian-American Writers*, these writers and co-editors deplored "the lack of a recognized style of Asian-American manhood." In a forthcoming sequel entitled *The Big Aiiieeeee! An Anthology of Asian American Writers*, they attempt to revive an Asian heroic tradition, celebrating Chinese and Japanese classics such as *The Art of War, Water Margin, Romance of the Three Kingdoms, Journey to the West,* and *Chushingura,* and honoring the renowned heroes and outlaws featured therein.[11]

The editors seem to be working in an opposite direction from that of an increasing number of feminists. While these Asian American spokesmen are recuperating a heroic tradition of their own, many women writers and scholars, building on existentialist and modernist insights, are reassessing the entire Western code of heroism. While feminists question such traditional values as competitive individualism and martial valor, the editors seize on selected maxims, purportedly derived from Chinese epics and war manuals, such as "I am the law," "life is war," "personal integrity and honor is the highest value," and affirm the "ethic of private revenge."[12]

The *Aiiieeeee!* editors and feminist critics also differ on the question of genre. According to Chin, the literary genre that is most antithetical to the heroic tradition is autobiography, which he categorically denounces as a form of Christian confession:

> . . . the fighter writer uses literary forms as weapons of war, not the expression of ego alone, and does not [waste] time with dandyish expressions of feeling and psychological attitudinizing. . . . A Chinese Christian is like a Nazi Jew. Confession and autobiography celebrate the process of conversion from an object of contempt to an object of acceptance. You love the personal experience of it, the oozings of viscous putrescence and luminous radiant guilt. . . . It's the quality of submission, not assertion that counts, in the confession and the autobiography. The autobiography combines the thrills and guilt of masturbation and the porno movie.[13]

Feminist critics, many of whom are skeptical of either/or dichotomies (in this instance fighting vs. feeling) and are impatient with normative definitions of genre (not that Chin's criteria are normative), believe that women have always appropriated autobiography as a vehicle for *asserting,* however tentatively, their subjectivity. Celeste Schenck writes:

> . . . the poetics of women's autobiography issues from its concern with constituting a female subject—a precarious operation, which . . . requires working on two fronts at once, *both* occupying a kind of center, assuming a subjectivity long denied, *and* maintaining the vigilant, disruptive stance that speaking from the postmodern margin provides—the autobiographical genre may be paradigmatic of all women's writing.[14]

Given these divergent views, the stage is set for a confrontation between "heroism" and "feminism" in Chinese American letters.

II

The advent of feminism, far from checking Asian American chauvinism, has in a sense fueled gender antagonism, at least in the literary realm. Nowhere is this antagonism reflected more clearly than in the controversy that has erupted over Maxine Hong Kingston's *The Woman Warrior.* Classified as autobiography, the work describes the protagonist's struggle for self-definition amid Cantonese sayings such as "Girls are maggots in the rice," "It is more profitable to raise geese than daughters," "Feeding girls is feeding cowbirds" (51, 54). While the book has received popular acclaim, especially among feminist critics, it has been censured by several Chinese American critics—mostly male but also some female—who tax Kingston for misrepresenting Chinese and Chinese American culture, and for passing fiction for autobiography. Chin (whose revulsion against autobiography we already know) wrote a satirical parody of *The Woman Warrior;* he casts aspersions on its historical status and places Kingston in the same company as the authors of Fu Manchu and Charlie Chan for confirming "the white fantasy that everything sick and sickening about the white self-image is really Chinese."[15] Jeffery Paul Chan castigates Knopf for publishing the book as "biography rather than fiction (which it obviously is)" and insinuates that a white female reviewer praises the book indiscriminately because it expresses "female anger."[16] Benjamin Tong openly calls it a "fashionably feminist work written with white acceptance in mind."[17] As Sau-ling Wong points out, "According to Kingston's critics, the most pernicious of the stereotypes which might be supported by *The Woman Warrior* is that of Chinese American men as sexist," and yet some Chinese American women "think highly of *The Woman Warrior* because it confirms their personal experiences with sexism."[18] In sum, Kingston is accused of falsifying culture and of reinforcing stereotype in the name of feminism.

At first glance the claim that Kingston should not have taken the liberty to infuse autobiography with fiction may seem to be merely a generic, gender-neutral criticism, but as Susan Stanford Friedman has pointed out, genre is all too often gendered.[19] Feminist scholars of autobiography have suggested that women writers often shy away from "objective" autobiography and prefer to use the form to reflect a private world, a subjective vision, and the life of the imagination. *The Woman Warrior,* though it departs from most "public" self-representations by men, is quite in line with such an autobiographical tradition. Yet for a "minority" author to exercise such artistic freedom is perilous business because white critics and reviewers persist in seeing creative expressions by her as no more than cultural history.[20] Members from the ethnic community are in turn upset if they feel that they have been "misrepresented" by one of their own. Thus where Kingston insists on shuttling between the world of facts and the world of fantasy, on giving multiple versions of "truth" as subjectively perceived, her Chinese American detractors demand generic purity and historical accuracy. Perhaps precisely because this author is female, writing amid discouraging realities, she can only forge a viable and expansive identity by refashioning patriarchal myths and invoking imaginative possibilities.[21] Kingston's autobiographical act, far from betokening submission, as Chin believes, turns the self into a "heroine" and is in a sense an act of "revenge" (a word represented in Chinese by two ideographs which Kingston loosely translates as "report a crime") against both the Chinese and the white cultures that undermine her self-esteem. Discrediting her for taking poetic licence is reminiscent of those white reviewers who reduce works of art by ethnic authors to sociohistorical documentary.

The second charge concerning stereotype is more overtly gender-based. It is hardly coincidental that the most unrelenting critics (whose grievance is not only against Kingston but also against feminists in general) have also been the most ardent champions of Chinese American "manhood." Their response is understandable. Asian American men have suffered deeply from racial oppression. When Asian American women seek to expose anti-female prejudices in their own ethnic community, the men are likely to feel betrayed.[22] Yet it is also undeniable that sexism still lingers as part of the Asian legacy in Chinese America and that many American-born daughters still feel its sting. Chinese American women may be at once sympathetic and angry toward the men in their ethnic community: sensitive to the marginality of these men but resentful of their male privilege.

III

Kingston herself seems to be in the grips of these conflicting emotions. The opening legend of *China Men* captures through myth some of the baffling intersections of gender and ethnicity in Chinese America and reveals the author's own double allegiance. The legend is borrowed and adapted from an eighteenth-century Chinese novel entitled *Flowers in the Mirror,* itself a fascinating work and probably one of the first "feminist" novels written by a man.[23] The male protagonist of this novel is Tang Ao, who in Kingston's version is captured in the Land of Women, where he is forced to have his feet bound, his ears pierced, his facial hair plucked, his cheeks and lips painted red—in short, to be transformed into an Oriental courtesan.

Since Kingston explicitly points out at the end of her legend that the Land of Women was in North America, critics familiar with Chinese American history will readily see that the ignominy suffered by Tang Ao in a foreign land symbolizes the emasculation of Chinamen by the dominant culture. Men of Chinese descent have encountered racial violence in the U.S., both in the past and even recently.[24] Kingston's myth is indeed intimating that the physical torment in their peculiar case is often tied to an affront to their manhood.

But in making women the captors of Tang Ao and in deliberately reversing masculine and feminine roles, Kingston also foregrounds constructions of gender. I cannot but see this legend as double-edged, pointing not only to the mortification of Chinese men in the new world but also to the subjugation of women both in old China and in America. Although the tortures suffered by Tang Ao seem palpably cruel, many Chinese women had for centuries been obliged to undergo similar mutilation. By having a man go through these ordeals instead, Kingston, following the author of *Flowers in the Mirror,* disrupts the familiar and commonplace acceptance of Chinese women as sexual objects. Her myth deplores on the one hand the racist debasement of Chinese American men and on the other hand the sexist objectification of Chinese women. Although *China Men* mostly commemorates the founding fathers of Chinese America, this companion volume to *The Woman Warrior* is also suffused with "feminist anger." The opening myth suggests that the author objects as strenuously to the patriarchal practices of her ancestral culture as to the racist treatment of her forefathers in their adopted country.

Kingston reveals not only the similarities between Chinamen's and Chinese women's suffering but also the correlation between these men's umbrage at racism and their misogynist behavior. In one episode, the narrator's immigrant father, a laundryman who seldom opens his mouth except to utter obscenities about women, is cheated by a gypsy and harassed by a white policeman:

> When the gypsy baggage and the police pig left, we were careful not to be bad or noisy so that you [father] would not turn on us. We knew that it was to feed us you had to endure demons and physical labor. You screamed wordless male screams that jolted the house upright . . . Worse than the swearing and the nightly screams were your silences when you punished us by not talking. You rendered us invisible, gone. (8)

Even as the daughter deplores the father's "male screams" and brooding silences, she attributes his bad temper to his sense of frustration and emasculation in a white society. As in analogous situations of Cholly Breedlove in Toni Morrison's *The Bluest Eye* and Grange Copeland in Alice Walker's *The Third Life of Grange Copeland,* what seems to be male tyranny must be viewed within the context of racial inequality. Men of color who have been abused in a white society are likely to attempt to restore their sense of masculinity by venting their anger at those who are even more powerless—the women and children in their families.

Kingston's attempt to write about the opposite sex in *China Men* is perhaps a tacit call for mutual empathy between Chinese American men and women. In an interview, the author likens herself to Tang Ao: just as Tang Ao enters the Land of Women and is made to feel what it means to be of the other gender, so Kingston, in writing *China Men,* enters the realm of men and, in her own words, becomes "the kind of woman who loves men and who can tell their stories." Perhaps, to extend the analogy further, she is trying to prompt her male readers to participate in and empathize with the experiences of women.[25] Where Tang Ao is made to feel what his female contemporaries felt, Chinese American men are urged to see parallels between their plight and that of Chinese American women. If Asian men have been emasculated in America, as the aforementioned male critics have themselves argued, they can best attest to the oppression of women who have long been denied male privilege.

IV

An ongoing effort to revamp Chinese American literary history will surely be more compelling if it is informed by mutual empathy between men and women. To return to an earlier point, I am of two minds about the ambitious attempt of the *Aiiieeeee!* editors to restore and espouse an Asian American heroic tradition. Born and raised in Hong Kong, I grew up reading many of the Chinese heroic epics—along with works of less heroic modes—and can appreciate the rigorous effort of the editors to introduce them to Asian American and non-Asian readers alike.[26] But the literary values they assign to the heroic canon also function as ideology. Having spoken out against the emasculation of Asian Americans in their introduction to *Aiiieeeee!,* they seem determined to show further that Chinese and Japanese Americans have a heroic—which is to say militant—heritage. Their propagation of the epic tradition appears inseparable from their earlier attempt to eradicate effeminate stereotypes and to emblazon Asian American manhood.[27] In this light, the special appeal held by the war heroes for the editors becomes rather obvious. Take, for example, Kwan Kung, in *Romance of the Three Kingdoms:* loud, passionate, and vengeful, this "heroic embodiment of martial self-sufficiency" is antithetical in every way to the image of the quiet, passive, and subservient Oriental houseboy. Perhaps the editors hope that the icon of this imposing Chinese hero will dispel myths about Chinese American tractability.

While acquaintance with some of the Chinese folk heroes may induce the American public to acknowledge that Chinese culture too has its Robin Hood and John Wayne, I remain uneasy about the masculist orientation of the heroic tradition, especially as expounded by the editors who see loyalty, revenge, and individaul honor as the overriding ethos which should be inculcated in (if not already absorbed by) Chinese Americans. If white media have chosen to highlight and applaud the submissive and nonthreatening characteristics of Asians, the Asian American editors are equally tendentious in underscoring the militant strain of their Asian literary heritage.[28] The refutation of effeminate stereotypes through the glorification of machismo merely perpetuates patriarchal terms and assumptions.

Is it not possible for Chinese American men to recover a cultural space without denigrating or erasing "the feminine"? Chin contends that "use of the heroic tradition in Chinese literature as the source of Chinese American moral, ethical and esthetic universals is not literary rhetoric and smartass cute tricks, not wishful thinking, not theory, not demagoguery and prescription, but simple history."[29] However, even history, which is also a form of social construct, is not exempt from critical scrutiny. The Asian heroic tradition, like its Western counterpart, must be re-evaluated so that both its strengths and limits can surface. The intellectual excitement and the emotional appeal of the tradition is indisputable: the strategic brilliance of characters such as Chou Yu and Chuko Liang in *Romance of the Three Kingdons* rivals that of Odysseus, and the fraternal bond between the three sworn brothers—Liu Pei, Chang Fei, and Kuan Yu (Kwan Kung)—is no less moving than that between Achilles and Patrocles. But just as I no longer believe that Homer speaks for humanity (or even all mankind), I hesitate to subscribe wholeheartedly to the *Aiiieeeee!* editors' claim that the Asian heroic canon (composed entirely of work written by men though it contains a handful of heroines) encompasses "Asian universals."

Nor do I concur with the editors that a truculent mentality pervades the Chinese heroic tradition, which generally places a higher premium on benevolence than on force and stresses the primacy of kinship and friendship over personal power. By way of illustration I will turn to the prototype for Kingston's "woman warrior"—Fa Mu Lan (also known as Hua Mulan and Fa Muk Lan). According to the original "Ballad of Mulan" (which most Chinese children, including myself, had to learn by heart) the heroine in joining the army is prompted neither by revenge nor by personal honor but by filial piety. She enlists under male disguise to take the place of her aged father. Instead of celebrating the glory of war, the poem describes the bleakness of the battlefield and the loneliness of the daughter (who sorely misses her parents). The use of understatement in such lines as "the general was killed after hundreds of combats" and "the warriors returned in ten years" (my translation) connotes the cost and duration of battles. The "Ballad of Mulan," though it commits the filial and courageous daughter to public memory, also contains a pacifist subtext—much in the way that the *Iliad* conceals an antiwar message beneath its martial trappings. A re-examination of the Asian heroic tradition may actually reveal that it is richer and more sophisticated than the *Aiiieeeee!* editors, bent on finding belligerent models, would allow.[30]

Kingston's adaptation of the legend in *The Woman Warrior* is equally multivalent. Fa Mu Lan as re-created in the protagonist's fantasy does excel in martial arts, but her power is derived as much from the words carved on her back as from her military skills. And the transformed heroine still proves problematic as a model since she can only exercise her power when in male armor. As I have argued elsewhere, her military distinction, insofar as it valorizes the ability to be ruthless and violent—"to fight like a man"—affirms rather than subverts patriarchal mores.[31] In fact, Kingston discloses in an interview that the publisher is the one who entitled the book "The Woman Warrior" while she herself (who is a pacifist) resists complete identification with the war heroine:

> I don't really like warriors. I wish I had not had a metaphor of a warrior, a person who uses weapons and goes to war. I guess I always have in my style a doubt about wars as a way of solving things.[32]

Aside from the fantasy connected with Fa Mu Lan the book has little to do with actual fighting. The real battle that runs through the work is one against silence and invisibility. Forbidden by her mother to tell a secret, unable to read aloud in English while first attending American school, and later fired for protesting against racism, the protagonist eventually speaks with a vengeance through writing—through a heroic act of self-expression. At the end of the book her tutelary genius has changed from Fa Mu Lan to Ts'ai Yen—from warrior to poet.

Kingston's commitment to pacifism—through re-visioning and re-contextualizing ancient "heroic" material—is even more evident in her most recent book, *Tripmaster Monkey*. As though anticipating the editors of *The Big Aiiieeeee!,* the author alludes recurrently to the Chinese heroic tradition, but always with a feminist twist. The protagonist of this novel, Wittman Ah Sing, is a playwright who loves *Romance of the Three Kingdoms* (one of the aforementioned epics espoused by Chin). Kingston's novel culminates with Wittman directing a marathon show which he has written based on the *Romance.* At the end of the show he has a rather surprising illumination:

> He had made up his mind: he will not go to Viet Nam or to any war. He had staged the War of the Three Kingdoms as heroically as he could, which made him start to understand: The three brothers and Cho Cho were masters of the war; they had worked out strategies and justifications for war so brilliantly that their policies and their tactics are used today, even by governments with nuclear-powered weapons. And they *lost.* The clanging and banging fooled us, but now we know—they lost. Studying the mightiest war epic of all time, Wittman changed—beeen!—into a pacifist. Dear American monkey, don't be afraid. Here, let us tweak your ear, and kiss your other ear.[33]

The seemingly easy transformation of Wittman—who is curiously evocative of Chin in speech and manner—is achieved through the pacifist author's sleight of hand. Nevertheless, the novel does show that it is possible to celebrate the ingenious strategies of the ancient warriors without embracing, wholesale, the heroic code that motivates their behavior and without endorsing violence as a positive expression of masculinity.[34]

Unfortunately, the ability to perform violent acts implied in the concepts of warrior and epic hero is still all too often mistaken for manly courage; and men who have been historically subjugated are all the more tempted to adopt a militant stance to manifest their masculinity. In the notorious Moynihan report on the black family, "military service for Negroes" was recommended as a means to potency:

> Given the strains of the disorganized and matrifocal family life in which so many Negro youth come of age, the Armed Forces are a dramatic and desperately needed change: a world away from women, a world run by strong men of unquestioned authority.[35]

Moynihan believed that placing black men in an "utterly masculine world" will strengthen them. The black men in the sixties who worshipped figures that exploited and brutalized women likewise conflated might and masculinity. Toni Cade, who cautions against "equating black liberation with black men gaining access to male privilege," offers an alternative to patriarchal prescriptions for manhood:

> Perhaps we need to let go of all notions of manhood and femininity and concentrate on Blackhood. . . . It perhaps takes less heart to pick up the gun than to face the task of creating a new identity, a self, perhaps an androgynous self. . . .[36]

If Chinese American men use the Asian heroic dispensation to promote male aggression, they may risk remaking themselves in the image of their oppressors—albeit under the guise of Asian panoply. Precisely because the racist treatment of Asians has taken the peculiar form of sexism—insofar as the indignities suffered by men of Chinese descent are analogous to those traditionally suffered by women—we must refrain from seeking antifeminist solutions to racism. To do otherwise reinforces not only patriarchy but also white supremacy.

Well worth heeding is Althusser's caveat that when a dominant ideology is integrated as common sense into the consciousness of the dominated, the dominant class will continue to prevail.[37] Instead of tailoring ourselves to white ideals, Asian Americans may insist on alternative habits and ways of seeing. Instead of drumming up support for Asian American "manhood," we may consider demystifying popular stereotypes while reappropriating what Stanford Lyman calls the "kernels of truth" in them that are indeed part of our ethnic heritage. For instance, we need not accept the Western association of Asian self-restraint with passivity and femininity. I, for one, believe that the respectful demeanor of many an Asian and Asian American indicates, among other things, a willingness to listen to others and to resolve conflict rationally or tactfully.[38] Such a collaborative disposition—be it Asian or non-Asian, feminine or masculine—is surely no less valid and viable than one that is vociferous and confrontational.

V

Although I have thus far concentrated on the gender issues in the Chinese American cultural domina, they do have provocative implications for feminist theory and criticism. As Elizabeth Spelman points out, "It is not easy to think about gender, race, and class in ways that don't obscure or underplay their effects on one another."[39] Still, the task is to develop paradigms that can admit these crosscurrents and that can reach out to women of color and perhaps also to men.

Women who value familial and ethnic solidarity may find it especially difficult to rally to the feminist cause without feeling divided or without being accused of betrayal, especially when the men in their ethnic groups also face social iniquities. Kingston, for instance, has tried throughout her work to mediate between affirming her ethnic heritage and undermining patriarchy. But she feels that identification with Asian men at times inhibits an equally strong feminist impulse. Such split loyalties apparently prompted her to publish *The Woman Warrior* and *China Men* separately, though they were conceived and written together as an "interlocking story." Lest the men's stories "undercut the feminist viewpoint," she separated the female and the male stories into two books. She says, "I care about men . . . as much as I care about women. . . . Given the present state of affairs, perhaps men's and women's experiences have to be dealt with separately for now, until more auspicious times are with us."[40]

Yet such separation has its dangers, particularly if it means that men and women will continue to work in opposing directions, as reflected in the divergences between the proponents of the Asian heroic tradition and Asian American feminists. Feminist ideas have made little inroad in the writing of the *Aiiieeeee!* editors, who contine to operate within patriarchal grids. White feminists, on the other hand, are often oblivious to the fact that there are other groups besides women who have been "feminized" and puzzled when women of color do not readily rally to their camp.

The recent shift from feminist studies to gender studies suggests that the time has come to look at women and men together. I hope that the shift will also entice both men and women to do the looking and, by so doing, strengthen the alliance between gender studies and ethnic studies. Lest feminist criticism remain in the wilderness, white scholars must reckon with race and class as integral experiences for both men and women, and acknowledge that not only female voices but the voices of many men of color have been historically silenced or dismissed. Expanding the feminist frame of reference will allow certain existing theories to be interrogated or reformulated.[41] Asian American men need to be wary of certain pitfalls in using what Foucault calls "reverse discourse," in demanding legitimacy "in the same vocabulary, using the same categories by which [they were] disqualified."[42] The ones who can be recruited into the field of gender studies may someday see feminists as allies rather than adversaries, and proceed to dismantle not just white but also male supremacy. Women of color should not have to undergo a self-division resulting from having to choose between female and ethnic identities. Chinese American women writers may find a way to negotiate the tangle of sexual and racial politics in all its intricacies, not just out of a desire for "revenge" but also out of a sense of "loyalty." If we ask them to write with a vigilant eye against possible misappropriation by white readers or against possible offense to "Asian American manhood," however, we will end up implicitly sustaining racial and sexual hierarchies. All of us need to be conscious of our "complicity with the gender ideologies" of patriarchy, whatever its origins, and to work toward notions of gender and ethnicity that are nonhierarchical, nonbinary, and nonprescriptive; that can embrace tensions rather than perpetuate divisions.[43] To reclaim cultural traditions without getting bogged down in the mire of traditional constraints, to attack stereotypes without falling prey to their binary opposites, to chart new topographies for manliness and womanliness, will surely demand genuine heroism.

Notes

1. Research for this essay is funded in part by an Academic Senate grant and a grant from the Institute of American Cultures and the Asian American Studies Center, UCLA. I wish to thank the many whose help, criticism, and encouragement have sustained me through the mentally embattled period of writing this essay: Kim Crenshaw, Donald Goellnicht, Marianne Hirsch, Evelyn Fox Keller, Elaine Kim, Elizabeth Kim, Ken Lincoln, Gerard Maré, Rosalind Melis, Jeff Spielberg, Sau-ling Wong, Richard Yarborough, and Stan Yogi.

A version of this article was delivered at the 1989 MLA Convention in Washington, DC. My title alludes not only to Maxine Hong Kingston's *The Woman Warrior* and *China Men* but also Frank Chin's *The Chickencoop Chinaman* and *The Chinaman Pacific & Frisco R. R. Co.* The term "Chinamen" has acquired diverse connotations through time: "In the early days of Chinese American history, men called themselves 'Chinamen' just as other newcomers called themselves 'Englishmen' or 'Frenchmen': the term distinguished them from the 'Chinese' who remained citizens of China, and also showed that they were not recognized as Americans. Later, of course, it became an insult. Young Chinese Americans today are reclaiming the word because of its political and historical precision, and are demanding that it be said with dignity and not for name-calling" (Kingston, "San Francisco's Chinatown: A View from the Other Side of Arnold Genthe's Camera," *American Heritage* [Dec. 1978]: 37). In my article the term refers exclusively to men.

2. The devaluation of daughters is a theme explored in *The Woman Warrior* (1976; New York: Vintage, 1977); as this book suggests, this aspect of patriarchy is upheld no less by women than by men. The "emasculation" of Chinese American men is addressed in *China Men* (1980; New York: Ballantine, 1981), in which Kingston attempts to reclaim the founders of Chinese America. Subsequent page references to these two books will appear in the text. Detailed accounts of early Chinese immigrant history can be found in Victor G. Nee and Brett De Bary Nee, *Longtime Californ': A Documentary Study of an American Chinatown* (1973; New York: Pantheon, 1981); and Ronald Takaki, *Strangers from a Different Shore: A History of Asian Americans* (Boston: Little Brown, 1989), 79–131.

3. See Edward Said, *Orientalism* (New York: Vintage, 1979). Although Said focuses on French and British representations of the Middle East, many of his insights also apply to American perceptions of the Far East.

4. "Asian American Writers: A Bibliographical Review," *American Studies International* 22.2 (Oct. 1984): 64.

5. "Confessions of the Chinatown Cowboy," *Bulletin of Concerned Asian Scholars* 4.3 (1972): 66.

6. "Racist Love," *Seeing through Shuck,* ed. Richard Kostelanetz (New York: Ballantine, 1972), 65, 79. Although the cinematic image of Bruce Lee as a Kung-fu master might have somewhat countered the feminine representations of Chinese American men, his role in the only one Hollywood film in which he appeared before he died was, in Elaine Kim's words, "less a human being than a fighting machine" ("Asian Americans and American popular Culture," *Dictionary of Asian American History,* ed. Hyung-Chan Kim [New York: Greenwood Press, 1986], 107).

7. "Racist Love," 69.

8. "Asian American Writers: A Bibliographical Review," 64.

9. "Racist Love," 68. The five writers under discussion are Pardee Lowe, Jade Snow Wong, Virginia Lee, Betty Lee Sung, and Diana Chang.

10. Similar objections to the passage have been raised by Merle Woo in "Letter to Ma," *This Bridge Called my Back: Writings by Radical Women of Color,* ed. Cherríe Moraga and Gloria Anzaldúa (1981; New York: Kitchen Table, 1983), 145; and Elaine Kim in *Asian American Literature: An Introduction to the Writings and Their Social Context* (Philadelphia: Temple UP, 1982), 189. Richard Yarborough delineates a somewhat parallel conundrum about manhood faced by African American writers in the nineteenth century and which, I believe, persists to some extent to this day; see "Race, Violence, and Manhood: The Masculine Ideal in Frederick Douglass's 'Heroic Slave,'" forthcoming in *Frederick Douglass: New Literary and Historical Essays,* ed. Eric J. Sundquist (Cambridge, MA: Cambridge UP). There is, however, an important difference between the dilemma faced by the African American men and that faced by Asian American men. While writers such as William Wells Brown and Frederick Douglass tried to reconcile the white inscription of the militant and sensual Negro and the white ideal of heroic manhood, several Chinese American male writers are trying to disprove the white stereotype of the passive and effeminate Asian by invoking its binary opposite.

11. *Aiiieeeee! An Anthology of Asian-American Writers* (1974; Washington: Howard UP, 1983), xxxviii; *The Big Aiiieeeee! An Anthology of Asian American Writers* (New York: New American Library, forthcoming). All the Asian classics cited are available in English translations: Sun Tzu, *The Art of War,* trans. Samuel B. Griffith (London: Oxford UP, 1963); Shi Nai'an and Luo Guanzhong, *Outlaws of the Marsh [The Water Margin],* trans. Sidney Shapiro (jointly published by Beijing: Foreign Language P and Bloomington: Indiana UP, 1981); Luo Guan-Zhong, *Romance of the Three Kingdoms,* trans. C. H. Brewitt-Taylor (Singapore: Graham Brash, 1986), 2 vols.; Wu Ch'eng-en, *Journey to the West,* trans. Anthony Yu (Chicago: U of Chicago P, 1980), 4 vols.; Takeda Izumo, Miyoshi Shoraku, and Namiki Senryu, *Chushingura (The Treasury of Loyal Retainers),* trans. Donald Keene (New York: Columbia UP, 1971). I would like to thank Frank Chin for allowing me to see an early draft of *The Big Aiiieeeee!.* For a foretaste of his exposition of the Chinese heroic tradition, see "This is Not an Autobiography," *Genre* 18 (1985): 109–30.

12. The feminist works that come to mind include Paula Gunn Allen, *The Sacred Hoop: Recovering the Feminine in American Indian Traditions* (Boston: Beacon, 1986); Nina Auerbach, *Communities of Women: An Idea in Fiction* (Cambridge: Harvard UP, 1978); Zillah R. Eisenstein, *The Radical Future of Liberal Feminism* (New York: Longman, 1981); Carol Gilligan, *In a Different Voice: Psychological Theory and Women's Development* (Cambridge: Harvard UP, 1982); Christa Wolf, *Cassandra: A Novel and Four Essays,* trans. Jan van Heurck (New York: Farrar, 1984). The Chinese maxims appear in the introduction to *The Big Aiiieeeee!* (draft) and are quoted with the editors' permission. The same maxims are cited in Frank Chin, "This Is Not an Autobiography."

13. Chin, "This Is Not An Autobiography," 112, 122, 130.

14. "All of a Piece: Women's Poetry and Autobiography," *Life/Lines: Theorizing Women's Autobiography,* ed. Bella Brodzki and Celeste Schenck (Ithaca: Cornell UP, 1988), 286. See also Estelle Jelinek, ed., *Women's Autobiography: Essays in Criticism* (Bloomington: Indiana UP, 1980); Donna Stanton, *The Female Autograph* (New York: New York Literary Forum, 1984); Sidonie Smith, *Poetics of Women's Autobiography: Marginality and the Fictions of Self-Representation* (Bloomington: Indiana UP, 1987).

15. "The Most Popular Book in China," *Quilt 4,* ed. Ishmael Reed and Al Young (Berkeley: Quilt, 1984), 12. The essay is republished as the "Afterword" in *The China-man Pacific & Frisco R. R. Co.* The literary duel between Chin, a self-styled "China-town Cowboy," and Kingston, an undisguised feminist, closely parallels the paper war between Ishmael Reed and Alice Walker.

16. "The Mysterious West," *New York Review of Books,* 28 April 1977: 41.

17. "Critic of Admirer Sees Dumb Racist," *San Francisco Journal,* 11 May 1977: 20.

18. "Autobiography as Guided Chinatown Tour?," *American Lives: Essays in Multi-cultural American Autobiography,* ed. James Robert Payne (Knoxville: U of Tennessee P, forthcoming). See also Deborah Woo, "The Ethnic Writer and the Burden of 'Dual Authenticity': The Dilemma of Maxine Hong Kingston," forthcoming in *Amerasia Journal.* Reviews by Chinese American women who identify strongly with Kingston's protagonist include Nellie Wong, "The Woman Warrior," *Bridge* (Winter 1978): 46–48; and Suzi Wong, review of *The Woman Warrior, Amerasia Journal* 4.1 (1977): 165–67.

19. "Gender and Genre Anxiety: Elizabeth Barrett Browning and H. D. as Epic Poets," *Tulsa Studies in Women's Literature* 5.2 (Fall 1986): 203–28.

20. Furthermore, a work highlighting sexism within an ethnic community is generally more palatable to the reading public than a work that condemns racism. *The Woman Warrior* addresses both forms of oppression, but critics have focused al-most exclusively on its feminist themes.

21. Susanne Juhasz argues that because women have traditionally lived a "kind of private life, that of the imagination, which has special significance due to the outright conflict between societal possibility and imaginative possibility, [Kingston] makes autobiography from fiction, from fantasy, from forms that have convention-ally belonged to the novel" ("Towards a Theory of Form in Feminist Autobiogra-phy." *International Journal of Women's Studies* 2.1 [1979]: 62).

22. Cf. similar critical responses in the African American community provoked by Alice Walker's *The Color Purple* and Toni Morrison's *Beloved.*
Although I limit my discussion to sexual politics in Chinese America, Asian American women are just as vulnerable to white sexism, as the denigrating stereo-types discussed by Kim earlier suggest.

23. Li Ju-Chen, *Flowers in the Mirror,* trans. and ed. Lin Tai-Yi (London: Peter Owen, 1965).

24. A recent case has been made into a powerful public television documentary: "Who Killed Vincent Chin?" (directed by Renee Tajima and Christine Choy, 1989). Chin, who punched a white auto-worker in Detroit in response to his racial slurs, was subsequently battered to death by the worker and his stepson with a baseball bat.

25. The interview was conducted by Kay Bonetti for the American Audio Prose Library (Columbia, MO, 1986).

Jonathan Culler has discussed the various implications, for both sexes, of "Reading as a Woman" (*On Deconstruction: Theory and Criticism after Structuralism* [Ithaca: Cornell UP, 1982], 43–64); see also *Men in Feminism,* ed. Alice Jardine and Paul Smith (New York: Methuen, 1987).

26. The other modes are found in works as diverse as T'ao Ch'ien's poems (pastoral), Ch'u Yuan's *Li sao* (elegiac), selected writing by Lao Tzu and Chuang Tzu (metaphysical), and P'u Sung-ling's *Liao-Chai Chih I* (Gothic). (My thanks to Shumei Shih and Adam Schorr for helping me with part of the romanization.) One must bear in mind, however, that Asian and Western generic terms often fail to correspond. For example, what the *Aiiieeeee!* editors call "epics" are loosely classified as "novels" in Chinese literature.

27. Epic heroes, according to C. M. Bowra, are "the champions of man's ambitions" seeking to "win as far as possible a self-sufficient manhood" (*Heroic Poetry* [London: Macmillan, 1952], 14). Their Chinese counterparts are no exception.

28. Benjamin R. Tong argues that the uneducated Cantonese peasants who comprised the majority of early Chinese immigrants were not docile but venturesome and rebellious, that putative Chinese traits such as meekness and obedience to authority were in fact "reactivated" in America in response to white racism ("The Ghetto of the Mind," *Amerasia Journal* 1.3 [1971]: 1–31). Chin, who basically agrees with Tong, also attributes the submissive and "unheroic" traits of Chinese Americans to Christianity ("This Is Not An Autobiography"). While Tong and Chin are right in distinguishing the Cantonese folk culture of the early immigrants from the classical tradition of the literati, they underestimate the extent to which mainstream Chinese thought infiltrated Cantonese folk imagination, wherein the heroic ethos coexists with Buddhist beliefs and Confucian teachings (which do counsel self-restraint and obedience to parental and state authority). To attribute the "submissive" traits of Chinese Americans entirely to white racism or to Christianity is to discount the complexity and the rich contradictions of the Cantonese culture and the resourceful flexibility and adaptability of the early immigrants.

29. "This Is Not an Autobiography," 127.

30. Conflicting attitudes toward Homeric war heroes are discussed in Katherine Callen King, *Achilles: Paradigms of the War Hero from Homer to the Middle Ages* (Berkeley: U of California P, 1987). Pacifist or at least anti-killing sentiments can be found

in the very works deemed "heroic" by Chin and the editors. *Romance of the Three Kingdoms* not only dramatizes the senseless deaths and the ravages of war but also betrays a wishful longing for peace and unity, impossible under the division of "three kingdoms." Even *The Art of War* sets benevolence above violence and discourages actual fighting and killing: "To subdue the enemy without fighting is the acme of skill" (77).

31. "'Don't Tell': Imposed Silences in *The Color Purple* and *The Woman Warrior*," *PMLA* (March 1988): 166. I must add, however, that paradoxes about manhood inform Chinese as well as American cultures. The "contradictions inherent in the bourgeois male ideal" is pointed out by Yarborough: "the use of physical force is, at some levels, antithetical to the middle-class privileging of self-restraint and reason: yet an important component of conventional concepts of male courage is the willingness to use force" ("Race, Violence, and Manhood: The Masculine Ideal in Frederick Douglass's 'Heroic Slave'"). Similarly, two opposing ideals of manhood coexist in Chinese culture, that of a civil scholar who would never stoop to violence and that of a fearless warrior who would not brook insult or injustice. Popular Cantonese maxims such as "a superior man would only move his mouth but not his hands" (i.e., would never resort to physical combat) and "he who does not take revenge is not a superior man" exemplify the contradictions.

32. Interview conducted by Kay Bonetti.

33. *Tripmaster Monkey: His Fake Book* (New York: Knopf, 1989), 348.

34. I am aware that a forceful response to oppression is sometimes necessary, that it is much easier for those who have never encountered physical blows and gunshots to maintain faith in nonviolent resistance. My own faith was somewhat shaken while watching the tragedy of Tiananmen on television; on the other hand, the image of the lone Chinese man standing in front of army tanks reinforced my belief that there is another form of heroism that far excels brute force.

35. Lee Rainwater and William L. Yancey, *The Moynihan Report and the Politics of Controversy* (Cambridge: M.I.T. Press, 1967), 88 (p. 42 in the original report by Daniel Patrick Moynihan).

36. "On the Issue of Roles," *The Black Woman: An Anthology*, ed. Toni Cade (York, ON: Mentor-NAL, 1970), 103; see also Bell Hooks, *Ain't I a Woman: Black Women and Feminism* (Boston: South End Press, 1981), 87–117.

37. *Lenin and Philosophy and Other Essays* (New York: Monthly Review Press, 1971), 174–83.

38. Of course, Asians are not all alike, and most generalizations are ultimately misleading. Elaine Kim pointed out to me that "It's popularly thought that Japanese strive for peaceful resolution of conflict and achievement of consensus while Koreans—for material as much as metaphysical reasons—seem at times to en-

courage combativeness in one another" (personal correspondence, quoted with permission). Differences within each national group are no less pronounced.

39. *Inessential Woman: Problems of Exclusion in Feminist Thought* (Boston: Beacon, 1988), 115. I omitted class from my discussion only because it is not at the center of the literary debate.

40. Elaine Kim, *Asian American Literature: An Introduction to the Writings and Their Social Context* (Philadelphia: Temple UP, 1982), 209.

41. Donald Goellnicht, for instance, has argued that a girl from a racial minority "experiences not a single, but a double subject split; first, when she becomes aware of the gendered position constructed for her by the symbolic language of patriarchy; and second, when she recognizes that discursively and socially constructed positions of racial difference also obtain . . . [that] the 'fathers' of her racial and cultural group are silenced and degraded by the Laws of the Ruling Fathers" ("Father Land and/or Mother Tongue: The Divided Female Subject in *The Woman Warrior* and *Obasan,"* paper delivered at the MLA Convention, 1988).

42. *The History of Sexuality*, vol. 1, trans. Robert Hurley (New York: Vintage, 1980), 101.

43. Teresa de Lauretis, *Technologies of Gender: Essays on Theory, Film, and Fiction* (Bloomington: Indiana UP, 1987), 11.

Chinese American Women Writers

The Tradition behind Maxine Hong Kingston

AMY LING

◆ ◆ ◆

WRITING IS AN ACT OF self-assertion, self-revelation, and self-preservation. One writes out of a delight in one's storytelling powers, out of a need to reveal and explain oneself, or from the desire to record and preserve experience. However, for women brought up in the old Chinese tradition that for eighteen hundred years codified their obedience and submission to the men in their lives—father, husband, son—a tradition that stressed female chastity, modesty, and restraint; that broke girls' toes and bound their feet as an ideal of beauty; that sold daughters into slavery in times of hardship; that encouraged and honored widow suicides—any writing at all was unusual, even an act of rebellion. Working-class women did not have the education or leisure, and upper-class women were taught that writing was "an unwomanly occupation, destructive of one's moral character, like acting" (Han Suyin, *Destination* 8; 1969). Furthermore, since it was the Chinese custom to leave the women at home when the men first immigrated, temporarily they thought, to the Gold Mountain to make their fortunes, the number of Chinese women in America was small. In 1852, for example, of the 11,794 Chinese in California, only 7 were women, and most of these were prostitutes. By the 1880s the ratio had risen to 1 woman for every 20 men (Hirata 226–28). Moreover, from 1924 to 1930, a law specifically prohibited Chinese women, including wives of American-born Chinese, from immigrating to this country. In 1930, the act was revised, and, for the next ten years, an average of 60 Chinese women entered the United States each year. The 1882 Chinese Exclusion Act was not repealed until 1943, and the numbers of Chinese women in the United States did not approach equality with Chinese men until 1954. Thus it is not surprising that we have so little writing by Chinese American women; it is notable that we have so much.

With the exception of Maxine Hong Kingston, most scholars of American literature are at a loss to name Chinese American women writers. Yet Kingston is not an isolated Athena (or Hua Mulan) springing full grown from Zeus's (or Buddha's) forehead. A line of Chinese American women writers dating back nearly a century preceded her. My term *Chinese American* is broadly inclusive, embracing people of full or half Chinese ancestry; American-born or naturalized immigrants; citizens and sojourners, who have published in the United States. Obviously, books written in Chinese by United States residents are also Chinese American, but since the Chinese language is accessible to so few Americans, this study will be limited to works in English and specifically to full-length works of prose. My definition will be stretched to include international figures like Han Suyin, now residing in Lausanne, Switzerland, and Lin Tai-yi, who lived in Hong Kong for many years, who may not consider themselves American and, in the case of the former, who may not even have lived any appreciable length of time in the United States. However, since they write in English and since their books are regularly published in this country, they certainly are addressing an American audience, and their voices, particularly Han Suyin's, have been heard here and have had an impact. Finally, as Vladimir Nabokov is considered "American" enough to be included in American literature anthologies, so Han Suyin and Lin Tai-yi are included here.

Using this definition, we find that the majority of Chinese American works are by immigrants and sojourners, daughters of diplomats and scholars, and those who have had contact with the West through missionaries or mission schools. For the immigrant, the very act of choosing to write in English, a second language, and thereby addressing a predominantly Caucasian audience is significant and colors the purpose and nature of the work. Though generalizations are always riddled with exceptions, we may say that immigrant and sojourner Chinese American writers, like Helena Kuo and Lin Tai-yi, seek primarily to explain and justify China and Chinese ways to the Western world. As their sensibilities were shaped in their homeland, they have what seems a stable, single center. Their upbringing, as Francis Hsu pointed out in his comparative study *Americans and Chinese,* gives them a strong group orientation, a concern for the good of the whole. Transplanted after their formative years, they see their role in the West as interpreters and ambassadors of good will and understanding for China; to borrow David Riesman's term, they are "other-directed."

American-born Chinese American writers, like Kingston, however, tend to be more individualistic and to have an inward focus. Because they have grown up as a racial minority, imbibing the customs of two cultures, their centers are not stable and single. Their consciousness, as W. E. B. Du Bois pointed out for African Americans, is double; their vision bifocal and fluctuating. Therefore, they look inward with an urgency to comprehend and balance the bicultural clashes they have known and must reconcile. That they write and publish is of course indicative of an awareness of an external world and a desire to communicate, but their initial impetus is primarily introspective. Their purpose is to explain themselves to themselves.

Eurasians and Amerasians may be said to combine the characteristics of immigrants and American-born Chinese Americans. They may, as in the case of Han Suyin and Edith Eaton, identify so strongly with the Chinese side of their ancestry that they have all the fervor, and sometimes more, of the Chinese-formed immigrant instructing and explaining her homeland to outsiders. And yet, at times, like the American-born Chinese American, they also look within and express the conflicts of the two cultures, in their cases particularly poignant, when warring factions are represented by the two heritages that are their own.

Apart from the sociological and psychological effects of birth and upbringing on the sense of self, and purpose in writing in relation to self or other, the highly diverse fifteen writers in this study may be roughly placed into three thematic or formal categories: delight in storytelling often mingled with nostalgia, protest against racial and sexual injustice, and experiment in language or structure. Many of the writers, depending on the time in their lives and on the individual work in question, move from one category to another, and often even a single work crosses categorical boundaries.

II

Chinese American literary history begins with two Eurasian sisters who responded to racism in divergent ways in their writing. Because they created paradigms followed by their successors, we shall examine them in some detail. Edith (1865–1914) and Winnifred (1875–1954) Eaton were two of fourteen surviving children born to an English landscape painter, Edward Eaton, and his Chinese wife, Grace Trefusis. The Eatons immigrated from England to America, living first in the United States and then settling in Montreal. Both sisters, as adults, moved to the United States—Edith lived briefly in the Midwest and for more than ten years in San Francisco and Seattle; Winnifred, in Chicago, New York, and Los Angeles.

Though initially shocked by the first Chinese workers she saw on her arrival in the United States, "uncouth specimens of their race, drest in working blouses and pantaloons with queues hanging down their backs" ("Leaves" 126), Edith Eaton later identified strongly with her mother's people, assumed a Cantonese pen name, Sui Sin Far (Narcissus), and wrote short stories and articles "to fight their battles in the papers" ("Leaves" 128).

At that time the Chinese had many battles to fight, for throughout the late nineteenth century and the early decades of the twentieth, anti-Chinese sentiment raced across the United States. Imported by the thousands for the construction of the railroads, Chinese workers remaining here were seen as a threat to white labor and became targets of mass vilification campaigns, physical abuse, and even murder. From 1882 until 1943, the Chinese Exclusion Act prohibited United States entry to all Chinese except teachers, students, merchants, and diplomats. Japan, by contrast—having won a war against China in 1895 and against Russia in 1904–05, and with few nationals in the United States to be a threat—was highly respected. A dialogue recounted by Edith Eaton in her autobiographical essay "Leaves from the Mental Portfolio of an Eurasian" demonstrates clearly the contrasting attitudes toward Chinese and Japanese in the United States at the turn of the century:

> "Somehow or other . . . I cannot reconcile myself to the thought that the Chinese are humans like ourselves." [Mr. K., her new employer]
> "A Chinaman is, in my eyes, more repulsive than a nigger." [the town clerk]
> "Now the Japanese are different altogether. There is something bright and likeable about those men." [Mr. K.] (129)

Though her facial features did not betray her racial background, Edith's response to this conversation was the courageous one of asserting her Chinese ethnicity at the expense of her job with Mr. K.

Winnifred, perhaps reasoning that few could tell the difference between Japanese and Chinese, decided to be the favored "Oriental." Exploiting the prejudices of her day, she invented a Japanese pen name, Onoto

Watanna, claimed a Japanese noblewoman for a mother and Nagasaki for a birthplace, and concocted tender romances set in Japan coupling charming Japanese or Eurasian heroines with American or English heroes. Winnifred's works were highly successful, exquisitely published with full-color illustrations by real Japanese artists, the text printed on decorated paper. They went through repeated printings, were translated into European languages, and were adapted for the stage. Winnifred went on to an exclusive contract with Hearst Publications and later became scriptwriter and editor for Universal Studios and MGM before retiring to an elegant home in Calgary, Alberta.

Assertion of her Chinese ethnicity was not easy for Edith Eaton, for initially the Chinese themselves did not recognize her as one of their own and were almost as ignorant and rude as her brief employer, Mr. K.:

> . . . save for a few phrases, I am unacquainted with my mother tongue. How, then, can I expect these people to accept me as their own countrywoman? The Americanized Chinamen actually laugh in my face when I tell them that I am one of their race. ("Leaves" 131)

Nonetheless, after a lifetime of stories and articles in defense of the Chinese, published in the leading magazines of the time, Sui Sin Far received the recognition and appreciation of the Chinese community in the form of an engraved memorial stone erected on her tomb in the Protestant Cemetery in Montreal.

Edith Eaton's collected stories, published under the title *Mrs. Spring Fragrance* (1912), are divided into tales for adults and those for children. They are simply told. Some are marked by a sentiment fashionable in her day. Others introduce themes and perspectives new to American literature. The following passage from the title story gives a sample of the irony Eaton employs in the cause of sexual and racial protest. Lively, independent Mrs. Spring Fragrance, on a visit to San Francisco, writes a letter in Chinese-flavored English to her husband in Seattle, about a lecture a Caucasian woman had taken her to, entitled "America the Protector of China":

> It was most exhilarating, and the effect of so much expression of benevolence leads me to beg of you to forget to remember that the barber charges you one dollar for a shave while he humbly submits to the American man a bill of fifteen cents. And murmur no more because your honored elder brother, on a visit to this country, is detained under the rooftree of this great Government instead of under your own humble roof. Console him with the reflection that he is protected under the wing of the Eagle, the Em-

blem of Liberty. What is the loss of ten hundred years or ten thousand times ten dollars compared with the happiness of knowing oneself so securely sheltered? All of this I have learned from Mrs. Samuel Smith, who is as brilliant and great of mind as one of your own superior sex. (8–9)

In Edith Eaton's stories the Chinese in America are presented sympathetically, not as one-dimensional heathens but as multidimensional humans, capable of suffering pain and of inflicting it, of living and being lovable, of being loyal as well as deceiving. Compared with most of the contemporaneous writing about Chinese by white authors, analyzed and discussed comprehensively by William Wu in *The Yellow Peril* (1982), or the writing by Christian missionaries, as represented by *The Lady of the Lily Feet,* by Helen Clark (1900), stressing the sensational, "heathenish" Chinese practices, Edith Eaton's stories give a balanced view, attempting to portray psychologically realistic conditions. She is most successful in presenting the inner condition of the Eurasian in a society hostile to one part of her heritage. In "Its Wavering Image," and particularly in "Story of One White Woman Who Married a Chinese," she examines the interracial anguish she personally knew. Though the white wife of a Chinese is despised by society for her marriage, she ignores others' opinions until the birth of her son:

> . . . as he stands between his father and myself, like yet unlike us both, so will he stand in after years between his father's and his mother's people. And if there is no kindliness nor understanding between them, what will my boy's fate be? (132)

Edith Eaton compared her own Eurasian identity with bearing a cross and hoped that by giving her right hand to the Occidentals and her left hand to the Orientals, she herself, "the insignificant connecting link," would not be "utterly" destroyed ("Leaves" 132). One has the impression that she felt the anti-Chinese sentiment of her day so strongly and so personally that in a sense (dying at forty-nine, unmarried) she was destroyed early by the strain of attempting to be a bridge.

Winnifred Eaton, in her "Japanese" novels, flourished. With her first book, *Miss Numé of Japan,* she discovered a formula that worked and used it in romance after romance filled with such exotic elements as showers of cherry blossoms, moonlit assignations in bamboo groves, childlike women in colorful kimonos, fragile shoji screens. The formula includes the following elements: the work is short and easily read in one sitting; the setting is exotic; the potential lovers are introduced, then estranged through an initial obstacle (a difference in class, religion, or party, a previous engagement, opposing families); that obstacle is overcome, only to be followed by another one (war, meddling third parties, misunderstnding, duty else-where); during the prolonged separation the lovers each suffer mental an-guish or physical hardship and illness; finally, by chance or fate or the kind offices of a friend, the lovers are reunited.

Winnifred Eaton's women are nearly always in an inferior, powerless position: social outcasts (*A Japanese Nightingale, The Wooing of Wisteria*), orphans (*Sunny-San* and *The Heart of Hyacinth*), an unwanted stepdaugher (*Love of Aza-lea*), a blind, homeless wood sprite (*Tama*), a geisha in bondage (*The Honorable Miss Moonlight*). Her men, in clear contrast, are invariably in positions of power and influence: princes, ministers, architects, and professors. The plot, reiterated in book after book, of the helpless, childlike, charming Japanese female looking up to the powerful white male, could not but ap-peal to the white audience's sense of superiority and generosity, supporting as it did the prevailing stereotypes and prejudices.

However—to give credit where it is due—despite their powerless posi-tions, her heroines are also vivid, witty, spirited. Their seductive powers are quite real, as are Winnifred Eaton's storytelling powers. Though the plots may be a touch melodramatic or may hinge on a coincidence, they are nearly always engrossing, appealing; there is a certain magic that draws the reader into their spell of delicate emotions, of poignant twists and turns. Winnifred Eaton is particularly skilled at depicting tremulous, protract-edly unconsummated virgin love. Even as sophisticated a reader as William Dean Howells praised *A Japanese Nightingale* in the *North American Review:* "There is a quite indescribable freshness in the art of this pretty novelette . . . which is like no other art except in the simplicity which is native to the best art everywhere." In an extraliterary way, he was particularly taken with the heroine: "Yuki herself is of a surpassing lovableness. Nothing but the irresistible charm of the American girl could, I should think, keep the young men who read Mrs. Watana's [*sic*] book from going out and marry-ing Japanese girls" (881). Even Japanese readers, though recognizing that Winnifred Eaton was not a writer of the first magnitude, nonetheless praised her work and found it worthy of study alongside the books of Laf-cadio Hearn and Pierre Loti for playing "an important role in introducing things Japanese to the American public." They ranked her even higher than Hearn and Loti in that "her descriptions of human feelings are more delicate than those of both famous writers" (Swann and Takeda 58). If the Japanese themselves found that their culture was "properly introduced to the West" through Winnifred Eaton's books, her credibility and accom-plishment were even further enhanced.

The paradigms presented by the Eaton sisters are what Shirley Lim in a talk at the 1982 MLA Annual Convention called "exotics" and "existentials." The former, "other-directed," like Winnifred Eaton, are keenly aware of the economic, political, and social climate around them and respond by producing work that conforms to or upholds prevalent stereotypes. The latter, "inner-directed," like Edith Eaton, are more concerned with definition of self and exploration of being. The other-directed may perpetuate untruths in an effort to preserve physical well-being and achieve social approval, while the inner-directed seek to clarify truths in an attempt to maintain psychological health.

Throughout her career, Edith Eaton used her pen to protest injustice and prejudice, whether racial or sexual. In addition to fighting battles for the Chinese, she also fought for women, particularly working-class women. Her feminism comes through in a number of stories. In the ironically titled "The Inferior Woman" she shows a woman earning her own living to be superior to one whose family has wealth and status. In "The Heart's Desire," nothing—fancy foods, clothes, doting father, mother, brother—can make a princess happy but the friendship of a poor girl.

Winnifred's writing was more a barometer of the status quo than a protest against it. Her storytelling powers shone through her ethnic camouflage, making her a successful professional writer. She evaded thorny issues and never dealt with her own ethnicity in her books, except for Chinese cooks, minor characters on the Alberta ranches of her last two novels. However, in one of the last novels, *Cattle,* she abandoned the romantic mode for a naturalist one and voiced a feminist protest. Orphaned at fifteen, Nettie Day is purchased, along with her parents' furniture, by Bull Langdon, a ruthless cattle baron, who later rapes her and inadvertently kills their child. Another woman helps Nettie stand up to Bull and eventually marry the man she loves.

Though Winnifred Eaton did not write of bicultural conflicts, her career and the contortions and distortions she went through to become acceptable—hence able to make a living—testify to the existence of such conflicts. At age forty she published, anonymously, an autobiographical work, *Me,* in which, to some extent, she clears her conscience. Although *A Japanese Nightingale* has been in lights on Broadway, she was clearsighted enough to realize how far she was from her youthful dreams:

> What then I ardently believed to be the divine sparks of genius, I now perceived to be nothing but a mediocre talent that could never carry me far. My success was founded upon a cheap and popular device, and that jumble

of sentimental moonshine that they called my play seemed to me the pathetic stamp of my inefficiency. Oh, I had sold my birthright for a mess of potage. (153–54)

III

Shortly before and particularly after Pearl Harbor, American opinion of the Chinese and Japanese underwent an about-face. The Japanese were now the enemy; the long-suffering Chinese—who had lost Formosa and Korea to Japan in 1895, Manchuria in 1905, Beijing and all the coastal cities by 1938—became a friend and ally. Books by American-born and Chinese-born Chinese Americans suddenly mushroomed. The former were encouraged to write by an American public eager to distinguish friend from foe; the latter were impelled by personal experiences of the horrors of war. *Our Family,* by Adet and Anor Lin, and *Dawn over Chungking,* by Adet, Anor, and Meimei Lin; *Destination Chungking,* by Han Suyin; *Flame from the Rock,* by Adet Lin (under the pseudonym Tan Yun); *War Tide,* by Anor Lin (under the pseudonym Lin Tai-yi); *I've Come a Long Way, Peach Path,* and *Westward to Chungking,* by Helena Kuo; *Fifth Chinese Daughter,* by Jade Snow Wong; and *Echo of a Cry,* by Mai-mai Sze—all appeared within a few years of each other. Though published years later, Janet Lim's *Sold for Silver* and Anna Chennault's *A Thousand Springs* and *Education of Anna* are primarily concerned with the same period.

The novels and autobiographies by the Chinese-born writers are moving accounts of women's firsthand experience of war. They describe the refugees waiting day and night outdoors for trains to take them from threatened cities; boats so crammed that people perished in the crush or were drowned trying to get aboard; the devastation of Japanese incendiary bombs flattening buildings, creating giant craters and walls of flame, leaving bloody corpses and charred bones. But these books are filled as well with a glowing nationalism, with a deep pride in China's spiritual resistance, its patient, persistent rebuilding, its survival and endurance.

Dawn over Chungking is an unusual book because of its authors' ages: Adet was seventeen, Anor fourteen, and Meimei ten. The three are daughters of Lin Yutang, well-known novelist, essayist, and explainer of China to the West. Their book describes a return visit to China after a four-year stay in the United States. Through their individual chapters, we see that Meimei is the most Americanized, for she misses American foods; Anor has the strongest sense of humor, for when the bombs destroy their house, she finds her checkers, which the rats had stolen, and concludes impishly that "the Japs were not only trying to gain our love by bombing us, but trying very hard to help us kill rats too!" (120); Adet is the most romantic, ardently patriotic and Chinese. Despite the horrifying sights of rotting corpses, burning buildings, cratered streets, air raids that kept them underground six hours at a stretch, Adet sees the war as a leveler, pulling rich and poor together for a common cause, and she is moved by the beauty of that bond. *Dawn over Chungking* has the poignant appeal, though not the tragic outcome, of *The Diary of Anne Frank*, for it too is an account of tender, idealistic youth confronted with the most brutal human behavior yet still believing in humanity's inherent goodness and still nurturing hope for the future.

The theme of wartime love pervades both *Destination Chungking* and *Flame from the Rock*. The first is a beautifully written, fictionalized autobiography recounting the relationship between Han Suyin, a Chinese-Belgian Eurasian originally named Rosalie Chou, and her first husband, Tang Pao-huang, an officer in the Kuomintang army. As children they played together in Beijing; as young adults Pao refuses an arranged marriage with Suyin sight unseen; as Chinese students in London, ironically, they meet and fall in love; as patriots they return to China; despite the interruption of an air raid, Suyin and Pao are married by a missionary in Hankow; despite a yearlong separation (after only two weeks of marriage) while he serves at the front and she works in a hospital, they are finally able to set up housekeeping—only to have their house leveled by a bomb. Ostensibly a love story between a man and a woman, *Destination Chungking* is actually about the love of one's country. Though Han Suyin, in a foreword to the 1953 edition, acknowledged an insecurity about her English, a third language for her, *Destination Chungking,* her first book, reads fluently and well. Its language is vivid and its details are sharp, giving promise of the brilliant and prolific writing career that Han Suyin has since fulfilled, relinquishing a medical career to do so. Han Suyin, like Edith Eaton, identifies most strongly with her Chinese half. *Destination Chungking* stresses the humor of the Chinese, their resilience, their courage, and their staying power.

Adet Lin's *Flame from the Rock,* in contrast, focuses on the romantic and tragic. In this novel, lively young Kuanpo Shen, niece of a professor, is wounded by a bomb and receives a lifesaving blood transfusion from a taciturn soldier. Though her family disapproves because of his peasant background, the young people are drawn to each other. He is killed in battle, however, and she eventually dies of grief. This work may be read as Adet Lin's disavowal of her professor father's retreat from the war to the safety of the United States, for the uncle's snobbery is presented in a highly unfavorable light, and the soldier, for his dogged strength and ultimate sacrifice, is shown as worthy of admiration and love. Skillfully written, *Flame from the Rock* seems much influenced by traditional Chinese novels in being unabashedly romantic; yet its assertion of the importance of an ordinary peasant soldier is extremely modern.

War Tide, by Lin Tai-yi (Anor Lin), and *Westward to Chungking,* by Helena Kuo, are both novels about the effects of war on family. Kuo's book focuses on the father, Lee Tien-men, the head of a multigenerational family, who not only gives away the stock of his shop so that it will not fall into Japanese hands but who also gives his five children to the war effort. With the help of an American friend, Sam Hupper, Lee Tien-men retreats inland from Soochow to a small mountain village near Chungking, where he helps the villagers build air-raid shelters and grows tomatoes. Though a few breaks in the narrative mar the novel's coherence, the variety of character and incident creates an interesting and vivid panorama. Multiply these people several million times, Kuo implies, and you will have a picture of China at war, of the heroism of ordinary men and women.

In *War Tide,* a fuller, richer book, Anor Lin, initiating her pen name Lin Tai-yi, displays her precocious talent and a vigorous, original mind, which would later produce four more novels. This book is peopled with a variety of believable characters but centers on the capable eighteen-year-old daughter. The dialogue is often witty and convincing, the inventive incidents organized around the principle of yin-yang, counterbalancing opposite forces: good fortune follows hard upon disaster, birth upon death, beauty upon ugliness. Although war deprives the Tai family of their livelihood, their home beside the beautiful West Lake, and their father's life, they remain undaunted. Lo-Yin has discovered inner resources strong enough to sustain her extended family.

The most remarkable element in *War Tide* is the experimental quality of its language. At moments of crisis, the writing becomes heightened, almost surreal, exaggerated, sometimes horrifying, a literary counterpart to expressionistic painting. Here, for example, suggesting the misanthropy of a Bosch canvas, is Lin Tai-yi's description of the Japanese invaders of Hangchow:

> They hobbled their way like monkeys hopping among trees, and their long, hairy hands were claws, and they let out monstrous sizzlings or shrieks; they opened their mouths wide and let out shrieks into the open purple winter air, shrieks into the white sky, and their bloody claws scratched over

everything they saw, and their eyes were lit by some evil green fire, evil, bitter fire. They scratched the winter sky and broke it like a crust, and from behind the sky rain had poured—black rain, blacker than blood, and the sky was bleeding. . . . When the devils were tired of scratching . . . they sought something warm, something warm and human because they were so afraid, and they sought and found the sight and touch of warm, pale, soft female flesh, and their dirty claws tore the flesh apart, screeching as they did—and the warmth in the flesh had gone with the tearing, and that was how they went. . . . And the city lay rotting, red, wasted, smelling and burning, and on the streets hungry devils and stray dogs hunted; the devils sought among both living and dead to shame them, but the dogs sought for a bone to gnaw from the dead only. (96–97)

The insistent repetition of "shrieks," "fire," "something warm," and "devils," the harsh animal imagery, the devastating final indictment, in which dogs are portrayed as superior to humans—this is powerful writing at any time, but extraordinary for a seventeen-year-old.

In these war books, we find an ulterior purpose: demonstration to the United States, a country superior in arms and supplies, that China was a worthy ally. The character of the adventurer Sam Hupper is an embodiment of United States aid to China as well as a winsome addition to make more palatable to Americans a tale of Chinese suffering. Lin Tai-yi, however, did not sugarcoat her material for her audience. With boldness and sarcasm, she attacks Americans for supplying Japan with materials used to bomb China and protests racism and greed in scathing terms:

"I'll tell you why I look sad, Mother!" Lo-Yin said. "Wipe the dust off your skin, for did you ever hear of the inferior yellow race, or white superiority, or race prejudice, or empire or trade relations or petty politics, Mother? Did you know of oil? Don't you know oil makes good trade, good profit? Ha! Ha, weak China, polite China, bully the four hundred million people, for they have no feelings, their skins are yellow, how can they feel the difference between life and death, or love of mother and son? Scrap iron, Mother, iron waste, iron—they can be burned into profit. Profit, Mother, profit—don't you know that's the most important thing in the world. . . . Don't you know, Mother, that the white man rules and governs by divine right? Heaven sent the Japs to us, but they forgot white men must make a profit. . . . Burn, burn! . . . Chinese blood is yellow, it is not red. Oh no! But it is good enough to sacrifice to fill the bellies of the red-blooded with gold and silver! So sing out the praises of democracy and equality, but who will pay for all these lives and this torture?" (*War Tide* 121)

With the fervor of Edith Eaton defending her Chinese heritage, with the bitterness of disillusioned idealism and the outspokenness of youth, Lin Tai-yi lashes out against injustice. It is to white America's credit that such words were printed in this country.

More popular by far, however, was homegrown "exotic" Jade Snow Wong's *Fifth Chinese Daughter,* for as Elaine Kim points out in her ground-breaking study *Asian American Literature:* "Bitterness against Asian cultures and values, and Asian American values and life styles, were far better tolerated by publishers and a predominantly white readership, which has been traditionally more receptive to expressions of self-contempt and self-negation on the part of members of racial minority people than to criticism of problems in American society" (59). Resentment of the Asian American community and low self-esteem among its members are very much part of *Fifth Chinese Daughter,* though the surface message, at least by the end of the book, seems to be pride in accomplishment and reconciliation with the author's past. In its day the work was a best-seller, and, under the auspices of the State Department, it was translated into Chinese, Japanese, Thai, German, Urdu, Burmese, and Indonesian (Chun-Hoon 125) and Jade Snow Wong was sent to Asia as a cultural ambassador. A documentary film was made about her as late as 1976, and, until the appearance of Kingston, Jade Snow Wong was the best-known Chinese American spokeswoman. Yet for contemporary readers the book is a stilted, emotionally strangled work, recounting rather spiritlessly and totally without humor Wong's strict, traditional upbringing in San Francisco's Chinatown, and her efforts to achieve self-determination. Overt expressions of resentment and anger are stifled but seethe under the surface of her girlhood memories of unjust parental punishment. As she mingles more with the mainstream community, Wong takes pride in her Chinese background, mainly by cooking Chinese dinners for friends and the dean with whom she lives as a servant. Having learned humility, as Kim points out, she seems unaware of the abnegation of coupling herself with her employer's pets: "All who lived in that home, including a pair of cocker spaniels named Pupuli and Papaia, a black cat named Bessie and Jade Snow, were recipients of the dean's kindness and consideration" (156). The book emphasizes the hurdles that her family set up on her road to self-fulfillment and downplays those erected by the larger society. Thus Wong's success may be attributable in large part to the same characteristics that made Winnifred Eaton's romances so popular: she caters to the stereotypes and myths of the majority about itself. *Fifth Chinese Daughter* is an ethnic Horatio Alger story bearing witness to the achievement of the American dream, in which even the

poorest and most unlikely (that is nonwhite) Cinderella may find her way
to the palace of the prince—in this case, gain recognition from the mainstream world by setting up a pottery business in Chinatown in San Francisco.

Contrary to Lowell Chun-Hoon's conclusion that Wong reconciled the
conflicts between the Chinese values of her parents and the values of the
larger society around her, it is actually her parents who come to accept
"their peculiar fifth daughter" and admire her success in making a living
through her ceramic business. At the end of the book, only Caucasians
flock to see her work; "the Chinese did not come to buy one piece from
her." Jade Snow Wong is as much a curiosity in Chinatown as she was at
Mills College. In the introduction to her second book, *No Chinese Stranger,*
she admits to feeling more at home in the People's Republic than she ever
felt in the land of her birth:

> During four weeks of travel in a land physically new to me, it was remark-
> able how very much I felt at home. Because of a radiance which enveloped
> me as I moved among the Chinese in the People's Republic of China, I dis-
> covered my comfortable bonds as one of them. Yet when I walk two familiar
> blocks between home and studio, in the freedom of the U.S., I am conscious
> of being a minority in a "white" or Western world. (xii)

Though she testified abroad that racism was no barrier to individual accomplishment in the United States, American intolerance of the Chinese
caused Wong to feel a divided loyalty and a split sense of self-awareness.

Autobiographical works of this period that did not cater to stereotypes
were neglected, despite the fact that some are livelier and better written.
Perhaps because the authors were born abroad, the American audience
found their experiences too foreign for popular consumption. At the same
time, however, Janet Lim's *Sold for Silver* appealed to Americans precisely because of the sensational aspects of her life story. Abandoned at age eight by
her mother, sold for $250 to a wealthy Singapore family, Lim had to defend
herself against the sexual advances of her master. Rescued by Anglican
missionaries, educated and trained as a nurse, she was later shipwrecked
and imprisoned by Japanese soldiers. The most striking characteristic of
the book is the matter-of-fact manner in which the most repellent events
are narrated.

More substantial is the work of Helena Kuo, a journalist, feminist, and
self-appointed cultural ambassador from China, as she put it, "a fragment
of old China come West." She was an embodiment of the new Chinese
woman, a result of the Revolution of 1911, which overthrew the three-

hundred-year-old Manchu dynasty, stopped footbinding, gave women the vote and equal education with men, and turned China's face toward Western progress. Kuo's first book, *Peach Path,* commissioned by Methuen, announces its feminist stance from the outset:

> This is a woman's book, written by a woman for women. To misquote St. Paul, and thus take revenge on the numerous well-meaning but unworthy translators of Confucius, when I became a woman I thought as a woman, I spoke as a woman, and I understand as a woman. So I write as a woman. (1)

The book is an uneven collage introducing to British and American readers the stories, legends, and maxims of old China—including the legend of Fa Mulan, the woman warrior who provides the central image of Kingston's book—as well as prescriptions for happiness from a young woman, sometimes preachy, sometimes whimsical and humorous, always confident and outspoken. Kuo's autobiography, *I've Come a Long Way,* is the story of an independent woman whose combination of good looks, fortunate contacts, personal integrity, and ingenuity did indeed bring her a long way, from war-torn China to a visit with Eleanor Roosevelt at the White House. Like Edith Eaton, Kuo used her skills and patriotic fervor to lecture on China's behalf, to write newspaper and magazine articles making the Chinese less strange to Westerners. Though her sensibilities were completely formed in China, Kuo confessed, after a few years in the United States, to an internal split:

> I live now in a happy if sometimes puzzling state of divided mind: the old Chinese mind and the new mind of the West. I am educated and progressive to the point of being aggressive, but always with me is my happy heritage of Chinese civilization which gives me a heaven-sent balance, and I believe I shall never be wholly westernized, even if sometimes I seem to be walking on the edge of a dangerous chasm. (4)

Since 1939, the United States has been her home; her occasional writing is devoted to books and articles about the work of her husband, the painter Dong Kingman.

By far the most introspective autobiography, delightfully illustrated by the author, is *Echo of a Cry* by Mai-mai Sze. Daughter of Alfred Sze, who was China's "Envoy Extraordinary and Minister Plenipotentiary to the Court of St. James" (16) and a 1902 graduate of Cornell, Sze recounts with humor her Anglicization as a young child, her summer with a religious Quaker family who punished any misbehavior or accident by forcing her to put her pennies into the China Inland Mission box decorated with a picture of a Chinese girl who looked like her. For high school and college, Sze came to the United States. At Wellesley College she encounters racism when white girls refuse to sit next to a black student at a lunch counter. After a conversation with the young black woman, Sze realizes that "we're cause people whether we like it or not" (165). While visiting France she is regarded as a Chinese, but when she visits China finds herself awkward and un-Chinese. Although one of the most privileged of the authors, Sze acknowledges "a funny mixed feeling of being given so much, yet feeling I've lost something" (164). The fragmentation of self resulting from the multiple "reshufflings," as she calls them, leads her to conclude poignantly:

> Fervently we have wanted to belong somewhere at the same time that we have often wanted to run away. We reached out for something, and when by chance we grasped it, we often found that it wasn't what we wanted at all. There is one part of us that is always lost and searching. It is an echo of a cry that was a longing for warmth and safety. And through our adolescent fantasies, and however our adult reasoning may disguise it, the search continues. (202)

As though in belated reaction to the Holocaust, Sze published *Silent Children,* the haunting allegory of a band of homeless children, orphaned by war, eking out a living by stealing. A surreal dimness permeates this book, set in an unnamed land, whose characters bear the unrecognizable names, Cruzz, Jolo, Worro, Toor, Lal. One of the boys steals a large trunk that contains not food but velvet gowns, lace parasols, and gold coins. Around the bonfire of their muddy camp, the half-starved children dress up and parade in a grotesque mockery of worldly splendor. Adult strangers intrude, and their greed and ineptness lead to several deaths and to the eventual scattering of the band of children. Sze is protesting the dehumanizing effects of war on the most innocent and powerless of society.

IV

With the repeal of the Chinese Exclusion Act, in 1943, the number of Chinese in America increased and, consequently, the number of Chinese American women writers. Yet, the literary scene through the next three decades was dominated by immigrant Chinese writers, and the traditions continued: explanation of China to the West; protest against discrimination; storytelling and experimentation.

Beijing-born Hazel Lin, who was one-quarter French, came to the

United States to study medicine in 1939 and lived here until her death. She juggled a dual career, a primary one as obstetrician-gynecologist and a secondary one as writer. She wrote four novels, all nostalgically set in China. Her best work, *The Physicians,* set in Beijing, recounts a young woman's determination to study Western medicine; eventually she wins the approval of her grandfather, who practices Chinese medicine. *The Moon Vow* is a somewhat sensational story of a young woman who cannot consummate her marriage because of a vow of celibacy to a secret lesbian society. In *House of Orchids* a young girl from a destitute family is sold into prostitution and falls in love with a student from a respectable family. Another novel, *Rachel Weeping for Her Children, Uncomforted,* tells of a Chinese medical student who has an affair with a much older American surgeon-missionary. Dreams, nightmares, and fears are interwoven into the narrative in an experimental fashion, but the book is overwritten in places and underdeveloped as a whole. *Weeping May Tarry* is a brief, moving diary of Lin's battle with cancer. She died of a sudden stroke at age 73 in 1986.

Anor Lin, author of *War Tide,* lived extensively in the United States in her youth, as noted, was for many years a resident of Hong Hong, and has recently moved to the Washington, D.C., area. Her later novels deal with serious, complex themes. *The Golden Coin* pits faith against cynicism in the intriguing story of a mismatched couple: a coldly scheming biology professor and an illiterate girl from the Shanghai slums. Although the author seems to sympathize with the heroine's faith in miracles, her joie de vivre, and capacity to love, Lin Tai-yi shows how misplaced such faith is and how it is ultimately destroyed. *The Eavesdropper* explores the tension between passivity and activity; the central character, a Chinese writer, moves back and forth between the United States and China, unattached to either world but in love with his older brother's tubercular wife. Class conflicts are dramatized in *The Lilacs Overgrow* and, in *Kampoon Street,* the effects of poverty. Though Lin Tai-yi does not discuss social issues directly, the Chinese political scene serves as the background for all the novels, and the events in the foreground parallel contemporaneous historical struggles in China. In *The Lilacs Overgrow,* for example, the marriages of the two nieces of a Nationalist Chinese official may represent the two forces that struggled for control of the country; the work, indeed, may well be a veiled criticism of both Nationalist and Communist excesses. One niece marries a wealthy man who turns out to be spoiled and spineless; the other weds a Communist, who is portrayed at first sympathetically and later as a fanatic. *Kampoon Street,* which has been translated and published in Brazil, Finland, Sweden, Denmark, and China, seems to indicate a leftward shift in the author's politics.

The work suggests that not only opportunities but even morality can be severely limited by poverty.

In these novels, particularly in *Kampoon Street,* Lin Tai-yi continues the expressionist strain she used to good purpose in *War Tide.* Here we find a character called Female One, who has a "frog-like face," and "holes . . . which served as eyes . . . so deep they were like tunnels" (98) and who does not know who she is because she has no identity card. Lin Tai-yi is a highly skilled writer, intelligent and observant, sympathetic as well as humorous, poetic as well as pointed, and deserving of much wider recognition.

V

By far the most versatile explainer of China to the West is Han Suyin, whose *Destination Chungking* is discussed above. Autobiographer, biographer, novelist, political analyst, chronicler and traveloguer, and medical doctor as well, she vies with Winnifred Eaton in being the most productive woman writer of Chinese ancestry with nearly twenty titles to her name. She received her higher education in Belgium and England, practiced medicine in Hong Kong and Singapore, and has lectured frequently in the United States.

Han Suyin is most widely known for *A Many-Splendored Thing* because of the popular movie based on her novel, and most controversial for her strong support for Mao Ze-dong and the Communist revolution, fully documented in *The Morning Deluge* and *Wind in the Tower,* almost a hagiography. Han Suyin's best work is *The Crippled Tree,* the first book of her four-volume autobiography. Like Kingston's *Woman Warrior,* this work is a mixed genre, combining history (in this case, China's from 1885 to 1928), reconstructed family history, and Han Suyin's personal memories presented in a novelistic mode. Often poetic and deeply felt, it recounts her parents' storybook courtship in Belgium and disillusioned marriage in China, intertwined with and paralleled by the history of a feudal, weak China, represented as a woman struggling to free herself from the economic stranglehold of imperialistic (male) Western powers. Also like *The Woman Warrior,* on a personal level, *The Crippled Tree* is a working out of a painful relationship, from initial rejection by the mother through resentment, anguish, and finally understanding by the daughter. The other volumes of the autobiography, *A Mortal Flower, Birdless Summer,* and *My House Has Two Doors,* seem gradually to lose power.

In its attitudes toward the Chinese, white society has apparently changed little since the time of the Eaton sisters; in a 1982 newspaper interview, Han Suyin made the following remark:

> As a Eurasian, I was always fighting. I am still fighting race prejudice today. I was told by people in the sphere of my young life that I was only good enough to be a prostitute. This situation made me strong. It was either show strength or go under. . . . A very important Swiss surgeon once said to me, "All Eurasians are degenerate, syphilitic." I said: "Me, degenerate? Me?" He said that I am the exception. When he was speaking these words, he was hitting the table with his thumb. I told him: "It is not necessary to hit the table." That got him! I was commenting on his bad manners. (Christy)

Han Suyin is more a citizen of the world than of any single nation. Her nonfiction works passionately depict China in English, a language she loves and calls "that rich and inexhaustible treasure of moods and music, feeling and thought, endless ambrosia, a firm enchantment, lifelong" (Wakeman 613). In her novels, the couples are often interracial: the doomed lovers in *A Many-Splendored Thing,* set in Hong Kong, are a Eurasian doctor, a widow, and a married English journalist; a happy ending is allowed an Englishwoman, a writer, and a dark-skinned Indian engineer in *The Mountain Is Young,* set in Nepal. Communist China is the setting of *Till Morning Comes,* in which a Texan journalist, daughter of a millionaire, marries a patriotic Chinese doctor, who is ultimately destroyed by his countrymen. In this novel, Han Suyin again interweaves a moving story of individuals trapped by historical and political forces over which they have no control. She manages to present the Communist revolution sympathetically and yet be critical of the excesses of the cultural revolution and of political fanaticism. China has few advocates more eloquent or passionate than Han Suyin. As a novelist, at her best, she creates engrossing characters whose passions and agonies are deeply moving.

VI

Two Chinese American women novelists born in the United States and educated here are Virginia Lee and Diana Chang. Lee's *House That Tai Ming Built* emphasizes the favorable aspects of the Chinese as a superior ancient culture, symbolized by exquisite artifacts, while gently protesting racial discrimination. Bo Lin, a third-generation Chinese American brought up in San Francisco's Chinatown, falls in love with Scott Hayes; however, the miscegenation laws of California, enforced in the early 1940s, the time of this story—and on the books until 1967 (Kim 97)—forbade marriages between Asians and Caucasians. Scott dies at the front in Europe.

With two exceptions, Diana Chang's books have nothing to do with Chinese or Chinese Americans. Her first work, *Frontiers of Love,* a rich, full novel set in Shanghai at the close of World War II, is the story of three young Eurasians, representing the spectrum of possibilities in the struggle to determine their identities. At one end of the spectrum is Mimi Lambert, who rejects the Asian part of herself, chooses a Caucasian lover, and, when he refuses to marry her, throws herself at any American who can offer what she thinks of as a lifeline: passage out of China. At the other end is Feng Huang, who rejects the European in him and joins the Communists, becoming so committed to their cause that he rationalizes the murder of his fiancée's cousin, in which he inadvertently takes part, as an unfortunate means to a desirable end. In the middle position is Sylvia Chen, who, after much agonizing, realizes that she is "an entity composed of both her parents, but ready to act and not merely react, for one individual—herself" (237). Chang, who is three-quarters Chinese and one-quarter Irish but by upbringing an American, also acts for herself instead of reacting and goes her own way in her other novels.

Chang chooses in her later books to focus on modern varieties of love: love after divorce, in *A Woman of Thirty;* love for an unborn child, even if it is the result of rape, in *A Passion for Life;* interracial love between a Caucasian Peace Corps volunteer and a Chinese Communist dancer, in the minor, farcical *The Only Game in Town;* love as a manifestation of neurosis, in the clever *Eye to Eye,* in which a married white Protestant artist falls in love with a Jewish writer and seeks the help of a psychiatrist; extramarital love between an older woman and a younger man, in *A Perfect Love.* She writes with great skill of Ivy League graduates, artists, writers, publishers, who inhabit the world of New York City, Long Island, Massachusetts. Her characters tend to be blue-eyed Anglo-Saxons; the outsiders are Jews. "Fitness, in evolutionary biology," says the biologist Lewis Thomas, "means fitting in with the rest of life. If a species is good at this, it tends to survive" (32). Like Winnifred Eaton, Diana Chang is conscious of her audience and wants to fit in, to survive; she "subsumes aspects of her background in the interests of other truths" (qtd. in Ling, "Writer" 75), truths she believes will have a broader appeal in the society in which she lives.

A work that incorporates all aspects of its author's background and blends them in a highly sophisticated way is *Crossings,* by Chuang Hua. In theme and style a forerunner of Kingston's *Woman Warrior, Crossings* is an experimental novel that requires and rewards the reader's closest concentration. The narrative thread traces the growth and decline of a love affair between a Chinese American woman and a European journalist, but the story is constantly interrupted by memories of childhood and family, by dreams, nightmares, images arresting and resonant. Fourth Jane is the middle child of seven in a well-to-do family that transplanted her, when a child, from China to England and then to the United States. Jane herself, as an adult, spends time in Paris but makes return visits to New York. In all, there are seven crossings of the ocean and four cultural adjustments; as in *Echo of a Cry,* though these travels may be enriching, they increase the protagonist's sense of fragmentation and her difficulty in determining her identity.

As *The Woman Warrior* is infused by the tension between the narrator and her mother, *Crossings* is dominated by the presence of the father, a surgeon in China, a stockbroker in New York, a strong man who is as tyrannical as he is loving. Central to the book is the anguish Jane experiences when, for her own psychological well-being, she must take a stand against him; her pain is intense when she remembers the joy he gave to her childhood. Magnifying the familial tension is the conflict between her two countries—China and America—during the Korean War:

> I saw with dread my two lives ebbing. Each additional day of estrangement increased the difficulty of eventual reconciliation, knowing the inflexibility of Chinese pride. In that paralysis I lived in no man's land, having also lost America since the loss of one entailed the loss of the other. Moments I thought of giving up one for the other, I had such longings to make a rumble in the silence. But both parts equally strong canceled out choice. (122)

Crossings abounds with images interwoven throughout the text, intricately echoing and reechoing one another. Some obviously advance the action, while others that at first seem to arrest the action also, on closer inspection, inform the narration. An example of the second type occurs in the middle of a conversation between the journalist and Jane on his initial visit to her apartment. He speaks first:

> Writers belong in the kitchen. Cooking is an essential part of their imaginative environment.
>
> Oh. You can put in the steak now.
>
> A bird plunged like dead weight ten stories from the roof. Two stories from the pavement, with a single flap of wings, it skimmed above the quivering treetops and took off in a sweeping spiral till it disappeared behind the rooftops.
>
> We can eat now. (24)

In the midst of preparations of an intimate meal, the bird falling "like dead weight" for eight stories is jarring. Then we realize that it is a willful fall, for the bird has wings it prefers not to use until the last minute, when it swoops up and takes off in a display of its flying prowess. Jane is like the bird, falling into a dead-end affair with a married man, trusting that her strength will enable her, when she so decides, to escape relatively un-scathed.

Chuang Hua is not afraid to see all sides of life, and, like Lin Tai-yi, she does not shrink from horrifying images: "And in the spring bloated corpses flowed in the current of the yellow river, bobbing among torn roots and bits of watermelon rinds gnawed to the skin" (48). These corpses float past the sugarcane plot where Jane's Chinese nurse cuts the reddest and sweet-est stalks for the children. The juxtaposition of negative and positive im-ages recurs often in *Crossings* and indicates a worldview that unflinchingly encompasses both good and bad. By coercing opposite-tending fragments into a whole, Chuang Hua creates an artistic coherence.

In *Crossings,* Chuang Hua has created a highly original expression of the Chinese American hyphenated condition. She has explored her past and made it central, plumbed the depths of her ethnic confusion, mixed mem-ory with fantasy, with reality, with matter-of-fact detail, stretched the lan-guage of the novel in the direction of poetry, fragmented the narrative for a kaleidoscopic effect—in short, written what may well be a small master-piece.

VII

Maxine Hong Kingston's *Woman Warrior* was deservedly recognized for its boldness, power, and beauty, its fullness of voice in expressing the hyphen-ated condition, but this work did not spring full blown from the empyrean. Most of the writers we have examined, despite the Chinese tra-dition of repression of women, were also outspoken and individualistic. Nearly all their works have been ignored—in many cases, as I hope to have shown, undeservedly so. Looking back, we find that the works that re-ceived accolades in their time—Winnifred Eaton's romantic confections, Jade Snow Wong's autobiography—reflected more their audience and its taste than the quality of the books themselves. The frail Japanese or Eurasian heroines romantically involved with dominant Caucasian men in high positions, the Chinese American success story at a time when the United States was at war with Japan, satisfied a public that sought to confirm its own myths, in stories about its superiority, generosity, and openness. It was not particularly interested in learning about the Chinese themselves or in dispelling stereotypes. In fact, to a large extent, it still finds them "inscrutable."

In "Cultural Mis-Readings by American Reviewers," Kingston expresses her frustration that two-thirds of the critics who praised her book could not see beyond their own stereotyped thinking; she cites examples of the painful "exotic-inscrutable-mysterious-oriental reviewing." Here is one example, from the *Chattanooga News-Free Press:*

> At her most obscure, though, as when telling about her dream of becoming a fabled "woman warrior" the author becomes as inscrutable as the East always seems to the West. In fact, this book seems to reinforce the feeling that "East is East and West is West and never the twain shall meet," or at any rate it will probably take more than one generation away from China. (63)

The inscrutableness, it seems to Kingston and to me, is in the eyes of the beholder, and the unbridgeable gulf as well. Chinese Americans have been explaining themselves for nearly a century, but their voices are either ignored or misunderstood.

A major theme in Kingston's *Woman Warrior* is the importance of articulateness. Finding one's voice and telling one's stories represents power, just as having one's stories buried is powerlessness. From the first episode, "No Name Woman," in which Kingston disobeys her mother's injunction and tells the story of the prodigal aunt whom she calls her "forerunner," through the accounts of her own childhood (her belief that her mother had cut her frenum, her silence in Caucasian school, her terrible bullying of a Chinese American classmate in an effort to make her speak—an act of self-hatred), to the last episode, "A Song for a Barbarian Reed Pipe," Kingston elaborates on this theme. Instead of the confusion and humiliation about her Chinese background that she felt as a child, she now finds, in the stories and customs that set her apart from her Caucasian classmates, her heritage and treasure, her strength and identity. Kingston's work combines the traits of the Chinese American writers who preceded her—protest, storytelling, nostalgia, and experimentation. The effect is one of surprising power and startling beauty.

DESPITE THE TRADITION of repression and devaluation—as Kingston's mother put it, "It's better to feed geese than girls"—Chinese American women writers have demonstrated their talents, have expressed their concerns and their creativity, and have contributed to American literature. As a nation of immigrants, the United States has the opportunity to become acquainted with the peoples of the world within its own borders and in its own language. In their books, the immigrants and their children are speaking, singing. Together they make up the great American chorus, and it is our special privilege, as teachers and students of literature, to listen.

Intelligibility and Meaningfulness in Multicultural Literature in English (Excerpts)

REED WAY DASENBROCK

◆ ◆ ◆

LITERATURE IN ENGLISH is an increasingly international, even global, phenomenon. Writers all over the world, from the Pacific, Asia, Africa, and the West Indies as well as from the traditional centers in the British Isles and the United States, use English as a medium for fiction and poetry. One consequence has been that literature in English has become increasingly cross- or multicultural, as writing about a given culture is destined—because of its language, English, and its place of publication, usually London or New York—to have readers of many other cultures. This is not simply a matter of readers in the traditional centers of the English language struggling to understand work rooted in other cultural traditions; a Kenyan reader of a Nigerian or Guyanese or Indian novel is caught up in the same multicultural dynamic as an American reader of that novel. Admittedly, previous writers in English have found themselves in similar situations: Sir Walter Scott, writing about Scotland for an audience of the English as well as his compatriots, offers an interesting parallel. But Scott's situation was hardly typical at the time; in contrast, over the last generation there has been such an explosion in writing from a global range of cultures that, arguably, multicultural literature dominates literature in English today. I use the term *multicultural literature* to include both works that are explicitly about multicultural societies and those that are implicitly multicultural in the sense of inscribing readers from other cultures inside their own textual dynamics. By examining aspects of four such multicultural narratives written in the last fifteen years—R. K. Narayan's *The Painter of Signs,* Maxine Hong Kingston's *The Woman Warrior,* Rudolfo Anaya's *Bless Me, Ultima,* and Witi Ihimaera's *Tangi*—I hope to show that explicitly multicultural texts are also implicitly multicultural.

The multiculturalism of contemporary world literature in English raises crucial issues that have not been dealt with by critics working with this body of material. As many linguists and discourse analysts argue, all units of language are necessarily incomplete or open. No utterance or written text is ever fully explicit, completely freestanding. To be understood, any text must be read in the light of prior knowledge, background information, expectations about genre and about sequence—all the aspects often considered together as "context."[1] Many of these factors are culturally specific, varying across languages and even within the various English-speaking communities and nations of the world. Oscar Wilde once called England and the United States "two countries divided by a common language," and any American who has ever been asked by an English host or hostess when he or she would like to be "knocked up in the morning" knows that the common language can divide and lead to some potentially disastrous misunderstandings. We expect problems when communicating with speakers of other languages; more startling, however, is that such problems often occur between speakers of the same language.

These problems grow more acute when one is dealing with written texts since the opportunity for clarifying discussion disappears, and they grow yet more acute with literary texts, which tend to lack some of the specifying contexts that head off misunderstandings in nonliterary forms of discourse. Thus, the multicultural writer and his or her audience may indeed be divided by a common language, and the greater the gap between the two, the more open to misconstrual the multicultural work of literature becomes. This should not be ignored, for while some of the greatest writing being done in English today is coming from outside the traditional Anglo-American mainstream, there would seem to be real barriers to a broad understanding and appreciation of that literature.

The criticism that has responded to this issue has overwhelmingly tended to concentrate on the criterion of intelligibility. This emphasis is a little surprising, since poststructuralists might be expected to find such literature interesting precisely because of its potential undecidability and unintelligibility. But most deconstructive criticism has stayed within the confines of a traditional canon, and the Nigerian Sunday O. Anozie, in his work on African literature in English, is the only prominent critic attempting to argue for a deconstructive reading of any of the new literatures in English (but see Appiah). Virtually every other critic working in this field has seen misunderstanding or unintelligibility as the danger to be avoided at all costs. I argue, in contrast, that intelligibility cannot be made the sole criterion in our understanding and evaluation of multicultural texts. Ready intelligibility is not always what the writer is striving for; it therefore cannot be what the critic always demands.

TWO CRITICAL APPROACHES that use the criterion of intelligibility can be differentiated both according to how they use it and according to the body of literature each approach champions. On one side are the so-called universalist critics, who argue that writers should appeal to a universal audience—or, more precisely, a global audience in English—and that therefore barriers to ready intelligibility are flaws. John Updike, in reviewing *Petals of Blood,* by the Kenyan novelist Ngugi, complains of the profusion of untranslated Swahili and Kikuyu words in the novel, obviously preferring a novel without any such barriers to intelligibility for a non-East African audience. A number of academic critics, such as M. M. Mahood and Charles Larson, have given a more sophisticated formulation to this view, praising those "Third World" writers who have addressed a "universal" audience. Mahood writes, "I should be very happy if my juxtapositions did something to persuade the guardians of the pure English tradition of fiction that we do not need to change our criteria in approaching Third World novels" (2). Analogously, Larson praises the work of the African novelist Lenrie Peters for "its universality, its very limited concern with Africa itself" (229). Unlike Updike, these critics tend to commend works for avoiding barriers to intelligibility, like Ngugi's use of Swahili, instead of criticizing works for having them, but implicit in their praise is a stance that is one with Updike's.

This view has not passed without comment or indeed without counter-attack. And though the issue of universality is one faced—implicitly or explicitly—in the criticism of all the new literatures in English, it has inspired the most controversy in the criticism of African literature. African writers and critics have argued that the supposedly universal standards the critics appeal to are simply white, European ones, standards and values the Africans deliberately reject. As Chinua Achebe puts it, "I should like to see the word *universal* banned altogether from discussions of African literature until such time as people cease to use it as a synonym for the narrow, self-serving parochialism of Europe" (11). The criticism of Charles Larson has come under particular attack, the Ghanaian novelist Ayi Kwei Armah describing it as "Larsony" (14). Ironically, Larson praised Armah highly, and in fact was attacked by Achebe for that praise. Achebe in turn has cited Larson as one of a number of "colonialist critics" who, he says, are doing the same thing to African literature that the colonizing whites earlier did to African society (7, 10–12).[2] Other European and American critics have also been taken to task by Africans for their "Eurocentric" and colonialist approaches to African literature.[3]

This African critical position insists therefore on African literature's being African first and universal only second, if at all. In rejecting the tenets of "universalist" criticism, Achebe calls his vision "necessarily local and particular" (69). This stance determines a very different attitude toward the barriers to global intelligibility that Updike complains about. To understand African literature, readers need to be informed so that they can come to the texts with at least some of the necessary context of expectations. The reader who is interested in a work should expect to do some work to appreciate it. In an article entitled "The Limitations of Universal Critical Criteria," the Nigerian critic Donatus Nwoga argues that "there is not much of Soyinka that can be understood without a deep knowledge of Yoruba mythology and oral tradition literature" (627).[4] Similarly, the Ghanaian writer Kofi Awoonor comments that the Nigerian novelist Tutuola "is a writer whose art rests and has meaning only within the larger world construct of Yoruba thought and ontology" (667). These critics imply that Soyinka and Tutuola are not to be faulted because their work is rooted in their traditional culture.[5] On the contrary, the use they make of that tradition is part of their strength as artists. Consequently, one must know something about Yoruba culture to understand their work, and from this one can draw the general proposition that one must know something about the culture of any African writer to understand his or her work. It is therefore up to the reader, not the author, to do the work necessary to make the literature intelligible.

Nwoga's "localist" or contextualist position is more fruitful for a critic than the universalist or acontextualist one, if only because it makes the critic's role much more interesting and powerful. Both approaches are deeply prescriptive: the universalist praises works without a density of local reference difficult for outsiders to follow; the localist praises precisely the opposite. But if readers need to know about Yoruba culture to understand Soyinka, then critics have a job to do beyond simply praising or attacking him: they can provide the uninformed with the needed contextual background. Some of the best criticism of the new literatures in English has been of this explanatory kind, filling in the gaps between author and reader and offering information that makes the text intelligible.[6] Thus an informed guide helps the foreign reader open a door that had previously seemed closed and enter into the world of the text. In the localist view, however, the door still seems firmly closed against foreign critics, who can presumably never have the local competence needed for elucidation.

But the localist and universalist approaches to these new literatures in English share a great deal more than they recognize. Both feel that a work must be readily intelligible to be of value, that Ngugi's use of Swahili in *Petals of Blood* or Soyinka's use of Yoruba mythology is a problem if it is not understood. The difference is that they assign blame differently, the one blaming the writer who will not explain, the other the reader who thinks everything should be made easy to understand. But they are one in their dislike of, and desire to head off, any moments of openness in the text, in their denial of any value to difficult passages or failures of understanding. The reader, they seem to say, must have everything understood; if the author does not make everything clear, that simply defines the task of the critic.

IN SUCH AN UNCRITICAL acceptance of intelligibility as an absolute value, these different (or not so different) approaches are not proving adequate to the literature they purport to describe. The universalist approach seems an unworkable ideal for a writer, for only a writer of allegory such as J. M. Coetzee can successfully avoid specific, local references of the kind that fill any novel. But if the universalist position is unworkable for the writer, the localist position is equally unworkable for the reader. If we must be or become expert in the culture of any book we read, then we will tend to limit ourselves to our own literature. This would probably suit many African critics perfectly, since they seem to resent any outside interest in African literature. But surely it is foolish to confine each reader in a prison of only the literature that can be read expertly and surely. There is something wrong with a critical position that deprives a literature of much of its potential readership.

What these critics have failed to grasp is that intelligible and meaningful are not completely overlapping, synonymus terms. Indeed, the meaningfulness of multicultural works is in large measure a function of their unintelligibility for part of their audience. Multicultural literature offers us above all an experience of multiculturalism, in which not everything is likely to be wholly understood by every reader. The texts often only mirror the misunderstandings and failures of intelligibility in the multicultural situations they depict, as I hope to show by analyzing four works, each set in a different cultural milieu. My examples deliberately come from a range of cultures, none of them African, so as to indicate how the issues I have traced in African criticism are an integral part of all multicultural literatures in English.

Ready intelligibility, then, is far from crucial to the understanding of a multicultural text; in fact, the reader's ready assumption of understanding can itself be misleading, in just the way that American guests in Britain can be disconcerted because they think they know what "knocked up" means. Readers of multicultural literature can miss the point precisely where they think they get it (or fail to notice anything "to get" at all). In this case, the writer must disturb that assumption in order to be read correctly. . . .

. . . Maxine Hong Kingston's *The Woman Warrior,* an autobiographical account of growing up Chinese American in Stockton, California, is subtitled *Memoir of a Childhood among Ghosts.* In the third chapter, "Shame" [sic; should be "Shaman"], we hear a good deal about ghosts, in particular about a ghost that plagued the author's mother in medical school. A few pages later, the author herself seems to live among ghosts:

> But America has always been full of machines and ghosts—Taxi Ghosts, Bus Ghosts, Police Ghosts, Meter Reader Ghosts, Tree Trimming Ghosts, Five-and-Dime Ghosts. Once upon a time the world was so thick with ghosts, I could hardly breathe; I could hardly walk, limping my way around the White Ghosts and their cars. There were Black Ghosts too, but they were open eyed and full of laughter, more distinct than White Ghosts. (113)

Thereafter the book is littered with references to "Grocery Ghosts," "Social Worker Ghosts," "Jesus Ghosts," "Mail Ghosts," "Druggist Ghosts," and so on. Now a reader quickly figures out that *ghost* here doesn't mean what it does to most English speakers; instead, it means non-Chinese or non-Oriental. Indeed, before *ghost* is used in this sense, we are told: "The Japanese, though 'little,' were not ghosts, the only foreigners considered not ghosts by the Chinese" (109). But just as we think we have a firm criterion for distinguishing ghosts from ghosts, we encounter passages where it is genuinely difficult to tell: "But how can I have that memory when I couldn't talk? My mother says that we, like the ghosts, have no memories" (194). Or, "That ghost! That dead ghost! How dare he come to the wrong house" (196). Or again, "They would not tell us children because we had been born among ghosts, were taught by ghosts, and were ourselves ghostlike. They called us a kind of ghost. Ghosts are noisy and full of air; they talk during meals" (213–14).

If one insists that the word *ghost* must mean either a spirit ("our" meaning) or a non-Oriental ("their" meaning), in all these passages it is possible to decide that the second meaning is intended, that the object referred to by the word *ghost* is indeed an animate, corporeal one. But the effect of these passages, reinforced by the constant reiteration of the tag *ghost* ("Hobo Ghosts," "Delivery Ghost," "Sales Ghosts") is to show the reader a way of using the word and of seeing the world in which that distinction is not made. The "Delivery Ghost" is indeed a ghost for the author's mother, and he takes on a spectral quality in these pages, even for "ghost" readers of *The Woman Warrior.* My point is not that we cannot decide which meaning of the word *ghost* is intended; my point is that after a while, we do not bother to decide, as we enter into the semantic world of the book.

. . . The meaning of the word *ghost* as Kingston uses it is not hard to figure out and is not a serious or insuperable barrier to intelligibility (though the number of students who have asked me, "What are all these ghosts doing in the book?" indicates that a significant percentage of the book's readers may be confused longer than a careful reader might think probable). But it is worth inquiring for a moment why Kingston might want to make non-Chinese readers do that work.

One motive is simply a realistic one, for the Chinese do refer to outsiders by a word most closely translated as ghost, even though, as we have seen, the English word does not have quite the same semantic field. But the second, more important reason is that the reiteration of *ghost* confronts those of us who are not Chinese with the different way of using the word and hence with a different way of seeing the world. To understand *ghost* in *The Woman Warrior,* non-Chinese readers need to understand the Chinese use of the word, which means that we must, momentarily at least, learn to see ourselves as ghosts. As we experience the word, we also experience a perception and a category of thought, and in so doing we learn a good deal about Chinese perceptions of us.

Even if the task is not that difficult, it is still something we have to work at. The writer has deliberately made her text more difficult, blocking automatic intelligibility by using *ghost* in a less broadly available sense, in a way that makes a "ghost" reader pause and think. This . . . is a Shklovskian defamiliarization, not so much of the word as of our self-concept. And . . . it is a culturally specific defamiliarization, one that would not take effect on a Chinese or Chinese American reader. Yet this split effect . . . leads ultimately to a reconciliation, since the net effect is that a non-Chinese reader can understand Chinese cultural horizons more expertly than before.

This effect is of course a major theme of the book itself, which is multicultural in that it deals with multiculturalism, addresses a multicultural audience, both Chinese and non-Chinese, and above all imbues that audience with at least a measure of multiculturalism, making non-Chinese readers more aware of, and sensitive to, Chinese and Chinese American culture.

Writers can therefore choose to make moments of their work more difficult to understand, less immediately intelligible, because they know that the reader will work for their meaning. One could say, adapting the language of Paul Grice, that there is implicit in any act of reading a maxim of intelligibility, which is that readers—like speakers and listeners—will work to make texts as intelligible as possible.[9] Assuming that a work makes sense and has significance, the reader will try to find that sense and significance even when they are not readily apparent. Obviously writers also work most of the time to maximize the intelligibility of their texts. But aware that readers will go on obeying the maxim even if writers do not, an author may flout the maxim so as to exploit it, to make the reader work harder at certain moments. This principle can be abused, but a skillful writer will make the reader work hard only at those moments where the work is meaningful. If we are not already informed about Chinese culture, we work to understand the meaning of *ghost* in *The Woman Warrior* and thus come to understand the book's subtitle and a great deal about the form of life the book seeks to represent. Only by doing that work, by striving to understand a different mode of expression, are we brought up against the fact of cultural difference. If everything is translated into our terms and made readily intelligible, then our cultural categories will be reinforced, not challenged. So the work the reader does when encountering a different mode of expression can be a crucial part of a book's meaning, since the book may have been designed to make the reader do that work.

. . . Multicultural works of literature are multicultural, not only in having multiculturalism as part of their subject matter and theme, but also in allowing for readers from a range of cultures. . . . We have seen how differently informed and less informed readers experience all such multicultural works. But critics of these works have erred in thinking that one of these experiences must be the right one. The difficulty experienced by a less informed reader, far from preventing that reader from experiencing the work justly, is what creates meaning for that reader. A full or even adequate understanding of another culture is never to be gained by translating it entirely into one's own terms. It is different and that difference must be respected. In multicultural literature in English today, that difference is primarily established by barriers to intelligibility being strategically and selectively raised for the less informed reader, forcing the reader to do work that then becomes part of the book's meaning. It is not as if the author could have made things easy but refused. Making things easy would have denied the reader the experience needed to come to an understanding of the culture . . .

Difficulties in a text cannot simply be attacked as destroying the "universality" of a work or celebrated as establishing its "localism," as closing the text to outsiders. The critic needs to decide whether unintelligibility exists merely for its own sake or for the sake of the work the reader must do to make the text intelligible. Writers accommodate themselves to their readers' horizons as much as they can; where they honestly cannot, the reader must take over. Attention paid to moments where the reader must work to broaden his or her horizon of understanding tells us more than anything else does about a work's locus of meaning and values.[11]

Notes

1. A great deal of work could be cited here, including J. L. Austin's on speech acts and Paul Grice's on "conversational implicatures." Many scholars have tried to carry on the work of Austin and Grice; for the initial attempt to apply Gricean pragmatics to literary theory, see Mary Louise Pratt (152–200).

2. Achebe's charge seems unfair in the sense that Larson does attempt to identify distinctively African characteristics of the novels he studies. But Larson has a disconcerting habit of viewing these differences as elements of the European novel that the African novel lacks rather than as positive elements in their own right, and he posits that the African novel of the future will be less and less distinctively African. He likes the fiction of Armah because he considers that it represents this trend; Achebe dislikes it for the same reason and dislikes Larson's singling it out for praise; and Armah himself disagrees with Larson's praise, disdaining the critics' "obsessive, blind need to annihilate whatever is African in me and my work" (9).

3. For a typical attack on non-African critics of African literature, particularly Bernth Lindfors, see Emenyonu. See Lindfors for his response to attacks on his criticism by Emenyonu and others.

4. Nwoga's words are closely echoed by the European critic Albert Gerard: "Likewise no one can hope to have anything truly meaningful to say about Wole Soyinka, even when he is adapting Euripides or Gay or Brecht, unless the analyst is aware of the particulars of Yoruba culture" (20).

5. In fact, Soyinka has been widely attacked for not being "African" enough, for being a "eurocentric modernist." See Chinweizu et al., but also see Soyinka's response to an earlier version of these critics' attacks on him.

6. E.g., see A. Afolayan, who compares Tutuola's syntax to the syntactic structures of the novelist's native language, Yoruba.

. . . .

9. See Grice (45–46). My maxim combines aspects of two separate maxims in Grice's taxonomy: the maxim of quantity, that one should make one's contribution as informative as is required, and the maxim of manner, that one should avoid obscurity of expression.

. . . .

11. I should like to thank first of all the National Endowment for the Humanities for granting me a Fellowship for College Teachers, during which this essay was written; second, Andy Wiget, my colleague at New Mexico State, for a helpful reading of an earlier draft; finally and most important, my wife, Feroza Jussawalla, for, among many other things, reading and criticizing successive drafts of this essay, lending me the Paul Sharrad essay that initially drew the work of Ihimaera to my attention, and teaching me most of what I know about multilingualism, multiculturalism, and Indian writing in English.

Works Cited

Achebe, Chinua. *Morning Yet on Creation Day.* Garden City: Doubleday, 1976.

Afolayan, A. "Language and Sources of Amos Tutuola." *Perspectives on African Literature: Selections from the Proceedings of the Conference on African Literature held at the University of Ife, 1968.* Ed. Christopher Heywood. London: Heinemann, 1971. 49–63.

Anaya, Rudolfo. *Bless Me, Ultima.* Berkeley: Tonatiuh, 1972.

Anozie, Sunday O. "Negritude, Structuralism, Deconstruction." *Black Literature and Literary Theory.* Ed. Henry Louis Gates. New York: Methuen, 1984. 105–25.

Appiah, Anthony. "Strictures on Structures: The Prospects for a Structuralist Poetics of African Fiction." *Black Literature and Literary Theory.* Ed. Henry Louis Gates. New York: Methuen, 1984. 127–50.

Armah, Ayi Kwei. "Larsony: Or, Fiction as Criticism of Fiction." *Asemka* 4 (1976): 1–14.

Austin, J. L. *How to Do Things with Words.* 1962. Ed. J. O. Urmson. New York: Oxford UP, 1965.

Awoonor, Kofi. "Tradition and Continuity in African Literature." *Dalhousie Review* 53 (1973–74): 665–71.

Chinweizu, Onwuchekwa Jemie, and Ihechukwu Madubuike. *Toward the Decolonization of African Literature.* 1980. Washington: Howard UP, 1984.

Emenyonu, Ernest. "African Literature: What Does It Take to Be Its Critic?" *African Literature Today* 5. New York: Africana, 1971. 1–11.

Gerard, Albert. "Is Anything Wrong with African Literary Studies?" *African Literature*

Studies: The Present State/L'état present. Ed. Stephen Arnold. Washington: Three Continents, 1985. 17–26.

Gingerich, Willard. "Aspects of Prose Style in Three Chicano Novels: *Pocho; Bless Me, Ultima;* and *The Road to Tamazunchale,*" *Form and Function in Chicano English.* Ed. Jacob Ornstein-Galicia. Rowley: Newbury, 1984. 206–28.

Grice, Paul. "Logic and Conversation." *Speech Acts: Syntax and Semantics.* Ed. Peter Cole and Jerry L. Morgan. New York: Academic, 1975. 41–58.

Ihimaera, Witi. *Tangi.* 1973. Auckland: Heinemann NZ, 1984.

Jameson, Fredric. *The Prison-House of Language.* Princeton: Princeton UP, 1972.

Jussawalla, Feroza. *Family Quarrels: Towards a Criticism of Indian Writing in English.* Berne: Lang, 1985.

Kingston, Maxine Hong. *The Woman Warrior.* 1976. New York: Vintage, 1977.

Larson, Charles. *The Emergence of African Fiction.* 1971. Bloomington: Indiana UP, 1972.

Lindfors, Bernth. "The Blind Men and the Elephant." *African Literature Today* 7. New York: Africana, 1975. 53–64.

Mahood, M. M. *The Colonial Encounter: A Reading of Six Novels.* Totowa: Rowman, 1977.

Narayan, R. K. *The Painter of Signs.* New York: Viking, 1976.

Nwoga, D. Ibe. "The Limitations of Universal Critical Criteria." *Dalhousie Review* 53 (1973–74): 608–30.

Pratt, Mary Louise. *Toward a Speech Act Theory of Literary Discourse.* Bloomington: Indiana UP, 1977.

Sharrad, Paul. "A Rhetoric of Sentiment: Thoughts on Maori Writing with Reference to the Short-Stories of Witi Ihimaera." Unpublished ms., 1985.

Soyinka, Wole. "Neo-Tarzanism: The Poetics of Pseudo Tradition." *Transition* 48 (1975): 38–44.

Updike, John. Rev. of *Petals of Blood,* by Ngugi. *Hugging the Shore: Essays and Criticism.* New York: Knopf, 1983. 697–701.

PART IV

An Interview

Susan Brownmiller Talks with Maxine Hong Kingston, Author of *The Woman Warrior*

SUSAN BROWNMILLER

✦　✦　✦

H ER VOICE IS NOT THE dried-duck voice of her childhood nightmares; it is, rather, a polite little girl's voice—perhaps her "American-feminine" voice—and it giggles. I giggle too. We gravely compliment each other's work as "powerful" and agree to meet on Friday at 3. She and her husband will pick me up at the hotel.

On Thursday night I have dinner with my Honolulu friends Diane Morisato and Susan Yim who are appropriately envious that I am getting to meet Maxine Hong Kingston before they do since, after all, it's *their* city. *The Woman Warrior* has just been published, to rave reviews. Five thousand miles away in New York City it has been instantly celebrated with drums and smoke signals peculiar to the trade. "Who *is* Maxine Kingston?" people have asked in print. Who is this unknown Chinese-American woman who has dropped a brilliant, polished gemstone in our midst?

Susan Yim writes for the Honolulu *Star-Bulletin* but another local reporter got the assignment to interview Maxine. "The piece ran yesterday but it got buried in the election coverage," she tells me. "If you meet her son, tell him you don't think he's small. That's how the book jacket described him. 'She lives in Honolulu with her husband and small son,' but I hear he's thirteen and resents the description." (I make a mental note of this insider's tip and shamelessly use it at the opportune time.)

She stands, looking hesitant, at the pink hotel phone. I cross the plush, red-carpeted lobby and shyly say hello. From the book jacket picture I was expecting someone tough and strong, a woman warrior, but Maxine Kingston is tiny, doll-like in an ankle-length purple and white dress that is minutely patterned. But she is no porcelain China doll. At 36 her face is the face of a woman who has known hard work, whose childhood was bur-dened with grown-up responsibility. (The theme of hard work, of feeling uneasy guilt when one is not at work, dominates our time together.)

She puts a *lei* of purple orchids around my neck and I have to bend low to receive it. At 5'6" I am suddenly conscious of being big, awkward and lum-bering, a strapping mainland American. I don't think I have ever been in the presence of a towering talent so physically small in size. She is all of 4'9" and I can't help but comment as I write this detail in my reporter's notebook.

"Charlotte Brontë was 4'9"," she informs me. "She and I are *both* 4'9". Emily *towered* over Charlotte, and *she* was 5'3"." She has a way of emphasiz-ing certain key words in a sentence, with wonderment.

We leave the pink palace that is the Royal Hawaiian Hotel and look for Earl Kingston, who has been circling around in the car. Soon the three of us are driving past the University of Hawaii's Manoa campus to the grounds of the Mid-Pacific Institute, a boarding-in private high school were Maxine teaches creative writing and where the Kingstons have their apartment. "It used to be rent-free," Maxine tells me, "but then they raised our salaries and made us pay." Earl points out a redeeming feature—a huge monkeypod tree that blooms in the front yard.

The apartment is friendly and Paris-poster bohemian. Maxine's beat-up wooden desk and old Underwood take up a corner of the living room. ". . . but I can write anywhere," she proudly confesses, "down at the beach, at the picnic table under the monkeypod tree." Scott passes through just long enough for me to tell him he's not a small child at all, and then Earl, Maxine and I settle around the kitchen table for the after-noon's work.

Work for me at the table is getting the 'facts, ma'm.' Maxine and Earl occupy themselves cutting strips of chicken and sausage and aluminum foil, for individually wrapped portions of a popular Cantonese dish that they had modernized and given the name of Chicken in a Jet. The recipe comes from the Stockton, California, Chinese community where Maxine grew up and that evening we will carry over piping hot plates of it to the apartment of Beverly and Roger, the Kingstons' best friends and fellow teachers at Mid-Pacific. It is an Hawaiian Island custom to contribute a dish when you are invited to dinner.

In Island terminology, Earl is a *haole,* which means Caucasian. More specifically, he is half Jewish, one-quarter Portuguese, and one-quarter Irish. This means, he says, helping me get the spelling right, that Scott is colloquially called a *hapa-haole* (half-white). Scott has been known to pose as Japanese or Hawaiian, depending on his set of friends at school. Maxine bought Scott an electric typewriter for his birthday—"to start him off on his writing career," she laughs—but it is Earl's profession, acting, that seems to draw him.

Theater is central to the Kingston family life. Earl met Max, as he and her friends call her, when they each had bit parts in a production of Brecht's *Galileo* at Berkeley. They have been married for fourteen years, the last ten of them living in Hawaii. Earl works with a theater company that tours the high school circuit and the week before my visit he snared a one-shot on *Hawaii Five-O.* His voice resonates nicely, befitting an actor who prefers doing Shakespeare to commercial T.V.

It is a warm, lovely feeling, like the surf at Waikiki, to immerse myself in the wave of Maxine Kingston's success as it is happening. I have barely given her a Xerox copy of Jane Kramer's front-page rave review from *The New York Times,* which she has not yet seen, when Chuck Elliot, her editor at Knopf whom she has never met, calls from New York with the latest news about the paperback sale. Should she go with Vintage or Bantam? I can't help chiming in on the discussion.

"Listen, Maxine," I say a few moments later, "do you consider *The Woman Warrior* to be fiction or nonfiction? The reviewers seem confused. It's a memoir, but it's very artful."

"The bookstores seem confused too," she giggles. "I've seen it placed in the anthropology section. Oh, I guess I do think it's closer to fiction, but whatever sells. . . ." She lets the sentence trail off. We agree that the title (not her first choice) is mildly deceiving, since it bespeaks of battles and militance while the book is a mystical evocation of her childhood spent among the "ghosts" of her mother's ancestors and the "ghosts" that are the white people with foreign ways that she must get used to in Stockton, California, while she washes and irons in the family laundry.

"The laundry sounded like awfully hard work," I say with embarrassment. I am one of those ghosts who takes clothes in and out, who interrupts families trying to finish a meal by arguing about a missing pillow case.

"It was *awfully* hard work," she sighs. "I used to make up kid games to keep going. If I did ten T-shirts I'd allow myself to take a break, okay? The laundry also influenced how I thought about money. Twenty-five cents was one white starched shirt."

Could I dare ask a genuine source why so many Chinese went into the laundry or restaurant business? "It was the work ethic. The important thing was to own your own business."

Before the Stockton laundry, Maxine's father had worked as the manager of a gambling house. This was while Brave Orchid, Maxine's incredible mother whose presence dominates *The Woman Warrior*, was pregnant. "I got my name from the gambling house. There was a big blond American lady who came in named Maxine and she *won* all the time!" She tells me this triumphantly, with great glee. Maxine Hong Kingston has been trained from infancy to work and win.

But surely, I demand to know, even if the Hong family ran a laundry, they couldn't be called typical, could they? She answers slowly, "My father was a poet, and my aunts and mother could read, that was unusual, okay? You know, people ask me is Brave Orchid truly that large in real life, or is that my poetic license. But in truth I calmed her down for the book. She is even larger than that. Sometimes I wonder, do I come from a normal family or do I come from a family that is *very irrational?*"

Earl laughs, but does not offer his opinion. "Uhm, Maxine," I nervily inquire, "how did Brave Orchid take to your marrying a Caucasian?"

Earl, cutting squares of aluminum foil to Maxine's specifications, answers this one. "For years she referred to me as The Boyfriend—this is after we were married."

"But she loved your curly hair."

"Yes, she did."

"How old is Brave Orchid now?" I ask.

"I don't know," Maxine says simply, showing me a color snapshot of a recent Hong family reunion and pointing out her sisters, their husbands and kids. Everyone looks quite rational—and Westernized—to me, but Brave Orchid herself is enigmatically absent from the posed and smiling family grouping. "What *was* she doing that day, Earl?" Maxine questions, but Earl shakes his head. More Brave Orchid mystery.

From the steaming laundry to radicalizing Berkeley, hotbed of the free-speech movement of the early 1960s. "I had eleven scholarships," Maxine tells me. "I wouldn't have been able to do it without them." She started out majoring in engineering because she was good in math, but eventually switched to the English department.

"I wanted to be a writer since I was nine years old," she says, methodically cutting up the chicken. "When I was a child I was writing book-length things. Writing was like *breathing,* but I never thought about making a living from it." She sighs, "Berkeley was such a giant; there was so little contact between the students and the teachers. Maybe there wouldn't have been all those riots if there'd been more contact. I was homesick all the time at Berkeley. I couldn't figure out the day-to-day practical things like washing my clothes. I couldn't do anything. And majoring in English interfered with my writing. It was all I could do to write those formal papers on literary criticism. I felt that if I stayed to get a master's degree it would *destroy* the writing. Formal literary criticism made me look at my own writing too critically. I would tear the page apart before I created it."

We are quiet for a moment as we ponder this terrible truth. I know, too, that I could never have written my book within the academic discipline of a university. Formal education does seem to crush a writer by imposing rigidities of form and thought. I also briefly flash on those Berkeley mafiosi, so prominent then in student politics, some of them so prominent now in New York publishing. Are they wondering whether they ever sat next to a shy Chinese girl named Maxine Hong in a huge lecture hall?

As for the contact between students and teachers, this has remained a preoccupation for Maxine. Before moving to Honolulu she and Earl both taught in a ghetto school in Hayward, California. She still feels twinges of guilt for abandoning the ghetto kids for the middle-class boarding students at Mid-Pacific. "But I said to myself when I left," she soliloquizes, "what's the use? Math and English are such small weapons against what they have to deal with."

So now she teaches creative writing to prep school kids and wonders about the value of that. "Can one actually *teach* writing?" she gloomily worries. "I try to take a look at where they are and move them up a little. That's about all you can do."

I tell Maxine that the craft of *The Woman Warrior* impressed me enormously—in particular her unique sentence structure that strikes me as an artful combination of Chinese rhythms and American slang. She nods her understanding of what I am trying to say. "My subconscious is Chinese, isn't that weird? At night in my dreams I speak to Earl in Chinese."

"And here and there you throw in a deliberately naïve sentence, a young girl's sentence—is that your writer's guile masquerading as guilelessness?"

"Yes, several times I did that quite consciously. Do you remember where I say 'I read in an anthropology book . . .'? Oh, but I, the bookworm, went through *piles* of anthropology books. That sentence is a lot more naïve than I am."

It was her conscious writer's craft that led her to use an English word—"ghosts"—to represent both the spirit demons that haunt her Chinese ancestors and the paleface Americans that her uprooted family must cope

with in California. And it was her conscious writer's craft that led her to select the magical phrase "talk-story," to describe the passing down of tales
from the old generation to the young. "Talk-story," I learn in Maxine's
kitchen, is actually an Hawaiian pidgin phrase, borrowed street language
from her adopted city.

In Maxine's conversation her father is very much a presence, yet *The
Woman Warrior* tells a matriarchal story, of Brave Orchid, of Aunt Moon Orchid and the rest, I learn to my surprise that this too was a strictly professional craft decision: "This was a book that I started to write when I was ten
years old, but I didn't have the words. Twenty-five years later I was able to
do it. In 1973 Earl and I took a vacation on Lanai—it's a very small pineapple
island with one hotel and *just twelve* rooms. One night we were expecting to
watch a movie, but the hotel's projector broke down! I had nothing to
do—so I wrote out a two-page outline for the book, in pencil! At first I
thought I could do it all in one volume, the men and the women, but the
men's stories didn't fit in with the women's stories. The mythology is so
different—the men's stories were in *conflict* with the women's stories. So I
decided that the men's book would be a companion volume."

And how does an unpublished Chinese-American novelist living in
Honolulu make the connection with the prestigious New York publishing
firm of Alfred A. Knopf? "Well, I looked up a list of New York literary
agents at the University of Hawaii library and I picked out a name quite
blindly and sent off the manuscript."

"Hold on. Did you know that most agents don't even consider unso-
licited manuscripts?"

"Yes, but I didn't have any choice, did I? I sent a covering letter explaining that I wasn't a complete amateur—I'd had some articles published in
academic journals. But actually the first two packages mailed came back
marked 'addressee unknown.' I began to think this is a very unstable business, this literary agenting. The third name I chose from the list wrote to
say he'd be very happy to represent me. Then while he was sending it
around I wrote him to stop. I wanted to make some revisions. I had been
explaining too much intellectually at the beginning of the book, instead of
letting it happen. After I rewrote the beginning he sent it to Knopf and
they took it immediately."

"So you have your work cut out for you. Now you're going to start on
the men's story?"

Her face lights up. "I already have more than 200 pages of the men's
story," she says proudly. "On paper. Typed."

It is time to go next door for dinner and meet Roger and Beverly and their friends. The Chicken in a Jet gets added to roast beef, French bread, salad, lots of wine and ice cream for dessert, and the easy, pleasant conversation is about ecology, Hawaiian pidgin, Shakespeare and *minehunes,* little spirit folk that appear to abound on the islands. Midway through the evening I realize that only I, the mainland *haole* didn't take her shoes off at the door.

On Saturday Maxine and I meet again on my temporary turf, the Royal Hawaiian, for lunch. We watch the colorful sails of an International Hobie Cat Competition and mug shamelessly on the beach for a free-lance photographer. This is work, too, and Maxine understands it: part of the publicity machinery in which writers pretend to be starlets in order to keep a book afloat. But I sense she is eager to get home. "I've had a recurring dream lately," she confides. "About my typewriter disintegrating. Have you ever had that?" I shake my head no. My dreams are rarely poetically symbolic. "Sometimes I feel like I'm a crazy old lady who can't put two sentences together," she continues. This is a condition I understand.

We discuss a trip to China she would like to take. To answer some of the questions she poses in her book: "I'd like to go to China and see those people and find out what's a cheat story and what's not," she wrote. "Did my grandmother really live to be ninety-nine? Or did they string us along all those years to get our money? Do the babies wear a Mao button like a drop of blood on their jumpsuits? When we overseas Chinese send money, do the relatives divide it evenly among the commune? Or do they really pay 2 percent tax and keep the rest? It would be good if the Communists were taking care of themselves; then I could buy a color T.V."

There is something in Hawaii, I'm told, called Island fever, in which the afflicted person, a transplanted mainlander, grows dizzy and weak. The cure is a trip home. Poised between the megaliths of China and the United States, Maxine Hong Kingston has two mainlands tugging at her. The gravitational pull must be tremendous. It created her art.

Annotated Select Bibliography

❖　❖　❖

Allen (1996)

Narratologically analyzing traditional and contemporary Chinese versions of the Mulan story, argues that *The Woman Warrior* follows a pattern of return to "domestication." Examines cross-dressing motif to show a historical shift from "sartorial" to "corporeal" signs of gender. Reads the woman warrior's slaying of the baron after baring her breast as a transformation from "woman-as-warrior" to "woman-within-the-family." Many illustrations.

Blinde (1979)

Among the earliest scholarly studies of *The Woman Warrior*, places it in an Asian American literary tradition. Covers many of the issues that preoccupy later poststructuralist critics (e.g., fragmented subjectivity, epistemological uncertainty, formal hybridity), but uses a vocabulary associated more with the critical tradition on modernism. Kingston is said to achieve transcendence as an individual artist by radically combining a Chinese American woman's experiences with the Western literary forms available to her (52). Contrasts this correlation between form and life situation with that found in Jade Snow Wong's more conventional 1945 autobiography, *Fifth Chinese Daughter.*

Cheung (1988)

One of a handful of cross-ethnic readings available, beginning from the premise that both Walker and Kingston are female "minority" American writers. Raises questions about both the promises and the pitfalls of comparative approaches. Close readings reveal numerous, sometimes uncanny, textual parallels between the two works on feminist themes. Cheung concedes that the situations of African Americans and Chinese Americans are very different, but refrains from exploring or drawing generalizations about the sociopolitical conditions of the two groups. Instead, focuses on the personal triumphs of the characters as well as the authors in overcoming the difficulties of being "female and colored" in the United States.

M. Chin (1989–90)

Occasioned immediately by the publication of *Tripmaster Monkey,* but because the interviewer is Marilyn Chin, a prominent Chinese American poet who shares much in Kingston's background (and has been personally inspired by *The Woman Warrior*), the conversation ranges widely over many topics—perhaps more so than when the interviewer is someone unfamiliar with matters Chinese American. Topics relevant to *The Woman Warrior* include the striking realism of Kingston's stories to "cultural insiders," cultural and gender politics in the Chinese American community, struggles with "personal pronouns" and problems of self-centeredness in writing, and the impact of both classical Chinese literature and Western "canonical" literature on Kingston's writing.

Chu (1992)

Draws attention to Kingston's familiarity with Anglo-American literature (a fact often overlooked when critics focus on her "Chineseness") and argues that Kingston is a "feminist practitioner of the female bildungsroman," at once invoking and resisting its plot conventions on romance, marriage, domesticity. Also relates *The Woman Warrior* to the kunstlerroman genre. Calls Kingston a "cultural double agent, shuttling between cultures" and "draw[ing] upon the feminist elements of each tradition to challenge the patriarchal ideology she finds in another" (99).

Eakin (1985)

Part of a far-ranging, book-length theoretical study of autobiography premised on the notion that storytelling is both a crucial mode of existence and a literary form—that autobiographical "truth" is a matter of self-invention. *The Woman Warrior* "confirms both as theme and gesture that in our life in culture the self and language exist in an irreducible relation of mutually constituting interdependence" (256). Close-reads many sections of *The Woman Warrior* dealing with speech and writing to highlight Kingston's investigations of the autobiographical act.

Goellnicht (1991)

Using Kingston's *The Woman Warrior* and Joy Kogawa's *Obasan* as examples, criticizes Lacanian-influenced academic feminist criticism for overlooking material conditions, especially race, in its privileging of pre-Oedipal/semiotic mother–daughter language over the father's phallic/symbolic language. Argues that in these works the protagonists experience a "double subject split" because of both patriarchy and racism. This complicates their attempts to achieve radical agency between "mother tongue" and "father land."

Holaday (1978)

At first sight Pound and Kingston make an "odd couple," until one sees that, at such an early stage in the development of Asian Americn literature and criticism, Holaday needs a canonical figure as a "hook" of sorts to make a case for *The Woman Warrior*'s importance: "While Pound used Chinese literature mainly to fill gaps in Western tradition, Kingston gives a voice to a new tradition growing out of the meeting of East and West" (23). Denaturalizes professional literary criticism, especially the notion of what constitutes legitimate topics of comparison or critical dialog. Among the first to address issues that have become staples in Kingston criticism: sources, cultural authority, "voice," and in particular, Orientalism.

Hutcheon (1988)

Kingston is discussed on only a few pages, but this is typical of Hutcheon's aim and method: to set forth a comprehensive theory of postmodernist poetics by identifying themes and forms—marginality, rupture, multiplicity, self-reflexiveness, etc.—shared by artists of diverse backgrounds (e.g., '60s countercultural, "postcolonial," Chinese American) in diverse media (e.g., architecture, film, literature, etc.). Makes a case for the political subversiveness of postmodernism and defends its usefulness for racial minorities and women, using, among others, *The Woman Warrior* as example. Reveals Kingston as a product of her times in the broadest sense of the term. At the same time, Hutcheon's detection of "the same" ideas everywhere (even as these all, presumably, express an attunement to "difference") paradoxically creates a difference-leveling theoretical juggernaut of its own. The issues raised by Hutcheon can be transposed into various contexts in Kingston scholarship (e.g., see Lee 1995).

Juhasz (1979)

Contends that Millet and Kingston exemplify two kinds of formal experimentation in feminist autobiography based respectively on "dailiness" and "fantasy" (or "the life of the imagination"). Both are said to construct female identity in resistance to the criteria of "significance, objectivity, distance" governing men's lives and men's autobiographies. One of the earlier studies of how women's life writing might be shaped by gender; many refinements on the gender/genre connection have been made since.

Kim (1982)

A section in the "Chinatown Cowboys and Warrior Women: Searching for a New Self-Image" chapter in Kim's pioneering study of Asian American literature. Emphasizes the work's American context, in particular, the historical determinants of the American-born narrator's confusion over identity. At the same time, juxtaposition of *The Woman Warrior* against the works of Frank Chin and Shawn Wong brings out the gender dimension that Kim explores extensively elsewhere. Useful to contrast this highly "located" interpretation with the "universalist" manner in which *The Woman Warrior* has frequently been read.

Lee (1995)

Points out a central contradiction in the American academy, which "ironically wishes to posit its critical endeavors as a champion of marginality, even when the institution itself is a legitimating discourse" (157–58). Within this framework, contends that because *The Woman Warrior* appears less threatening than *China Men* (which highlights "racial oppression over intraracial sexism"), the former has been successfully incorporated into American academic institutions, whereas the latter still "sits uncomfortably between English literature and Ethnic Studies programs" (157). Addresses a neglected topic in Kingston studies: the politics of canon formation and academic professionalization.

Li (1988)

Uses an approach combining "native" knowledge of Chinese culture, especially of the Chinese language, with poststructuralist theory and Geertzian concepts of culture. For example, examines Kingston's differing presentation of the characters' Chinese names (e.g., phonetic transcription versus semantic translation) in order to uncover Kingston's "hidden ideological agenda" (501). Demonstrates Kingston's "revisionist mythmaking" to negotiate an "interface of cultures upon which new knowledge generates" and a nonhyphenated Chinese American self (511).

Lim (1991)

Part of the Modern Language Association's *Approaches to Teaching World Literature* series—one indication of the work's status in the American literary canon. (*The Woman Warrior* is the only Asian American work in the series.) Provides information on editions and anthologies, other works by Kingston, and courses and contexts; a review of relevant readings for instructors; a list of audio/visual aids; a personal statement by Kingston; and 17 brief essays by teachers and scholars on cultural and historical contexts, pedagogical contexts, and critical contexts. Apart from being useful, the volume illustrates the wide range of critical responses to *The Woman Warrior* and the institutional uses to which it has been put.

Lim (1992)

Writing against the devaluation of Asian American women's writing by masculinist critics, Lim seeks to establish a tradition of Chinese American women's "lifestories" extending back to the early twentieth century. Discusses several early examples of the tradition; in particular, contrasts *The*

Woman Warrior with Jade Snow Wong's *Fifth Chinese Daughter,* which also engages race and gender issues but in a form (linear, "objectified" narrative) suppressive of her ambivalences on these issues.

Ludwig (1996b)

Part of a book-length study (Ludwig 1996a) of intercultural communication based on the comprehensibility of metaphors organizing human experience (what George Lakoff and Mark Johnson call "metaphors we live by"). Kingston's autobiography about an intercultural existence coincides with "the situation of the extracultural reader." "Focusing on self-attributed metaphors in the text may indicate a way of overcoming communicative problems of authenticism and absolute cultural relativism." Develops this thesis through the "monkey feast" section in *The Woman Warrior.*

Myers (1986)

Attempts to arrive at an understanding of fictivity in autobiography through the speech act theory of J. L. Austin, John R. Searle, and Paul Grice (and through Mary Louise Pratt's application of it to literary analysis). Argues that "the autobiographer is not originally a maker *of* speech acts, but an audience *for* speech acts"; she is a member of the community into which she is trying to assimilate and from which she also needs to extricate her voice. By mixing myths with "factual" language, Kingston flouts speech act rules, but through this draws attention to the process whereby meaning is constructed in a cultural context.

Quinby (1992)

In a Foucauldian vein, argues that we take seriously the word *memoirs* in the subtitle of *The Woman Warrior.* Whereas autobiography (even if "postmodern") has historically promoted an interior, "normalizing and disciplinary form of subjectivity," the subjectivity promoted in memoirs is "externalized," "overtly dialogic," "multiple and discontinuous" (298–99). Examines the nexus of "two patriarchal technologies of power" in *The Woman Warrior:* the deployment of alliance, associated with the protagonist's Chinese heritage, and the deployment of sexuality, associated with hegemonic American culture. Details how she constructs an alternative technology of "ideographic" (as opposed to "alphabetic") selfhood to resist such social constraints. Can be compared to and contrasted with other studies claiming various types of radical subjectivity for *The Woman Warrior;* or read against Lee's (1995) views on institutional legitimation of "subversive" literature.

Schueller (1989)

Presented as a corrective to some feminist critics' tendency to ignore questions of national and racial identity in *The Woman Warrior* (e.g., neglecting folkloric elements or Chinese American immigrant concerns). Reviews theorists like Cixous, Kristeva, and Bakhtin to develop a framework in which oppressions are seen as interlinked and singular categories in need of challenge. Argues that Kingston's book is a "sustained subversion of cultural, racial, and gender definitions and an affirmation of a radical intersubjectivity as the basis of articulation" (422).

Bibliography

✦ ✦ ✦

Allen, Joseph R. 1996. "Dressing and Undressing the Chinese Woman Warrior." *positions: east asia cultures critique* 4 (2): 343–79.

Blinde, Patricia Lin. 1979. "The Icicle in the Desert: Perspective and Form in the Works of Two Chinese-American Women Writers." *MELUS* 6 (3): 51–71.

Brownmiller, Susan. 1977. "Susan Brownmiller Talks with Maxine Wong Kingston, author of *The Woman Warrior.*" *Mademoiselle* Mar.: 148–49, 210–11, 214–16.

Carabi, Angeles. 1989. Interview with Maxine Hong Kingston. *Belles Lettres* (Winter): 10–11.

Cheung, King-Kok. 1988. "'Don't Tell': Imposed Silences in *The Color Purple* and *The Woman Warrior.*" *PMLA* 103 (2): 162–74.

————. 1990. "The Woman Warrior versus the Chinaman Pacific: Must a Chinese American Critic Choose between Feminism and Heroism?" In *Conflicts in Feminism.* Edited by Marianne Hirsch and Evelyn Fox Keller. New York: Routledge. 234–51.

————. 1993. *Articulate Silences: Hisaye Yamamoto, Maxine Hong Kingston, Joy Kogawa.* Ithaca and London: Cornell University Press.

————. 1997. "Re-viewing Asian American Literary Studies." In *An Interethnic Companion to Asian American Literature.* Edited by King-Kok Cheung. Cambridge, Mass.: Cambridge University Press. 1–36.

Chin, Frank. 1984. "The Most Popular Book in China." *Quilt* 4: 6–12. Reprinted as

"Afterword" in *Chinaman Pacific and Frisco R.R. Co.:" Eight Short Stories by Frank Chin.* Minneapolis: Coffee House Press, 1988. I–IV.

———. 1991. *Donald Duk.* Minneapolis: Coffee House Press.

Chin, Frank, Jeffery Paul Chan, Lawson Fusao Inada, and Shawn Wong, eds. 1974. *Aiiieeeee! An Anthology of Asian-American Writers.* Washington, D.C.: Howard University Press, 1983.

Chin, Marilyn. 1989–90. "A MELUS Interview: Maxine Hong Kingston." *MELUS* 16 (4): 57–74.

Christian, Barbara. 1990. "The Race for Theory." In *The Nature and Context of Minority Discourse.* Edited by Abdul R. JanMohamed and David Lloyd. New York and Oxford: Oxford University Press. 37–49.

Chu, Patricia. 1992. "'The Invisible World the Emigrants Built': Cultural Self-inscription and the Antiromantic Plots of *The Woman Warrior." Diaspora: Journal of Transnational Studies* 2 (1): 95–115.

———. Forthcoming. "Maxine Hong Kingston, *The Woman Warrior."* In *The MLA Resource Guide to Asian American Literature.* Edited by Stephen H. Sumida and Sau-ling C. Wong. New York: The Modern Language Association of America.

Dasenbrock, Reed Way. 1987. "Intelligibility and Meaningfulness in Multicultural Literature in English." *PMLA* 102 (1): 10–19.

Davis, Rocio, ed. 1996. *European Perspectives on Asian American Literature.* A special issue of *Hitting Critical Mass: A Journal of Asian American Cultural Criticism.* 4 (1).

Deeney, John J. 1993. "Of Monkeys and Butterflies: Transformation in M. H. Kingston's *Tripmaster Monkey* and D. H. Hwang's *M. Butterfly." MELUS* 18 (4): 21–39.

Eakin, Paul John. 1985. "Maxine Hong Kingston: 'I Had to Tell My Mother So That She Would Know the True Things about Me and to Stop the Pain in My Throat.'" *Fictions in Autobiography: Studies in the Art of Self-invention.* Princeton, N.J.: Princeton University Press. 255–75.

Fishkin, Shelley Fisher. 1991. "Interview with Maxine Hong Kingston." *American Literary History* 3 (4): 782–91.

Frankenberg, Ruth. 1993. *The Social Construction of Whiteness: White Women, Race Matters.* Minneapolis: University of Minnesota Press.

Goellnicht, Donald C. 1991. "Father Land and/or Mother Tongue: The Divided Female Subject in Kogawa's *Obasan* and Hong Kingston's *The Woman Warrior."* In *Redefining Autobiography in Twentieth-century Women's Fiction: An Essay Collection.* Edited by Janice Morgan and Colette T. Hall. New York: Garland. 119–34.

Goldberg, David Theo, ed. 1994. *Multiculturalism: A Critical Reader.* London and Cambridge, Mass.: Blackwell.

Ho, Wen-ching. 1987. "In Search of a Female Self: Toni Morrison's *The Bluest Eye* and Maxine Hong Kingston's *The Woman Warrior.*" *American Studies* 17 (3): 1–44.

Holaday, Woon-Ping Chin. 1978. "From Ezra Pound to Maxine Hong Kingston: Expressions of Chinese Thought in American Literature." *MELUS* 5 (2): 15–24.

Homsher, Deborah. 1979. "*The Woman Warrior,* by Maxine Hong Kingston: A Bridging of Autobiography and Fiction." *Iowa Review* 10: 93–98.

Hornung, Alfred, and Ernstpeter Ruhe, eds. 1992. *Autobiographie & Avant-garde.* Tubingen: Gunter Narr Verlag Tubingen.

Hunt, Linda. 1985. "'I Could Not Figure Out What Was My Village': Gender vs. Ethnicity in Maxine Hong Kingston's *The Woman Warrior.*" *MELUS* 12 (3): 5–12.

Hutcheon, Linda. 1988. "Decentering the Postmodern: The Ex-Centric." In *A Poetics of Postmodernism: History, Theory, Fiction.* London and New York: 1988. 57–73.

Juhasz, Susan. 1979. "Towards a Theory of Form in Feminist Autobiography: Kate Millet's *Fear of Flying* and *Sita;* Maxine Hong Kingston's *The Woman Warrior.*" *International Journal of Women's Studies* 2 (1): 62–75.

Kang, Laura Hyan Yi. 1995. "Compositional Subjects: Enfiguring Asian/American Women." Ph.D. diss. University of California, Santa Cruz.

Kim, Elaine H. 1982. *Asian American Literature: An Introduction to the Writings and Their Social Context.* Philadelphia: Temple University Press.

Kingston, Maxine Hong. 1976. *The Woman Warrior: Memoirs of a Girlhood among Ghosts.* New York: Vintage Books, 1977.

———. 1980. *China Men.* New York: Ballantine, 1981.

———. 1982. "Cultural Mis-readings by American Reviewers." In *Asian and Western Writers in Dialogue: New Cultural Identities.* Edited by Guy Amirthanayagam. London: Macmillan. 55–65.

———. 1989. *Tripmaster Monkey: His Fake Book.* New York: Knopf.

Lee, Rachel. 1995. "Claiming Land, Claiming Voice, Claiming Canon: Institutionalized Challenges in Kingston's *China Men* and *The Woman Warrior.*" In *Reviewing Asian America: Locating Diversity.* Edited by Wendy L. Ng, Soo-Young Chin, James S. Moy, and Gary Y. Okihiro. Pullman: Washington State University Press. 147–59.

Li, David Leiwei. 1988. "The Naming of a Chinese American 'I': Cross-Cultural Sign/ification in *The Woman Warrior.*" *Criticism* 30 (4): 497–515.

Lim, Shirley Geok-lin, ed. 1991. *Approaches to Teaching Kingston's "The Woman Warrior."* New York: The Modern Language Association of America.

———. 1992. "The Tradition of Chinese American Women's Life Stories: Thematics of Race and Gender in Jade Snow Wong's *Fifth Chinese Daughter* and Maxine Hong Kingston's *The Woman Warrior.* In *American Women's Autobiography: Fea(s)ts of Memory.* Edited by Margo Culley. Madison: University of Wisconsin Press. 252–67.

Ling, Amy. 1990a. "Chinese American Women Writers: The Tradition behind Maxine Hong Kingston." In *Redefining American Literary History.* Edited by A. LaVonne Brown Ruoff and Jerry W. Ward, Jr. New York: The Modern Language Association of America. 219–36.

———. 1990b. *Between Worlds: Women Writers of Chinese Ancestry.* New York: Pergamon Press.

Ludwig, Sämi. 1996a. *Concrete Language: Intercultural Communication in Maxine Hong Kingston's "The Woman Warrior: Memoirs of a Girlhood among Ghosts" and Ishmael Reed's "Mumbo Jumbo."* Frankfurt am Main, Bern, New York: Peter Lang.

———. 1996b. "'You Can See behind You Like a Bat': Metaphorical Constructions and Intercultural Understanding in Maxine Hong Kingston's *The Woman Warrior."* In Davis 81–102.

Myers, Victoria. 1986. "The Significant Fictivity of Maxine Hong Kingston's *The Woman Warrior." Biography* 9 (2): 112–25.

Palumbo-Liu, David, ed. 1995a. *The Ethnic Canon: Histories, Institutions, and Interventions.* Minneapolis and London: University of Minnesota Press.

———. 1995b. "The Ethnic as 'Post': Reading *the Literatures of Asian America." American Literary History* 7 (1): 161–68.

Quinby, Lee. 1992. "The Subject of Memoirs: *The Woman Warrior's* Technology of Ideographic Selfhood." In *De/Colonizing the Subject: The Politics of Gender in Women's Autobiography.* Edited by Sidonie Smith and Julia Watson. Minneapolis: University of Minnesota Press, 297–320.

Rabine, Leslie W. 1987. "No Lost Paradise: Social Gender and Symbolic Gender in the Writings of Maxine Hong Kingston." *Signs: Journal of Women in Culture and Society* 12 (3): 471–92.

Rubenstein, Roberta. 1987. "Bridging Two Cultures: Maxine Hong Kingston." In *Boundaries of the Self: Gender, Culture, Fiction.* Urbana: University of Illinois Press. 164–89.

Scalise, Kathleen. 1997. "The Humanities Medal for Kingston." *Berkeleyan* 26 (8): 1–2.

Schueller, Malini. 1989. "Questioning Race and Gender Definitions: Dialogic Subversions in *The Woman Warrior." Criticism* 31 (4): 421–37.

Smith, Sidonie. 1987. "Maxine Hong Kingston's *The Woman Warrior:* Filiality and Woman's Autobiographical Storytelling." In *A Poetics of Women's Autobiography: Marginality and the Fictions of Self-representation.* Bloomington and Indianapolis: Indiana University Press. 150–73.

Wong, Sau-ling Cynthia. 1992a. "Autobiography as Guided Chinatown Tour? Maxine Hong Kingston's *The Woman Warrior* and the Chinese-American Autobiography Controversy." In *Multicultural Autobiography: American Lives.* Edited by James Robert Payne. Knoxville: University of Tennessee Press. 248–79.

———. 1992b. "Ethnic Dimensions of Postmodern Indeterminacy: Maxine Hong

Kingston's *The Woman Warrior* as Avant-garde Autobiography." In Hornung and Ruhe. 273–84.

———. 1993. *Reading Asian American Literature: From Necessity to Extravagance.* Princeton, N.J.: Princeton University Press.

Woo, Deborah. 1990. "Maxine Hong Kingston: The Ethnic Writer and the Burden of Dual Authenticity." *Amerasia Journal* 16 (1): 173–200.

Wu, Qing-yun. 1991–92. "A Chinese Reader's Response to Maxine Hong Kingston's *China Men." MELUS* 17 (3): 85–94.

Zhang, Ya-jie. 1986. "A Chinese Woman's Response to Maxine Hong Kingston's *The Woman Warrior." MELUS* 13 (3 & 4): 103–7.